BUT FOR OUR GRIEF

To Margaret
with love,

June Filkin Taylor

June Filkin Taylor

BUT FOR

OUR GRIEF

How Comfort Comes

A. J. HOLMAN COMPANY
Division of J. B. Lippincott Company
Philadelphia and New York

Scripture quotations marked NAS are from the New
American Standard Bible, © The Lockman Foundation
1960, 1962, 1963, 1968, 1971, 1972, 1973, 1975, and
are used by permission.

The poems on pages 14, 26, 28–29, 33, 38, 46, 55, 59–
60, 61, 67, 74, 95, 104, 107, 110, 113–14, and 124 are
from *I Need a Miracle Today, Lord* by Wilma Burton.
Copyright 1976. Moody Press, Moody Bible Institute of
Chicago. Used by permission.

The quotation on pages 82–83 is from *Mr. Jones, Meet
the Master* by Peter Marshall. Copyright © 1949, 1950
by Fleming H. Revell Company.

The song "Angels Are Always Smiling" on page 85 is
© Copyright 1975 by Singspiration, Division of the
Zondervan Corporation. All rights reserved. Used by
permission. The lyrics on pages 74 and 109 are copyright © 1977 by Nancy Woods Harrison.

U.S. Library of Congress Cataloging in Publication Data

Taylor, June Filkin, birth date
    But for our grief.

    Includes bibliographical references.
    1. Grief.   2. Consolation.   3. Taylor, June
Filkin, birth date   I. Title.
BJ1487.T375   242'.4   77-3345
ISBN-0-87981-078-5

*Dedicated to my family
and to fellow travelers in grief*

Contents

Foreword 9

No Utopia, This 11

OUR NEED

1. "I Want to Go Home" 15
2. A Turn for the Worse 19
3. "May I Help You?" 21

HELP FROM HEAVEN

HIS STILL, SMALL VOICE

4. Where's Heaven? Is She There?
   (For Assurance of Heaven) 27
5. Dear God, How Do You View This?
   (For Emotional Stress) 30
6. Satan on the Prowl
   (For Satanic Oppression) 34
7. Please Tell Her Something for Me
   (For Guilt) 39
8. Thank You, Lord, for Sondra
   (For Painful Memories) 43

HIS WRITTEN WORD

9. Needed: A New View of Death 48
10. Death Is Deliverance 52
11. Jesus' Words 55

HELP FROM EARTH

12. *Ties That Bind*   65
13. *Grief's First Stages and Delays*   68
14. *Grief Work Begins*   75
15. *Angels Aren't Always Smiling*   81
16. *"Dear Sondra"*   95
17. *Reentry*   105
18. *Out of the Valley at Last*   119

Epilogue: In a Capsule   125

Notes   127

Foreword

When I was a little girl, I thought it must be fun to be an author. Now I think it must be terrible. To put yourself on paper for anyone to see—why would any person ever do that to himself?

I have written about grief and death so that I will never forget the beautiful help that came to me when our ten-year-old Sondra died. I share these gleanings from my grieving on the outside chance that it might help someone else. I hope that whoever reads it will find God in it.

—*June Taylor*

No Utopia, This

"Dear God, please help the doctors to run out of customers." It was the prayer of a three-year-old for several weeks after her sister had died from complications of pneumonia. Her five-year-old brother would often pray, "Dear God, please keep the streets of Rockford clear from robbers, kidnappers, and stranglers."

Should I have told them that, for now, their prayers are all but useless because trouble is here to stay? Or should I have told them, as R. A. Torrey once said, that the main purpose of prayer is that God be glorified in the answer and not that you get what you want? I didn't tell them either one, because faith can move mountains; God still heals and can be glorified that way, too. I quietly listened to their prayers and hoped that their faith would remain firm all through their lives even as troubles came upon them.

For sure, trouble is ahead for them as it is for all of us. Sickness, tormenting evil by human hands, natural disaster—it is out there and it will come for all of us. Sometimes God will intervene with a miracle, but many times He won't.

Jesus knew all about our troubles. "In the world ye shall have tribulation," He said, adding, "but be of good cheer; I have overcome the world" (John 16:33 KJV). He could say those words "that [we] might have peace" because

He knew where the power was coming from to give us that peace.

We desperately need to tap into God's peace, all of us—because until Jesus comes again, the streets will have their robbers and the doctors will have their "customers."

OUR NEED

PRAYER IN ISOLATION ROOM 4205

Fill this room
with the aura of Your presence:
let no evil here remain.
  Every microbe on the rampant
  let it not enchain the one
  who lies here comatose
  beyond the reach of human voice
  or pain.
You are love, love, love
and Your slightest touch
can heal, can heal, can heal.
  A greening leaf glistening
  in a gentle rain,
  the flutter of a firefly's
  illumined wing
  know You.
And this flesh
invaded by a strange virus
let it mirror once again
Your perfect image.
Here, Lord, be glorified.
                    —Wilma Burton

And, behold, there cometh one of the rulers of the
synagogue, Jairus by name; And when he saw
[Jesus], he fell at his feet, and besought him greatly,
saying, "My little daughter lieth at the point of
death: I pray thee, come and lay thy hands on her,
that she may be healed; and she shall live."
                    —Mark 5:22, 23 KJV

1

"I Want to Go Home"

And He called a child to Himself . . .
—Matthew 18:2 NAS

It was cold that February 2, 1974—very cold. Sondra, who would be eleven in two months and five days, had come in shivering, her new purple coat with its cozy gray fur hood not keeping out enough of the winter cold. One week later she would be in heaven.

It had been a good day. She had sold over fifty boxes of Girl Scout cookies and was looking forward to spending the night at her girl friend's. She did not feel sick until Monday after school, and then only a little dizzy. I kept her home on Tuesday, a snow-covered, school-canceled day, and hoped she would not have to spoil her perfect attendance record. Surely she would be better by Friday for a swimming party.

Wednesday morning was spent watching TV and making an oatmeal box into a knitting box for Valentine's Day, her last love gift to me. After a long nap that afternoon, she coughed a strange cough and had a fever of 105 degrees.

The doctor met my husband and Sondra at the emergency room and diagnosed pneumonia. He told Walt that, because of the danger of cross-infection, home would be the best place for her. So we started her on antibiotics, moved her bed downstairs, and elevated the mattress. Her breathing was labored, so I stayed in the TV room with her all night waiting for the medication to do its work.

It didn't. Treating infection is somewhat hit-and-miss. While waiting for the culture studies to identify the culprit, doctors try various antibiotics, beginning with the one which is usually effective against the widest range of bacteria—the so-called "broad-spectrum" antibiotics—and continuing with other antibiotics if needed. It was the last antibiotic tried that would have worked against Sondra's infection, but it would be tried too late.

Her fever stayed high all night, and by morning nausea and diarrhea were added to her discomforts. By Thursday afternoon the fever still had not gone down and the doctor had her admitted into the hospital.

"Are you going to die there?" Jon asked her as she left. She smiled at her little brother to let him know what a funny joke *that* was. She had asked me earlier if they would "cut" her and I had assured her that oxygen and maybe an intravenous feeding would be all that would happen. I reminded her that I had had pneumonia when I was only three and remembered so well how my daddy did magic to entertain me and I got "all well."

Her time in the hospital that evening and all through the night was spent in panic at not being able to breathe comfortably, even in the oxygen tent, and then in further discomfort from the ice baths which were administered in an attempt to lower her temperature. Someone came in to have her cough up a sputum culture; nurses were in and out taking her temperature and replacing the needle of her IV feeding after it had worked its way out of her arm. Her temperature stayed high, but by early morning she was finally more comfortable in the oxygen tent.

"Well, at least I've learned about hospitals in here," she said. "I can tell the kids when I get home that they don't hurt you here. You can trust the people up here."

A second doctor was called in for his opinion. He looked in her throat and then shook his head. "How long have you been sick?" he asked. I replied that we had just noticed the dizziness on Monday, but I wondered if she had been sick longer. I asked him how long it would be until Sondra recovered, and he answered that it would be a long time for an infection that was this bad. Or did the shake of his head mean she wouldn't make it? (I wished doctors would tell more, or at least say if they didn't know.) I phoned my husband, Walt, from Sondra's room; and though the news I had to tell him was not good, I could not relay it, so I simply asked him if he wanted to come up to replace me. He did. Sondra did not want me to leave but was happy to have her dad come. I would see her again later that day and even communicate with her again, but her good-bye that morning was the last time I would ever hear her voice.

At home the phone rang a little before noon. It was Walt —and it was bad news. Sondra had turned blue from a lack of oxygen and had been rushed into surgery for an emergency tracheotomy. They *had* cut her.

She was still in surgery when I arrived. Would she make it? Walt and I sat and waited together in the waiting room. He told me how Sondra had panicked and fought against being taken to surgery, how she had insisted she had to make a "decision." Did she believe that death was ahead of her?

"If she can come through this," Walt was saying, "I think she has a chance." *Has a chance!* Was it that bad? I could not imagine that she wouldn't make it.

Within the hour the hospital chaplain came walking toward us and my heart sank. "Is she gone?" I asked.

"No," he said, "but she is a very sick little girl."

The chaplain told us that Sondra was out of surgery and in intensive care now but was still fighting the nurses, trying to get away. How I wanted to see her to try to calm her! I asked him to tell her that we were nearby and would see her soon. The chaplain left but was quickly back with permission for us to come down for just five minutes.

She was relieved to see us but panicked again when she saw that we were not going to get her out of the hospital.

"I want to go home!" She could only mouth the words. "*Home!*"

It was an easy word to whisper. With the oxygen going down the tube in her neck she couldn't talk. Added to her pain and panic was this new frustration: even her parents were not going to help her. Walt and I helped to hold her down and tried to convince her that the people were trying to help her, that they knew all about all of her hurting but could only fix one thing at a time.

She mouthed, "In the ground," and I wondered if she thought she was already dead.

"No," I told her. "You are in the hospital. This is just a different room and the sides on this bed keep you from falling out." I remembered that the sides of a hospital bed seem quite coffinlike after surgery.

She asked us to count, and I did, but it wasn't what she wanted. Was she remembering some relief from anesthesia during surgery and connecting it with a countdown before a release from her pain?

Sondra was still trying to get the oxygen mask from her face, probably blaming it for the suffocation and not realizing that it was giving her life. Walt noticed that her legs had a bluish color and he knew right then that she would probably die. I would not let myself think such a thing.

2
A Turn for the Worse

We stayed with her for a little over two hours. She was calmer with us there talking to her, touching her, so the doctors allowed us to remain. Her fever was still high. She could have no painkillers because of her respiratory difficulty. Dark fluid was being syringed from the tube in her trachea—and still she was fighting. I looked at our little girl, her lips cracked and sore, her golden hair wet with perspiration, her face pale and eyes bloodshot and wondered how a nurse could remark "how very pretty she was." I knew, because I could still see underneath her sweet, little-girl body. She was a bud ready to blossom into a woman; but we would never see her flower.

Should we be preparing her for what might be coming? We did not want to risk frightening her more. "Lots of people are praying for you, honey," I said. "And you know that Jesus loves you. You know that, don't you?"

She shook her head no, quite violently.

"Yes, He does," I assured her with great conviction.

It was soon after that that something good seemed to happen in her mind. Her little body relaxed somewhat and she turned toward the window, almost as if she were staring at something out there. I asked her what she saw, but she was far away.

Someone decided that we should leave. I asked Sondra if she thought she would rest now, and she nodded yes. I told her how much we loved her and kissed her eyelids shut. We left the room. I never saw her alive again.

Down the long hall we waited and prayed silently. "May your will be done, dear Lord, but oh, please, let it be a miracle. We know you have the power. Please make her well."

Friends came to be with us, each one for a short time. Our parents came for a while; then my mother went to our home to be with the other children.

About ten thirty that night we heard good news. A nurse came down to tell us that Sondra's fever was finally down, that there did not seem to be any brain damage, and that she was resting quite comfortably. She suggested that one of us go down to see for ourselves. Walt went just to peek, but Sondra saw him through the open door and sat straight up in bed, her arms raised, begging him to take her home. Walt ached for her, but he came back to the waiting room encouraged that she would actually recover.

I shed my first tears. We were going to get her back. "Thank you, Lord; we're going to get her back!"

At our doctor's urging, I ended my vigil there for some sleep at home. Mother and I prayed by the bed, "Whether a long or short life, let her spend it in Your peace and joy."

We slept until 2:45 A.M., when the phone jolted us into the awful news that Sondra was dead. Walt did not say it that way. He repeated the nurse's words to him, "She's taken a turn for the worse." Her heart had stopped, and a health-care team was even then trying to get it started again.

3
"May I Help You?"

"May I help you?"

It was the voice on the speaker outside the night entrance to the hospital. How I wished that someone could help. "My little girl is dying," I replied, and the buzzer let us in.

The night was cold. It would not be dawn for two more hours. Mom and I had quickly dressed and driven the four miles to the hospital and then made our way through a maze of boards on the construction site. Now someone was meeting us to lead us up a back way to the intensive-care unit.

None of them could help. It was over only minutes after we arrived, and now the seven people in white who had tried to save her were slowly filing out of the room. We saw their downcast faces, some wet with tears, and were sorry they had to see us sitting there, knowing they had failed.

Our doctor asked us if we wanted an autopsy. He did not think it necessary because they knew the cause of death —a staph infection in the epiglottis had blocked the passage of oxygen to her lungs. After giving Walt and me some antibiotics to fight off possible infection, he left.

None of us went into her room. Sondra was not there anymore. All my energy and reason for living had gone with her. We stood to leave and walked a few steps. I stooped to the floor, unable to go on; but then, from somewhere, the energy came for a step at a time as we left the hospital. God's help has often come that way; when I am at the end of my resources, He provides His— enough for a step at a time as needed.

There would be many needs. Immediately ahead would be a similar illness among the other three little children. Within the next forty-eight hours we would be rushing Jon to the hospital with breathing difficulties and hearing ourselves say in the emergency room, "His sister died here two days ago."

There would be the pain of grief's first duties—selecting her clothes for burial, cleaning out drawers of clothes and keepsakes, answering her mail and an occasional phone call, setting the table without her place, cooking her favorite foods and shopping at our favorite stores alone.

There would be that painful awakening each morning and suddenly remembering that she was gone, and wishing desperately that it hadn't happened. There would be a reliving, over and over, of her final hours of terror and pain.

Physical distress would seem minor by comparison, but it would be there, too—the loss of appetite, the sleeplessness, the heaviness of a despair that understands life to be terribly, terribly hard.

All those needs and more. But I did not know about the myriad of help ahead, and that slowly but surely every hurt would be healed. I did not know that one day I would look back knowing God better and loving Him more and thanking Him for the comfort that was soon to come from so many directions.

We passed the next hours in quiet disbelief, driving home in the still darkness—had it been only minutes before that Mom and I had driven toward her? How could we just leave her like this, with nobody to take care of her ever again? I couldn't fathom death.

We met our seventeen-year-old son, Brian, at the door

and hugged him as he sobbed his "Oh, no!" His ten-year-old sister had been a good friend, one with whom he had shared his confidences and dreams, and who had even beaten him in chess. His natural mother had died thirteen years before—and now Sondra. He went to his room to bear it alone.

Walt and I drank the tea Mom urged on us and laid ourselves down, calling her to be with us to wait for morning, when we would break the news as gently as possible to the other children. Janna, at three, wept quietly; Jon, five, sobbed loud and long; and Kristi, at seven, shed her tears alone, as Brian had done, behind closed doors.

HELP FROM
HEAVEN

HIS STILL, SMALL VOICE

I NEED A MIRACLE TODAY, LORD

no cheap magician trick
of rabbit/hat or bird/cage
or whirling dervish/scarves
   I need the sudden crimson
   of a sunset cutting through
   the dark travail of cobra heads
   that hood and veil, torment the sky
I am choking
on the fork-tongued
question—WHY?
   Death comes pushing rudely—
   speechless—I wait, O Lord,
   for Your reply.
               —Wilma Burton

4

Where's Heaven? Is She There? (For Assurance of Heaven)

People began to come to our door, dear friends who wanted to comfort but who didn't know what to say. I'm glad they did not come with all sorts of wisdom and reasons why this had happened. A tear and a hug and silent caring are much better than saying too much and answering questions that no one is yet asking. Job's friends did not bother us.

What I found distressing, however, was that their concern was for *us* and not for Sondra. I was not yet ready to worry about our grieving, or even to admit that was what we were doing. I just wanted to know all about my little girl. But I did not ask and no one could read my mind. How could they know that one's concern for a child is not easily turned off, not even when that child is in the care of Jesus Himself?

Weeks later I was to learn in every fiber of my being the things that God has let us know about heaven. Scripture's wisdom pierced my heart with truth as I studied the Bible with a new passion. But now I panicked.

The first chance I had to be alone in our room, I began to quietly sob out all of my questions to God. That was my first experience with God's special comfort, and by it I found that God is always there, just as He has promised to be.

"Is she really there, dear God? Is she happy? Does she remember all the suffering? Are you *sure* she is there?"

I asked my tortured questions and spilled out my agonizing thoughts. If there were nothing after death, it would be easier. A different plane of existence must be terrifying in its newness for a little girl. I wanted desperately to be with Sondra, to hold her and to comfort her in her new confusion. Was there anyone there to welcome her that she knew? She doesn't know anyone there, I thought.

I said it all and finally stopped. And then, unmasked as I was before the living God, I began to be filled with His peace. I became so strangely quiet that it was as if all time and space were inside me. And out of the silence of my quieted mind came some words, slowly as if by teletype:

AT MY RIGHT HAND THERE ARE PLEASURES FOR EVERMORE.

Out of my panic and into His peace. So that is what the saints could give their lives for! My heart was full during those moments of love and thanks to God for a glimpse into His truth.

One day I was to find those words in the Bible—in Psalm 16—but until that day when I would find truth straight from God's Word, He answered many more heart cries with His still, small voice.

YOU

I am at ease with You,
my Creator, for You
knew me in my womb-days,
knew my bare and unsure foot,
knew my school-door shyness,
knew my first-kiss quiver.
    You are Family.
    There is no need for woman-flutter
preparing for You as Guest.

You cannot be kept in Book,
or Mosque, or Crucifix.
You are the Chrysalis Cocoon
waiting to release the gift of wings.
—Wilma Burton

5

Dear God, How Do You View This? (For Emotional Stress)

The answer to that first prayer about heaven's reality taught me something in addition to what heaven is like. It taught me that I must be totally honest with God if I want correct answers. He answers what I ask. I must present my worst self as well as my best self and then let Him work, whether to cleanse, direct, comfort, or answer my questions. As Catherine Marshall [1] says, Jesus "tolerates no generalities, no fuzziness." She reminds us how He asked the two blind beggars who wanted sympathy from Him to spell out their request: "What do you wish Me to do for you?" (Matthew 20:29–34 NAS). We need to tell God what we want Him to do for us, too.

David knew about this. His confessions of an ugly and unbelieving spirit were honest statements of his true need. But those statements change almost as if by magic into overflowing, sincere songs of joy and thanksgiving (Psalm 13, for example). I think the reason for that change is David's honesty before God.

All of us need to practice such honesty. All of us know the grief of disappointment and loss: an unwanted move, the loss of job or limb or house, an unfaithful husband or wife. These disappointments take over our minds in much the same way as the loss of a loved one does, filling them completely. Change of any kind seems to trigger responses in us that are similar to grief. We turn inward and everything looks bad.

30

In *None of These Diseases*, Dr. S. I. McMillen points out that stress in our lives produces more than mental disturbance. Physical distresses, such as ulcers, colitis, and arthritis, come upon us when our bodies react chemically to the stress put upon them.[2] In fact, "medical science recognizes that emotions such as fear, sorrow, envy, resentment and hatred are responsible for the majority of our sicknesses. Estimates vary from 60 per cent to nearly 100 per cent."

Studies presently being done support the theory that unrelieved emotional stress can even cause cancer. The reason for this is that stress or anxiety can cause toxins—harmful chemicals—to poison our systems. The harmful effects stress may have on the heart have long been recognized.

A startling illustration of this can be seen in the results of an experiment with a prisoner. The volunteer for the experiment was told that his blood would be drained from his body in order to test his emotional response. He was blindfolded and a needle was injected into his arm. A simulation of blood dripping was made as water slowly dripped into a bucket. The man's pulse became slower and slower and he became weaker and weaker until finally he went into shock and died of a heart attack—from stress. He never lost a drop of blood. The tragic and unexpected results of this experiment with stress show that extreme anxiety can actually bring about death.

Little study has been done to correlate the particular relationship between the stress of grief and physical and mental disorders. Common observation leads one to believe that there is a definite connection. It is not uncommon to find that, within six months of the death of a beloved husband or wife, the spouse develops a serious and often fatal illness. Whether stress is the cause or whether one just loses the will to live is not easily determined, but there is a definite connection between the mind and the body with regard to illness.

C. M. Parkes has begun a pioneering work to determine the effects of stress on the bereaved. Admittedly it is difficult to impose upon the bereaved for purposes of research, but Parkes was able to study some twenty-six widows, selected at random through London physicians, for the purpose of detecting what physical distress might have come upon them during their first year of bereavement. In this and in other studies, one among psychotic patients, Parkes found a high correlation between physical and mental distress and unresolved grief.[3]

Studies like this are warnings to those of us in grief; but just knowing that stress is harmful does not cause it to magically disappear. We must recognize God as the source of help in time of trouble. We need to avail ourselves of His help, to come to Him with our honest condition—whether fear, doubt, anxiety, or anger—and let Him replace our way of feeling with His way.

Often during the early days I received help from the "honest prayer" (is there any other kind?). I still find immediate help when and if I remember to pray it. The text of the prayer is as individual as the specific trouble. We must spell out the trouble and tell exactly how we feel about it, going on and on until it is all out, and then—this is the most important part of all—we must ask God how He sees it all, in words like this: ". . . But Father in heaven, I know that you do not see things the way I do. How do you view all of this?"

While we wait, His answer fills us. We may receive wisdom for what to do or how to communicate, but for sure we will receive God's point of view. With His attitude controlling us, we become more forgiving, or more patient and loving. And the emotions which could have left an overload of stress in our systems have vanished.

God's ways are not our ways and His thoughts are not our thoughts. What a richness we tap into when we finally remember to ask for His view! He does not fail to answer the honest prayer.

During these past two years I have wondered if some severe illness would burst upon me. Up until now it hasn't, but stress from our conflicts, whether from grief or from something else, is real; and I know I do not always do the right thing with it. God has a perfect way of taking care of all our stress if only we let Him.

WHEN PRAYER HOLDS SO MANY ANSWERS

why am I so prayerless, Lord?
Why do I try to untangle
my own yarns, flounder
in mazes, dangle in endless webs
before I turn to You?
Will I never learn
to pray first—*before* I act?
Must I contend with horses
before I learn first to walk
with the horsemen?
        Prayer
is your mighty flaming sword
against the rulers of darkness,
why then dare I the battle,
unarmed and trembling—
    when the mighty unseen hosts
    that were Elijah's can be mine,
    if I will but call, Lord,
    in Jesus' Name.
                            —Wilma Burton

6

Satan on the Prowl
(For Satanic Oppression)

I almost didn't tell God about this.

I had been waking up in the night off and on for several months. It seemed that an inner clock startled me to consciousness just at the time Sondra had died. That's why I was awake to hear the cat.

Is there any more mournful sound than a cat's yowl in the night? This one would climb the fence near our bedroom window and then cry out *"Mama"*—or that's what it sounded like. Dark thoughts entered my mind. What if Sondra's spirit is in that cat? I would lie awake wondering. During the daytime, I knew what was happening: with or without Satan our minds can play tricks on us, and Satan would love to have us think we can communicate with our dead loved ones. So I put the night yowling out of my mind as best I could—until a daytime cat began to challenge my thinking.

I am not one that animals take to, because I'm afraid of them, so it seemed strange to me that a cat would follow me home on my morning walks from the children's school. It seemed even stranger when one nuzzled up to me on the porch. After about three days of trying to forget my weird wonderings, I decided to ask God what was what. Maybe He knew about things like that. It had taken those three days for me to realize that there is nothing hidden from God's knowing. I had flirted with the notion that maybe

Satan knew something that God didn't know and so it wouldn't do much good to go to God. Sweeping away the rankling doubt, I finally prayed, "Please, Father, if Satan has anything to do with any of this, get him out of here. In the name of *Jesus* get him out of here."

No cat has ever wakened or followed me since. I saw one the next day, but it just arched its back and hissed. I am not saying what was or was not with regard to a cat or cats. It, or they, may have been innocent bystanders in the little coincidental drama of my mind. But certainly God immediately eased my mental anguish about Sondra the moment I realized again that nothing is hidden from Him.

A person who is grieving is an excellent target for Satan. Through the eyes of our depression, Satan looks like the victor. Death has happened and Satan has won. We desperately want to believe in an afterlife, but we begin to wonder, "What if the Bible is wrong?" Frantically we carry on a search for more positive proof, for extra wisdom. Satan does have extra wisdom: he misuses it in trickery against us, but it is available from him. Many of us fall into his traps during our susceptible times of grieving.

Some look to mediums or black magic; others try forms of meditation-minus-God; but even activities such as reading the horoscope for fun or playing a ouija board seem to open us up for Satanic invasion. In all those activities we are saying, "I need more than God can give me." And yet by the very act of such seeking we separate ourselves from the greatest power in the Universe—God's!

During the low times that grief imposes, we are also extra vulnerable to religious sects—groups which emphasize one part of God's way but often leave out or destroy much that is basic. A Jehovah's Witness chose the time of Sondra's death to appear at the funeral home and then later at our home, trying to convince me that my understanding of death and the afterlife was wrong. Though she did not convince me, she probably realized that a person in grief is quite ready for answers. If only those answers were always the right ones.

Satan has many devices. Anyone suffering from a trauma looks for escapes. Certainly when we turn to God we are making a kind of escape from our sea of troubles. Vance Havner has said that in his grief he was "shipwrecked on God and stranded on omnipotence." [4] But there is a large difference between finding refuge in God and other escapes. Many other escapes make us less able to function and only postpone the inevitable facing of our problems. But with God we function even better than we ordinarily would: He makes us more than we are and all that we were meant to be. And with Him, our problems are not put off; His wisdom for action comes even during the times of peace.

There may be times when some human forms of escape and painkilling are in order. When one's mind, emotions, or body function so poorly that God's peace is just not penetrating, a "vacation by drugs" may well be medically indicated. But we must view with suspicion what looks like a help for any of our traumas. Those helps may be terrible hindrances. Alcohol, drugs, illicit sex may seem to help, but all command their own price. Satan does not have heavy work to do in the lives of those hooked on such deadly poisons.

Satan is as real as God is. He just won't last as long and his purpose is our damnation and destruction by whatever means he must use. Satan knows how much God loves us, how He longs for our good and eternal happiness, and it makes him furious. So Satan's revenge is to take as many of God's beloved creations with him as he can. He is powerless to take our salvation from us, but he would love to make us miserable and inoperable. We must guard against him and regard all his devices as the lethal time bombs that they are. Long ago God commanded the Israelites:

> There shall not be found among you anyone who makes his son or his daughter pass through the fire, one who uses divination, one who practices witchcraft, or one who interprets omens, or a sorcerer, or one who casts a spell, or a medium, or a spiritist, or one who calls up the dead.
>
> For whoever does these things is detestable to the Lord; and because of these detestable things the Lord your God will drive them out before you.
>
> —Deuteronomy 18:10 NAS

There *are* "secret things" that we do not know about. But we are not supposed to know about them. God says, "The secret things belong unto the Lord our God: but those things which are revealed belong unto us" (Deuteronomy 29:29 KJV).

If a child of God has unwittingly opened himself to oppression, the blood of Jesus is the greatest antitoxin in the Universe. When we command Satan to be gone because of the blood of Jesus, he is gone. Scars may be left from his past damage on us, but we will be spared from the future he had planned.

This is no small battle we are engaged in. Paul said:

> For we wrestle not against flesh and blood, but against principalities, against powers, against the rulers of the darkness of this world, against spiritual wickedness in high places.
>
> —Ephesians 6:12 KJV

But God is far greater than all the powers of darkness. He owns the Universe. And He will give us the discernment we need to see Satan for what he is.

WHEN THE TEMPTER COMES
in red tights and sprouting horns,
it is easy to cry,
"Get thee hence!"
  But when he comes
  in scintillating iridescence,
  softly, in ballet slippers
    or wearing shiny boots
    and an equally shiny smile,
    or riding a white horse
    with a silver saddle
    gleaming in the moonlight,
it is hard to recognize
and reprimand him.
  Give me discernment, Lord,
  and courage to send him
  fleeing down the road.
                    —Wilma Burton

7

Please Tell Her Something for Me (For Guilt)

Guilt is a by-product of all broken relationships, including death. Psychologists recognize guilt to be as much a culprit as stress in causing many emotional disturbances; and sometimes they try to eradicate that guilt by simply telling their patients to forget it. But no one can forget guilt, and God's answer is still the best one anyone has found. By Him we may be reconciled to God and man. By seeking His forgiveness and then forgiving others, we become free of guilt now and forever—free to live happy, whole, and healthy lives.[5]

But what if the guilt is produced from a relationship broken by death? How can we be reconciled and forgiven by one who has already died? The guilt in grief is normal, but how is it to be overcome? If it is dangerous for us to carry unforgiven guilt—Parkes for one found in a study of mental patients a high incidence of guilt and unresolved grief [6]—how can we finally resolve all the "if only's" we have about a lost loved one? We can make it right with God, but how can we ever make it right with our lost one?

Some have found help just by telling God the whole story and experiencing His forgiveness. Others have found help in also telling some other person, such as a pastor, substituting his hearing and understanding heart for the one who can no longer hear and understand. I was helped by imagining that God would make it right with Sondra for me. Even as I was praying my "Please tell her this for me" prayers, I realized that such passing of information probably does not go on in that burden-free place. (Our "mystic sweet communion" is our shared fellowship with our Savior.) The state of our loved ones there is surely one of deep contentment which would seem to be impossible without their oblivion to our troubles here. But I was helped by imagining that it was possible.

I gathered up all the guilts I could and asked God to talk to Sondra about them. I had not spent enough time with her. I had corrected her too often about her messy room, with anger and with little help to motivate her into better self-discipline. I had not baked enough cakes with her, or talked to her enough, or found out enough of her problems. Did she know how much I loved her? I wished I had sat by her bed during that last nap at home rather than taking a walk while Brian baby-sat. And I wished I had been more of a persistent mother at the hospital to check up on things better. I wished I had insisted that she be admitted sooner. I wished she had been better prepared for her trip to heaven. "Please tell her all of this for me, dear Lord in heaven," I prayed.

A strange prayer, perhaps, but no more strange than the good advice we hear to tell the deceased "Good-bye." Both are therapies only for us, to clear our minds of useless grief and harmful guilt. My prayer asking God to tell her things helped to ease my anguish.

Many of my prayers were written instead of spoken. I reread them now and recall the anguish. Though they appear exaggerated cries, my memory tells me that they were understatements.

> Thank you, Lord, that Jesus conquered death. Her change is so real. So recently warm and here and cuddling up for love. Then so sick. Why didn't we make sure they cared enough about her sore throat?

Or did they? They should treat everything. . . . But His peace is Real. And it passes understanding.

. . . Snow covers her "old home" while it waits for renewal. And life goes on. As she would wish. How tempting to just grieve and fade away and join her. Heaven sounds very good, Lord, and seems very near.

. . . O Lord, may I pray again on paper? It is still hard. Help me be patient. Tomorrow is Wednesday. I don't like Wednesdays. They are even worse than Fridays. I don't like my selfishness and all this pity I have for myself. . . .

How much may I think about her? Can I find out more about the end? Should I? I know this is useless. . . . Is there a schedule there? What are your people doing now? I wish for a glimpse. Just a glimpse. I know I can get it in your Book and from your Spirit's deposit in my life. Thank you . . . your peace comes. It is well with my soul. . . . Is it with hers? Oh to be fit and operable to do your will. I delight to do your will.

. . . Are a person's first ten years sometimes the best?

. . . Dear Lord, frustration seems to be mounting again. Panic sometimes sets in about her last hours. Finding out about that overwhelming infection that could not be stopped doesn't really help. Fever came down. Prayer perhaps was answered, and then her heart stopped. Something in me, the idealist, says, "God can answer this prayer, but this other way is His way and it is better." But what really happened was that air couldn't get down the infected windpipe and without oxygen her heart stopped.

. . . I wish I had gone down that hall to see her. Did part of me know she wouldn't make it? And in my weakness, did I know I couldn't bear it?

. . . You could raise her even now. It would be a bad idea; I understand that. And it would be awful on her to have to leave heaven. I know your ways are good. I wish wish wish I had told her that the mask wasn't her problem, that she would have been much worse without it.

. . . O Lord our Lord. How excellent is thy name in all the earth. And yet it is hard. Please show us how to bear it. Or to let you. Dr. Edman is there. She sure doesn't know many people there. I hope they are friendly to her.

. . . I wish I had been her nurse. I wish I could help sick children. I miss her, you know. . . . I wish there were more sensitive nurses. Someone should have told her about that mask. Why didn't I think of it? I was there.

. . . O Lord, how long till I care whether the sun is shining or not?

That in me that wants to claw the air and scream at separation was taught by things that only seem to be, not are. There is within a Spirit, striving quietly to tell my heart another thing. I listen and once again His truth does stop my clawing heart awhile.

"O Lord my God, I cried to Thee for help, and Thou didst heal me" (Psalm 30:2 NAS).

8

Thank You, Lord, for Sondra
(For Painful Memories)

I still see her everywhere. Her little treasures turn up at unexpected moments and memories crowd each room of the house.

—M. H. Read[7]

Memories stab with their own unique pain, but something Paul said in Philippians 1:3 helped me and is still helping me. He wrote to his friends, "I thank God upon every remembrance of you." The friends that Paul was thanking God for were still alive, but this principle of saying "thank you" works for the memories of one who is dead, too. When the pain of a memory strikes, we can purposely turn it into a prayer. Saying "Thank you, Lord, for Sondra" has helped turn many sad memories into thankful ones. God's voice is silent in that answer, but His presence is very real.

There is a principle here that goes beyond turning the sadnesses of memories into gratitude.

Paul said, "In everything give thanks; for this is God's will for you in Christ Jesus" (I Thessalonians 5:18 NAS). Giving thanks for everything—for the good and the bad—is just what the great Physician ordered. I will not pretend that I obeyed Him in thanking Him for Sondra's death. I have been terribly slow in believing God enough to do that. No wonder God had to command us to praise Him for everything. We just do not naturally do it.

43

But God knows that great benefits come to us when we thank Him. He knows that He made us to glorify Him and that we are happiest when we are doing that. He also knows how Satan has all but ruined us all. God's remedy, even for us who are now a part of His family because of Jesus, is for us to praise Him—to purposely remove our focus from the environment around us (or in us) that provokes our thanklessness and to focus on God, from whose hand come all things.

When we do that, God is free to work. Our bitterness is a wall that will not allow God's Spirit to flow through us, for God will not violate our free wills. But our thankfulness breaks down the walls. Our thankfulness is our acknowledgment that God is still God, that He has all the power and the love of the Universe. It is us resting in His ability to do right—to re-create if He sees best, or to do nothing we can see if He sees best.

We may choose bitterness or thankfulness. God does not force our responses. His Spirit in us prompts us to praise Him, but never—not in the Garden of Eden and not now —does He force us to do His will. Always we have a choice. It is a choice that should take little thought: Do we want bitterness, despair, and resulting sickness; or do we want thankfulness, hope, and health? For myself, I know what I should choose, but I don't always choose it. Too often I look at the trouble and refuse to praise God for it. Not only do I lose out on happiness but, worse, my attitude prevents God from even working on the difficulty.

I wanted to give Him freedom to work. I wanted to be done with bitterness and regrets. It was a long time coming, but finally I chose to praise Him.

> Thank you, God, for giving us Sondra: for her beauty and for her spirit of giving and for every memory that we will ever have of her. Thank you for trusting us to be her parents for almost eleven years.

Thank you, God, that in your wisdom you took her and spared her of the pain of living and the pain of perhaps dying a much harder death. Thank you for giving her now the pleasures of heaven. Thank you that for her dying is all over.

Thank you that I do not have to see reasons for things; that I can always know that You are in charge.

Thank you, God, that, because of Sondra, you have taught us how to live and how to die. For the peace and the comfort, as new as each day's needs. For the glimpse of heaven we have seen.

For the length of eternity we will all be spending with You—that forever that is now for Sondra and ahead of us.

And thank you, God, for the gift that I rediscover every time I believe you enough to thank you.

For anyone who has not by experience already learned God's secret of praise, Catherine Marshall will convince him in the praise chapter of her excellent book *Something More*.[8]

Giving thanks is not just the manner we come to God. It is the very method we enter into His gates (Psalm 100:4). Praise is the key that unlocks the doors of glory for us right now.

Communicating with God through prayer has been a most comforting experience for me. Answers that come, whether in times of desperately calling out for His help or in times of being still and knowing He is God, somehow prove God in a way that the finest logic cannot do. We ask and He answers; we seek Him and we know He is there; we thank Him and beautiful changes begin to happen:

YOU ARE THE FOUNTAIN, LORD

without You, I would be winter-grass
brown and lifeless.
   You keep me green
   as watercress in a flowing spring
   in late winter.
There is no yellow leafing
beneath the freshness of Your water.
   Every day is April,
   no summer draught,
   nights are wet dawns with dews,
   mornings are newborn.
Thank You for the coolness
of Your water from deep wells
giving abundance
to what would be paucity,
famine without You.

          —Wilma Burton

HIS WRITTEN WORD

My soul weeps because of grief;
Strengthen me according to Thy word.
        —Psalm 119:28 NAS

9
Needed: A New View of Death

Jesus became one of us "that through death He might render powerless him who had the power of death . . . and might deliver those who through fear of death were subject to slavery all their lives" (Hebrews 2:14, 15 NAS). At thirty-five, I was immature about death. Three grandparents had died in my lifetime; but though I loved them, I did not know them well. I don't recall ever attending anyone's funeral, not even Uncle Noel's.

Noel O. Lyons was my dad's best friend and was always as welcome in our home as we were. We loved him. We wouldn't believe that this big, virile, life-loving man had cancer. At eighteen I remember wishing and almost praying that it could have been me instead of him. Uncle Noel was the executive secretary for the Greater Europe Mission and was the financial lifeline for providing missionaries to that sadly neglected field. I couldn't imagine the work surviving without him. (It has; but there is still financial need for schools and churches.)

Uncle Noel did not get better. We knew it was to be our last visit with him that night in his apartment in Chicago. Aunt Billie was with him. It was hard on her and on all of us, seeing him so wasted. His body would not be fit for living in much longer.

Dying scared me. I hated to even look at Uncle Noel and hardly dared to talk to him. He died about two weeks later and I did not even go to the funeral.

That had been my one experience with death.

For a time in those same late teenage years I had toyed with the notion of reincarnation. I even found some Scripture, though taken out of context, that seemed to support what seemed to me to be an appealing possibility. Reincarnation would handle the problem of evil in the world quite neatly. I did much reading on the subject but finally put it away as a strange and unscriptural doctrine. Only occasionally would it slither out again, tempting my mind with its seeming mercy and logic.

But it has neither. Now that I have every hope of seeing and recognizing Sondra in heaven, I would hate to think that she is becoming someone else that I will never know. Nor do I see the logic of it as I look around at a world that keeps getting worse, not better. I believe that Jesus' teaching is crystal clear and that it does not indicate reincarnation for any of us.

My only other serious thinking about death was prompted by the "lump scare," as it is for so many other women (and for men with heart-attack-like chest pains). Three years before Sondra died I had a short hospital stay and some minor surgery. With the verdict that "all is well," I once again pushed the thought of my own death back into the Siberia of my mind. With it went all the contingent plans for the children, the review of a life that had accomplished so little, the thoughts about a funeral and the wondering how I would ever manage the slow and painful dying that was coming. Those were the thoughts, and I put them far away.

Except for the gnawing knowledge that someday my parents would die and that I knew I could never stand to lose them, I avoided as well as I could anything to do with death. I hated even to have an aquarium of fish in the house because I knew that they would die.

I needed to pray, as David had, "Lord, make me to know

mine end, and the measure of my days, what it is; that I may know how frail I am. Behold, thou hast made my days as an handbreadth; and mine age is as nothing before thee: verily every man at his best state is altogether vanity" (Psalm 39:4–5 KJV).

Several months before Sondra died I would periodically wake up in a cold sweat from a bad dream. I couldn't quite remember the dream, but I knew it was about dying and I was afraid. Wasn't I a Christian? Why was I afraid? Or was I only a phony? Why the night terror, the awful heaviness, the fear?

Whether my dreams were somehow a preparation or just a reflection of my fear of death, they showed me that my view needed some schooling. I was to receive the first of my new understanding from the S.O.S. prayers with their proof that God existed and that He cared and that death was not the end. But I would also need the deep and steady assurance that written facts can give. So now that death had stalked into our home and stolen our Sondra, I began an extensive search into God's written record.

I remember looking out into the snow-covered, star-studded silence that first night she had been buried and feeling lost and troubled. Where in the Universe were those "pleasures forevermore" that God had told me about just days before? It seemed that I could see and hear nothing from God. Even His beautiful creation was not piercing the doubt and sadness I was feeling. By the next morning the truth had slowly dawned on me that, as big as this death was to me, God was still on His throne; nothing had changed in heaven.

David, too, had had this feeling:

> Has God forgotten to be gracious? Or has He in anger withdrawn His compassion? Then I said, "It is my grief, that the right hand of the Most High has

changed." I shall remember the deeds of the Lord;
Surely I will remember Thy wonders of old. I will
meditate on all Thy work and muse on Thy deeds.
—Psalm 77:9-12 NAS

Like David, I began to look back to God's work in history,
back into the pages of Scripture.

10

Death Is Deliverance

Job

From Job I learned that bearing a loss is harder than dying. Job's family died and they were not even the ones being tested. This was new thinking for me. Between Sondra and me, perhaps my part now was the harder part. I thought back to her hospital suffering and knew that then her part had surely been hardest. How I had wished that I could have traded places with her. But what about now? Would I wish this grieving on her? Death was not unique with her, even the unpleasant way it happened. The process of dying is not pleasant for anyone. And unless Jesus returns first, there is not one of us who will be spared that termination of living as we know it. For Sondra it is all over —that hard part. She will never have to go through any struggles or dying ever again. Perhaps grieving is harder than dying. If it is, I would choose to be the one to do it instead of her. I will bear it for her.

Hezekiah

From Hezekiah I learned something, too. It was time for Hezekiah to die; but he pleaded with God for more time. And he got it: fifteen extra years. They were not good years, for Hezekiah behaved foolishly (Isaiah 38 and II Kings 20). Why did God answer Hezekiah's prayer? If the reason was Hezekiah's great faith, then Hezekiah would seem to be almost Godlike in his great achievement. I believe that God answered that prayer as a lesson to all of us not to bargain with God but to accept in trust God's way as best. Persistence in prayer is right only when we are certain that our request is in line with God's will.

Sometimes God's best way *is* more time. Healings do happen. But when they don't, *that* is God's best way. Satan would like to plague us with guilts: "If only you had more faith" or "If only you weren't such a sinner." But that is not God's way. He wants our complete trust; and He never asks of us more than He has given, so He would not require more faith than He had given us for our measure. Healing has nothing to do with us, really. If we think it does, if we become puffed up about our great faith, Satan has won an important victory.

That is what I learned from Hezekiah's extra fifteen years.

Lazarus's Silence and Jesus' Tears

How I wished that Lazarus had talked about where he had been while he was dead. And yet I learned as much from his silence as from what he might have said. He was silent, I think, because he could not speak of it. Either God had caused him to forget or else there were no words at all to describe his experience. How merciful of God to keep the beauty of heaven from us. We would not want to go on living here if we knew the experience that awaited us.

And I learned from Jesus' tears at Lazarus's grave (John 11:1–45). I don't think Jesus cried for the same reasons you and I cry at death. He knew He would see Lazarus soon even if He did not raise him; and He knew that Mary and Martha would see him soon because He was in fact going to raise him. I think Jesus wept for our human condition, the blindness that keeps us in the dark about how things really are. He wept because we could not see beyond death's heavy curtain. He wept because He knew He could heal our blindness if only we would believe, but so many of us will not believe. And perhaps He also wept because He had to call Lazarus back from a place that He Himself was missing greatly. I am thankful for Jesus' tears. They help me. They have helped to bring me to a new view of death.

Death is not the ogre we make it. Even in the psalms during times when most people did not understand or even believe in the afterlife, God's truth came through the Scripture. David writes, "But God will redeem my soul from the power of the grave: for he shall receive me" (Psalm 49:15 KJV).

11

Jesus' Words

Your fathers did eat manna in the wilderness and are dead.... I am the living bread which came down from heaven: if any man eat of this bread, he shall live for ever....

—John 6:49, 51 KJV

THIS LAZY MORNING

I do not feel like rising
to the small demands
that are my day.
  The phone, a silent raven
  on the wall, harbinger of more demands
  or gloom: I cringe to hear
  it ring. Keep it silent,
Lord, for at least a while.
I need to drink of Your sweet wine
and let the tentacles from Your green vine
  wind themselves around my soul.
Strengthen me with words
from men who knew You well.
Let this lassitude fall like sand
from feet that in Your Galilee
knew the lap of water's edge.
  —Wilma Burton

Jesus' words have comforted people through the ages, and they did their work for me. Even his harsh words "Let the dead bury their dead" (Matthew 8:22 KJV) show us death from God's vantage point. Jesus knew that no amount of our care can do a thing for them. The worlds are separate. Let the dead be in their world and let the living not fool themselves or waste their time here thinking that they can do anything for the dead.

I was beginning to learn that God does not see death the way we human beings do. We see this side and get the wrong picture. We fix up the leavings of death and pretend it does not smell or look bad; but it does. The part we can see is very bad. But God sees the eternal man, the personality that outlives the body, the soul and spirit that survive death for life eternal.

"Let not your heart be troubled," Jesus said, "neither let it be afraid. *I go to prepare a place for you . . . if it were not so, I would have told you*" (John 14:27, 2 KJV).

If it were not so He would have told us! There it is. God Himself just asking us to please believe Him. The place Jesus speaks of is beyond our capacity for understanding, but we can believe Him that it exists. He knows because He has been there and is about to return. If it were not so, He would have told us! His statement rings absolutely true to me.

"Come unto me, all ye that labor and are heavy laden, and I will give you rest. Take my yoke upon you, and learn of me; for I am meek and lowly in heart: and ye shall find rest unto your souls. For my yoke is easy, and my burden is light" (Matthew 11:28–30 KJV). I wondered how Jesus could say that. He had a yoke that was full of such sin-bearing agony that I couldn't fathom the mystery or horror of it, but He said that His yoke was easy and that you and I could have that yoke.

I found it was humility that made Jesus' yoke easy (Matthew 11:29). Jesus wore His humanity so lightly that life for Him, and even death, was really just a matter of thankfully accepting whatever came. Since He did not expect to be served, He happily served. Since He did not expect happiness as His right, He went about doing good. But in it all, He was also fulfilled and happy.

That was the yoke I needed. If I had it, grief would all but disappear. Not that I would be without hopes or dreams, but they would be at God's disposal, just as Jesus' hopes and dreams were. Jesus demonstrated the ultimate in humility when He gave up heaven for us (Philippians 2:6), and He "thought it not robbery." If I could take that yoke of humility in exchange for my heavy, ego-centered humanity, nothing could throw me. With the mind of Christ, I too would think it "not robbery" no matter what tragedy came into my life.

Jesus died so that all of us could have that mind; so we could live out the rest of our lives here by God's Spirit just as Jesus did, easy yoke and all. We who have come to Him for rest have already experienced His easy yoke at times, but we could wear it much more often. The choice is ours, whether to keep on carrying our own loads or to relinquish them to Him.

"Today you shall be with Me in Paradise" (Luke 23:43 NAS) were Jesus' words to a man being executed with Him. I love those words. Sometimes I wonder what other words they said later on that evening in Paradise.

If our loved one was not a believer, it would seem that heavenly comfort is most discomforting. However there is always the hope that some silent transaction of belief was made even at the point of dying when he had no strength to indicate his new life. I would far rather dwell on that possibility than on the despair that we will be forever separated from our loved one.

I wonder if anyone who heard the transaction between Jesus and the dying thief told his family about it—that God Himself had forgiven Him and assured Him of eternal life. How comforting that would have been for them to know.

> "Woman, behold, your son!" Then He said to the disciple, "Behold, your mother!"
> —John 19:26–27 NAS

It must have been horrible for Mary to watch her son die that terrible death. The Father in heaven must have suffered anguish, too, knowing that He could have stopped the agony but instead having to forsake His Son. But Mary in her humanity lacked God's understanding. Once I wondered how she ever stood it all.

Now I see how these words spoken from the cross helped Mary. I think they reminded her of something Jesus had been gently telling her throughout His life—that He was not really her son at all. He had given her this seemingly harsh message first in the temple when He was twelve (Luke 2:49), later while working a miracle (John 2:4), and again while speaking to the multitudes (Matthew 12:48–49). Now He was speaking the same message from the cross. Surely the angel who had told Mary that Jesus would be born had been right—this was the Son of God (Luke 1:35).

My sorrow for Mary and her unspeakable grief has turned to thankfulness to Jesus for the way He cares for. all of us. We are all His "mother and His brothers," and just as the Father had grieved, just as the angels in heaven and earth itself had grieved, so all of us who have come to know and love Jesus—to worship Him as Lord—have also grieved, no less than Mary herself. But memory's grief of Jesus' death is countered by our joy at His victory, by our

belief that Jesus is even now at the right hand of the Father
where He belongs, making intercession for each of us, for
our every need all of the time.

"Jesus . . . said . . . , 'Destroy this temple, and in three
days I will raise it up' . . . he spake of the temple of his
body" (John 2:19, 21 KJV). He did it. Jesus had prophe-
sied His resurrection and it had happened. He was really
raised from the dead.

Years ago I had studied all the gospel accounts of the
resurrection and was already convinced of their truth. In
the face of the evidence as reported by the apostles and
others, no theory of hallucination, stolen body, or any
other theory holds any weight at all. Those who reported
the resurrection were so thoroughly convinced that it had
happened that they willingly gave up their lives for their
beliefs. Jesus had risen and so would they; they were convinced, and so am I: "For we know that if the earthly tent
which is our house is torn down, we have a building from
God, a house not made with hands, eternal in the heavens"
(II Corinthians 5:1 NAS).

I THANK YOU, LORD, FOR BEING BORN

in the cold of Winter.
When death was evident
in brown of grass and tree
and overcast of sky,
You came.

I thank You, Lord,
that Your death-cross
was on Spring's hill
and when you rolled
the boulder alone,
said that first "Good Morning!"

to Your world, the dogwood
and the jonquils burst
through winter-gloves to bloom.

Thank You, Lord, for giving
to my leaf-brown heart
Your Eternal Spring.
                            —Wilma Burton

"He sent his word, and healed them, and delivered them
from their destructions" (Psalm 107:20 KJV). God's Word
brings healing to our hurts, wisdom and grace for our living
and dying. The truths that have been contained in God's
Word for years are modern answers to modern problems.
One has only to try them to prove them true. Some examples of these keys to mental health and successful living
are:

   to be forgiven, freed of guilt (Psalm 51, Psalm 32:2-5)
   to mourn and be comforted (Matthew 5:4)
   to not carry undue and continued stress (Matthew
      11:29)
   to examine yourself (I Corinthians 11:28)
   to share your true feelings (Ephesians 4:15)
   to be thankful (I Thessalonians 5:18)
   to reach out to others (Galatians 6:10).

The One who made us has given us many keys to understanding so that we may operate the way He meant us to.

Scripture is a gold mine of wisdom and understanding
about death and about life. We need it more than we need
bread. It is life for our souls. For me it is also armor
against the temptation not to believe. Thoughts often invade my mind, and though they are fleeting they sound so
right for a time:

"This God business is only psychological, just concocted
nonsense. People just fool themselves with it—and, worse,
they waste their time."

My only defense at those thoroughly frustrating times is to get God's Word in my head and to once again see life from His point of view. As I believe Him and discover again how beautifully His way works, falsehood is once again unmasked and the brainwashing of "things as they seem" is corrected by God's light of truth.

God's Word is highly potent for learning to die, for learning to live, and in it all for learning to really believe God.

I AM NOT SATISFIED WITH CRUMBS
from Your banquet table.
I would know Your full-course meal
complete with aperitif
of sweet communion wine
and over all the frescoed banner
of Your love
   stretching
from dawn to sunset
with the sunlit, starlit, moonlit
wonder of Your presence.
     —Wilma Burton

Through Scripture and prayer we have direct access to God's view, immediate help for any need. Let God be our first source of help, not our last. We can receive help from other books, too. They have many right answers. Our human condition has been well-observed and we human beings all have similar needs and responses. But the timing and intensity of those needs are different in each of us. God alone can give us each just the right answer at just the right time.

As we begin to practice God's presence through Scripture and prayer, more difficult portions of the Bible begin to make more and more sense. Words like these become the norm: "Rejoice evermore. Pray without ceasing. In every thing give thanks" (I Thessalonians 5:16–18 KJV). We can rejoice right now because God provides strength for our troubles and forever because of the place He is preparing for us. We can pray without ceasing as soon as we stop hiding anything from God. And we can give thanks in everything as we begin to see that God does know what He is about.

Exciting secrets begin to burst upon us as we open our Bibles and as we open our hearts in prayer to the God we find there.

HELP FROM EARTH

God speaks to us through the voice of the bells, and through the voice of his ministers. He speaks, as to Elijah, through the soft breath of the wind, and as to Job, through the clap of thunder. He speaks to us through our own thoughts when we submit them to Him, through our feelings and intuitions. We often ask him great questions to which he does not at once—or ever—reply. But he tells us day after day what we need to be told for the nurture and direction of our person. Grace is given drop by drop.

—Paul Tournier [9]

...He causes His sun to rise on the evil and the good, and sends rain on the righteous and the unrighteous.

—Matthew 5:45 NAS

12
Ties That Bind

God's peace is real, but rare is the one who is constantly claiming it. For me there were long, in-between times of being "down." It was during those times that I learned about the natural comforts that each of us may appropriate along that long, slow road of grief.

As I write this, I wonder, Why do we need all this help? Why cannot one idea that comforts, one activity, or one act of kindness be enough? Why do we keep going back into the depths of despair, always needing to be pulled back by someone or something?

And then I know: it is because our ties are so strong. They have bound us to our loved one in a thousand ways and they can never really be broken. As we try to leave, emotionally and mentally, our ties are like an elastic cord that quickly snaps us back at every reminder. That snapping back hurts. To leave, we need help over and over, until one day, though still connected, our cords lose some of their elasticity and we can return to the thoughts and memories at will, without so much grief. But for our grief, help is available. Grief is a process and processes take time. One way to describe this process is as if it were a long, hard climb from a deep, canyonlike valley. And though grief has its stages, they are never as evident as any book would indicate, at least not without time's perspective.

When a loved one dies, you enter the valley of the shadow of death. Over on the other side you can almost see through the haze the place where he is going and it is most beautiful. You may not follow him there; you must return to the flatlands above. The road you take is jagged, with many hairpin turns, and often you wonder if you are going up or down. You are so long in the dense growth of the foothills that you can't tell where you have been or where you are going and you wish you could see light somewhere.

Gradually you make progress. Manna, if you will, keeps you going with the various strengths it provides. Sometimes a fellow traveler keeps you company; and many are the people above calling down to you that you are coming along fine and soon you'll be there.

One day, as you rest, you look down at the road you have taken and you are startled by your progress. You wonder how you could ever have been way down there. You look up briefly as you rest, and there it is—the sun shining above you. You get up and continue on, always wondering where the road will turn next. Often you may feel as you did at the very beginning, that you are being lifted over some of the rough spots. Strength comes at those times in such proportion to make your feet almost like deer's feet (Habakkuk 3:19) and you know that it is heavenly manna giving you that different strength. Mostly you eat the daily bread along the way and are strengthened well for your journey.

The incline near the top is so gradual that you may not even know when you reach it, but one day you will look down and see most of your traveled road below and for the first time you will understand the way that you have taken out of that valley of the shadow of death.

Edgar Jackson describes our ties this way: "Our grief is rooted in emotions that reach out in all directions beyond our physical being. Only as we literally pull up by the roots the feelings that no longer have a soil to sustain them are we able to let them take root again elsewhere and be nurtured with life-giving experience." [10]

Some ties are stronger than others, so some roots are harder to pull than others. In parents who have lost a child, guilt and love combine in a strange mixture. Those parents were providers but they could not provide the normal threescore and ten. It was their love that brought life and thus made death a possibility. A mother, overwhelmed with awe at being a partner with God in birth's creation, looks on at death as only a helpless bystander. Those parental ties of helplessness, of love's awful and unabated missing, and the abrupt end of the great duty and pleasure of parenting—those ties are strong indeed.

But all ties are strong, welding each to his loved one in a unique relationship. We need help in our leaving. There is no easy formula for it all. Grief is hard work and takes a great deal of time, but there are unmistakable helps along the way.

I AM OUT OF STEP TODAY, LORD

in Your dance of life.
I am tripping over my own feet
in Eden-lost. Gone the minuet
that only yesterday
knew my curtsy.
   Let me know the rhythm
   of Your timpani, wind
   through the harp on the willow.
And though no ballet-joy
is mine today, let my movements
be in tune with the cricket song,
the meadowlark, the music
of Your world—and if I cannot
dance before Your Ark
in David-joy—let me
at least walk sedately.
            —Wilma Burton

13

Grief's First Stages and Delays

"And what stage of grief are you in? . . . Depression? How nice. I'm into anger. I'll be glad when I get as far as you."

The way the books read, we might expect such neat responses, but of course there is no tidy or exact stage that is recognizable to the one who is in it. For some, even the mention of stages is about as comforting as hearing a sales pitch for a trip to hell.

But grief does have stages, and in order for our healthy acceptance of death to happen, each of us must pass through those stages. In so doing we may be assured that "we happen to our grief rather than having our grief happen to us." [11] Elisabeth Kübler-Ross has done extensive and compassionate research among over two hundred terminal patients.[12] She finds that all have similar responses upon learning of their terminal illness, and that their responses are the same ones that the bereaved pass through in their grief. The stages are denial, anger, bargaining, depression, and acceptance. She feels that tranquilizing drugs only prolong the process, as each stage must eventually be faced. One must go through the stage of depression eventually, for there is in fact something to be depressed about.[13]

Others who have studied grief agree that grief is a process, though they may name the stages differently. Parkes describes the stages as denial, alarm, the urge to search, anger, guilt, feeling of internal loss or mutilation, identification phenomena, and acceptance.[14] In his helpful book

Good Grief, Granger Westberg names the stages shock, emotion, depression, panic, guilt, and hostility.[15]

Since everyone's experience within each of the stages is different, my own will serve only as an example, not a model.

I seemed to pass through the first three stages in the fifteen-minute interval between receiving Walt's phone call from the hospital and then hearing the final news with him there. I had relapses back into those stages, but most of my grief would be in dealing with the last stage before acceptance—depression. I am very well acquainted with that stage.

Denial comes upon all of us with the first news of a death and immediately produces a physical response that protects us for a while, normally from a few minutes to a few days. That response is shock. Our body responses slow down, we become weaker and for a time we are numbed against the reality that will demand deep and concentrated effort for the next months of our lives.

My fast-beating heart, aroused from a deep sleep, became almost stilled with Walt's news on the phone that night. I dressed quickly, but it felt like slow motion to me. I remember wondering, "Do you comb your hair when your daughter has just died?" Shock was protecting me from the onslaught of the truth, though even then it seemed to have completely settled in my head—Sondra was dead.

When the hospital chaplain came out of the intensive-care unit shaking his head that she had not made it, I remember whispering, "She is safe now." I think he bent down, probably wondering about my state of mind and how much care I would need. He seemed surprised and was wordless when all I said to him was, "She is safe in the arms of Jesus."

Shock is the first cushion of comfort. Anger is the next,

acting as a safety valve against emotional damage to our health.

All my energy seemed to have gone with hers, and I did not imagine I could even walk out of that building; I never benefited from the experience that railing anger brings. Mine would be the kind that sneaks out, and it would not come until later. Kübler-Ross suggests a "scream room" for the normal expression of anger at death. She does not advise tranquilizing the bereaved out of this normal and healthy response, hospital convenience notwithstanding.

My first anger came as a subtle and fleeting one, not at God but at the people who came to comfort us that morning. Though I did not lash out at anyone, I wished that they would feel sorry for the right person—not us, but Sondra. I was momentarily angered by their sympathy for us. Parkes speaks of the universality of that feeling: "Even talk about grief angers one who is still searching." [16]

But I did not experience the questioning anger that often asks, "Why did this happen to me?" Previously critical of that response to tragedy (would I wish my misfortune on someone else?), I was already deprogrammed from having that attitude.

Neither Walt nor I ever experienced any large anger. Beginning some six months after Sondra had died, we would find ourselves becoming extra angry at each other quite often. That may have been a delayed, pent-up anger about our daughter's death, but it passed as winter became spring.

Bargaining first came for me as I drove to the hospital and silently prayed for God to restore Sondra to life if it was His will. Bargaining would make a reappearance some six hours later. We had left the hospital in those dark hours before dawn with instructions for them to leave Sondra's body as it was until the undertaker came in the morning.

During all the time that her lifeless body was lying under the sheet, I often reminded God that if He wanted to He could bring her back again. That was my bargaining and denial too, perhaps, though I do not understand exactly how one bargains over one who is dead. Bargaining is quite natural for one who is terminally ill and still goes on hoping, but how does anyone think he can bargain for a dead body? Perhaps he hopes for a visit by the spirit or, as I had done, hopes against hope for that short time just after death for a return to life. My prayer was the only way I found myself bargaining.

Or was I exercising faith? Was it shock or was it faith that immediately knew that Sondra was dead and calmly accepted it? Was it shock or was it faith that helped me say she was safe in Jesus' arms? I do not know of any study that has been done to show the effect that God's Spirit has on grief's first stages. Perhaps such a study would not be possible, first, because relationships, guilt feelings, and personal temperaments all enter into our first reactions to a death, and, second, because it is difficult to measure or predict the length of the stages themselves.

I do not personally know much about shock, bargaining, or anger, but I make up for my ignorance there in all I know about depression.

Depression would become a new companion before the dawn of that first day. Life is so hard, I thought as I lay in bed waiting for morning. Life is good, too, much of the time; I knew that, but it can get so terribly hard. In later days depression would strike me more cynically as I would think, What a terrible trick life plays on all of us, looking as if it is so good but all the time poised and waiting to drop some tragedy on us. Trouble, to me, was a huge boulder held in the teeth of a giant crane—held until, when we least expected it, it would be dropped on us, smashing all our hopes and dreams and our love and trust in life itself. I feared future boulders poised against me and at times questioned the friendliness of whoever it was that worked the switches. There were others that I loved and someday I would lose them, too. How do all of us go on knowing all that? Why do we insist on acting as if life is fine and good when it isn't at all? I wondered during those times of depression. Guilt, of course, often accompanied that depression.

All the stages except shock must eventually be worked through. Shock is a delay to that work, and a welcome one; but there is another delay imposed on the bereaved, a respite to the work ahead: "busy-ness."

"Keep busy" is probably good advice, but it happens quite naturally in the first days after a loss. Perhaps that is the main advantage or reason for the funeral rites among us. Funeral preparations do keep one busy—selecting the casket, the clothes, the time and type of funeral, accommodations for the people who come from out of town.

If being busy is a help, Walt and I were fortunate indeed. Jon had become ill at my parents' home in Wheaton and was driven back to us along with the other children, who each took their turns being sick at home while Jon stayed out the week in the hospital in an oxygen tent. Our fears were heavy—would the same germs that killed Sondra take someone else? But our activity also provided respite from the grief work ahead.

Outside concerns and business do not cancel grief: they only delay it. But that delay is needed as it gives the mind a chance to catch up, to slowly adjust itself to the confronting reality.

Even as they delay our work, and replete as the funeral is with dignity, funeral preparations and all the imposed activities also usher in the reality of the loss. A body has to be disposed of. It is there and it is real. Plans and decisions must be made.

Walt and I discovered each other's feelings about funerals. For him, society's ways are all wrong. He did not even care to ever view Sondra's body or risk distorting the true living image he had of her. For me, a formal and final good-bye would be helpful. We compromised and had a private burial with a memorial service afterward in the funeral home. (It would be good if people would discuss their views and preferences about funerals before the time of need.)

I viewed her body the day before the service with my mom and sister and pastor and his wife. "Isn't death strange!" he had said. It is. That wasn't Sondra in there. She looked lovely, but much older than her almost eleven years. I wished I could have fixed her hair better, the way I always did it. But we left within minutes, without touching her and without shedding tears.

One is fortunate if he has a pastor guiding him in his decisions about the funeral. Ours, Gordon Hanstad, was most helpful. He was able to discern our needs and wishes and did not impose his own will on us at all. He arranged with the funeral director to come to our home, where they both helped us in our selections. Our pastor tries to be with all his bereaved families for that task so that they are not financially taken advantage of in time of need.

Our pastor also helped us plan a service we remember with gratitude for its peacefulness. He read some words that her Sunday school teacher had written about her—a beautiful tribute about her filled with the assurance that she was in fact one of God's children. I liked hearing someone else say that she had seen qualities in Sondra that I had so often prayed would become part of her—inner beauty, poise, helpfulness, gentleness. I also liked the singing of a beautiful song that had just been composed by my songwriter friend. Walt, for whom green things flourish and for whom God is almost visible in the garden, especially loved the chorus of that song:

> The grass will always wither,
> The flower it will fade.
> His love will last eternally;
> I shall not be dismayed.

I liked hearing our pastor's clear message of God's plan for all of us. I liked having the people come past us as they left. There was no casket, so we were able to experience God's love in extra measure in that hour in the quiet tears and hugs and in the sincere caring I saw in their eyes.

Since individuals have different needs and preferences, the funerals they plan should be tailored to meet their needs and not be bound by anyone's tradition.

I AM GLAD YOU SAID "GOOD MORNING"

on that first Easter.
 At the sound of Your voice
 flowers leaped from winter beds
 to festoon Your feet with golden heads
 while a hundred dawns
 gloried the eastern sky
 in one. Birds sang.
Death lost its stranglehold
on earth. The moment You spoke
the winter-stone rolled away.
 Today's "Good Morning"
 claims once more
the Triumph You knew that day
when over the chasm of the grave
You gave Forever Life
to fragmented, broken clay.
—Wilma Burton

14
Grief Work Begins

. . . put thou my tears into thy bottle.
—Psalm 56:8

"You mean God knows how much tears we will need for our whole life?"

It was Jon's question about the psalmist's belief that God keeps our tears in a bottle. The four younger children were talking one day not long before Sondra died. I was making supper and remember thinking how very charming children are and how much they teach us. Sondra told her brother and sisters that God probably did give us all the tears we needed because He knew all about us—how long we would live and all our reasons for crying.

"God sure is smart," Jon said, "to give us how much tears we need."

At that point Sondra's little bottle was almost full.

If God does keep our tears in a bottle, most of us must have a very large one. Tears announce that the reality of loss has hit and that denial and its accompanying shock and numbness are wearing off. Tears come frequently and uninvited for months and sometimes surprise one even years after a loss. I have talked to women whose loss has occurred twenty and even thirty years ago, and, in speaking of their child, the tears come freely. I can understand that. Although the immediate work of tears—of venting the hurt—is over, the memories of the times when tears were

75

needed release them again with the same ache as when they were first shed.

For me, tears came often at first. I did not try to hide them from the children, at least not the quiet ones. Jon and Janna and Kristi each needed to know that they, too, were important to me; and if I had not cried about losing Sondra, they might have decided that I wouldn't miss them either. They also needed to know that their own tears were natural and right. I saved my loud sobbing for the times alone—during a drive to the hospital or while filling a tub with water.

But you can't cry all the time. Tears must be dried and a hard look at the situation must begin. Freud rightly coined the phrase "grief work" long ago (1917). He found that people who had not done their grief work suffered from many various maladies. His interest in the responsibility of past problems for present problems led him to a lifelong interest in the interpretation of people's sexual past. His pioneering mind opened the door for many schools of thought, many of which are out of style now, but his work on grief still stands.

At first I was puzzled by the term "grief work." I had imagined that grief was something that happened to me and that I had nothing to do but bear it. I wondered what "work" I would have to do. Now I know. The work is the difficult mental labor of going over events and memories and trying to make them all fit together comfortably in your head.

This work is essential if we are to recover; for grief imposes an immense shock to the system—to the physical, emotional, mental, and spiritual system. New adjustment is required in every part of us. By an act of the will we might say that we accept the death, that our loved one is gone forever, but it will be a long time before the brain receives that information in every one of its cells.

Proof that this belief is slow in coming is in what happens in our first waking moments. For a few brief seconds we are oblivious to the fact of our loss, but it suddenly comes crashing into our conscious mind with full force, and once again the pain is as if all of it has just happened.

At certain times during the day, for very brief interludes, we may become so engrossed in a thought or an action that we momentarily forget our loss; but every time we remember, the hurt is back pounding its truth in us once again. Gradually and so slowly the loss becomes part of us, and one day we are able to put our total mind to a task and not suddenly be jolted back into a forgotten reality. Then we will know that we are accepting our loss in every cell of our brain.

That is the work ahead for everyone who experiences the loss of a loved one.

Grief work usually begins with the coping with death itself. Walt brought me to my first coping with some much needed stern words: "Look, Hon. Sondra is dead. But everyone has to die—you, me, everyone. With you moping around here it's as if you have already died. You're no good to anyone this way."

Harsh remarks like this, if we take them, can help us to face the reality of death. A friend who came to our door a few days later said, hugging me, "You will never see her again. I know it's hard, isn't it?" She later apologized for an unfeeling attitude she thought she had in that visit, but I know now that her words were most helpful. Dr. Ronald Ramsey, a psychologist who has had remarkable success in dealing with patients who have long-term symptoms of grief, will frequently confront them with those very words: "Your child is dead. You will never see your child again." (See Chapter 16.) That day my friend helped me begin to examine the truth of her words—in this life we will never see Sondra again. I needed help in facing that fact; and the sooner it was done, the better for my coping.

I tried to tell myself that maybe I was overreacting. Death does not excuse any of us. Only the time and manner of dying vary; so, in the larger view of it all, we need not mourn for anyone in particular but instead for everyone in general. I almost convinced myself.

Another friend in whom kindness is tightly bound with truth (Proverbs 3:3) gently reminded me that in a sense grief is selfish, and that, necessary as it is, grief can make us so inward that we become totally unconcerned about other people. I needed to be coaxed away from my sorrow by such reminders, to be prodded into the work ahead in my journey through grief. If Sondra was all right, and I believed that she was, then wasn't my extreme sadness just self-pity? That began to look ugly to me and I did not want to wallow in it.

Ann Landers helped a young man who "couldn't accept his brother's death" when she replied, in effect, "I'm afraid that you have no choice. He is gone. Nothing can bring him back, so you have to accept it." She helped me, too.

Harsh words sometimes do us more good in the long run than soothing ones.

Part of our coping with death is coping with the way our loved one died. To help in this, one should find out all he can about the end. There is much of it we may never know, but we should find out what we can. This is part of following our urge to search, and, though it is sometimes painful and difficult, it should be followed.

How awful for one whose child has been the victim of a brutal kidnap and murder. How those last moments before death must haunt a parent with all their unknown terror. But not knowing and imagining are usually much worse than knowing the truth. Even in such hard situations, and even if it means confronting a murderer, one should make every effort to find out exactly what the end was like.

For us, there was just the desire to know Sondra's level of consciousness, her awareness, her possible attempt at communication with the nurse as death closed in on her. Had she struggled? Panicked? Called out for us? It was more than imagination that we needed to tame. Walt's last view of his daughter was of the hospital team trying to pound and shock her lifeless body back to life. Discovering the truth about her last consciousness would surely help us. Knowing could not be worse than the fears of our imaginations.

I called nurses and doctors until finally I was satisfied. And, even though I realize that someone may have just told us what we wanted to hear, we chose to believe that it was as they had said: Sondra was in a comatose condition when her heart stopped. She died peacefully.

All the medical people I checked with were most sympathetic about my search. I have since read recommendations to visit the doctor six weeks after a child's illness and death in order to discuss the illness and be relieved of guilt and self-incrimination.[17] Even though one friend had chided me with, "What good would it do to know?" those who answered my questions thought that asking them was good.

The specialist who had been called in explained why the tracheotomy had not saved her life. He drew a diagram of the bronchial tubes and lungs showing how the tube inserted into her neck could deliver its oxygen only as far as the bronchial tubes. It could not make the turn down the V to her lungs, where infection had made passage all but impossible.

I had hoped to discover the cause of her illness, but that has remained a loose end. Our doctor explained that the bacteria infection that killed her is in all of us all the time and that we do not know the conditions that helped those bacteria breed the very life out of her. I would always wonder if we had failed in helping her establish the correct health habits, such as washing her hands frequently, or insisting that she tell the truth—was she sick longer than we knew? Walt would frequently wonder if he had somehow brought home an especially lively strain of virus or bacteria from the lab at the school where he teaches. But our doctor said all that he could say and he hoped we would believe him—that there was nothing anyone could do.

So we began to try to fit those last pieces of her little life and death together in order to get on with the grief work ahead. A few at a time the doors were closing. We would have to learn to keep them closed.

15
Angels Aren't Always Smiling

> For He will give His angels charge concerning you,
> to guard you in all your ways. They will bear you up
> in their hands, lest you strike your foot against a
> stone.
>
> —Psalm 91:11–12 NAS

The angels that came to our door were not smiling. They
were quite nervous, in fact. I would have felt the same way
coming to their doors on a similar mission. What does one
say? What can one do?

What they did was right. It was their silent caring that
helped the most during those first hours. They let us set
the pace of the conversation and just listened as we talked
about Sondra's death. We told the story over and over to
those who came, and in the telling we began to accept the
reality.

Eventually we found that their help took many other
forms. People are angels of mercy to those in grief. One of
the first things people do is pray. Believers and unbe-
lievers—all tap into God's help when someone begins to
pray. Though an unbeliever may separate himself from
God, he is not totally separated from God's people, and
so not from God's help. Someone who knows him also
knows God and carries his case to the highest throne in
the Universe. And help comes.

We can seek that help for ourselves if for some reason it
does not come easily. Books, Scripture, prayer, seeking out

other people—there is usually no excuse for any of us to be without comfort in our loss. But we are most fortunate when comfort comes to us—from people doing angel work to strengthen us and help to bear us up.

Walt and I experienced differing needs in the attention we were given. He most appreciated being left alone, while I felt buoyed up by any expressions of sympathy. Our friends sensed our differing personalities and helped me during the day but left us alone while Walt was home in the evening.

Those who would help a friend in grief are wise to find out what is needed before they rush in to help, and sometimes only God's Spirit can direct, for the one in grief may not always know what he needs.

Sympathy cards help, though perhaps they help women more than they help men. I read every word of the cards that came, but Walt only stared in amazement at the growing pile. The ones I appreciated most were those with personal notes on them, especially when those notes spoke about Sondra. I craved information about her. There were so many missing pieces about her life. I wished that more of her friends had told me more about her. The ones who did write to me about her are very special to me.

Several little boys showed that they felt the loss deeply, too, by biking the seven miles out to the cemetery daily for some time. Hearing or knowing of true sorrow in others lessens one's own sorrow somehow.

Teachers and other adults who had known Sondra were most complimentary and I loved it. I realized that when one speaks of the dead only the good is said, but I loved my collection of cards and messages.

One of my favorite cards had Peter Marshall's words: "Those we love are with the Lord, and the Lord has promised to be with us. If they are with Him, and He is with

us . . . they cannot be far away." Another one of my
favorites was this Helen Steiner Rice poem:

> When I must leave you for a little while
> Please do not grieve and shed wild tears
> And hug your sorrow to you through the years,
> But start out bravely with a gallant smile;
> And for my sake and in my name
> Live on and do all things the same,
> Feed not your loneliness on empty days,
> But fill each waking hour in useful ways. . . .

Everyone will find that he receives certain cards which are
especially meaningful. One friend collected all her own
most cherished poems about death and made a little scrapbook of them for me. It was a beautiful gift.

Most of the words that come to us in the mail are words
assuring us of the next life. As we grab onto them we may
think, "I'm not sure about this, but it is something to hang
onto for now." Later, as we think and study, we come up
with our true view of life after death. I have declared my
own understanding of this in the first section of this book.
Much later we must piece together our beliefs about the
meaning of life itself.

Seventeen days after Sondra died, I remember writing a
long sob to God that said, ". . . Help me. I am alone. With
this loss and with you. People want to help, but they
can't."

People cannot bring our lost one back, but loving acts by
friends certainly do cushion our hurting. Comforts may
come in a whirlwind of mail, food, visits, as well as in
specific missions of mercy. "Call me if you need anything"
is good, but even better are the acts—coming for the wash,
bringing in a meal, appearing at one's door to baby-sit.

I look back and remember gratefully the visits from my

brother and sisters, the long-distance calls from family and friends, the letters, flowers, growing plants, and gifts that were tangible evidence that people cared. I appreciated a tape my dad had sent of Vance Havner's real and difficult experience with grief and will always remember the gems from it: "I haven't lost her, of course, because I know where she is. . . ." [18] (Even though his words comforted, it seemed to me that a person in heaven *was* lost for a time to us. We have neither the permission nor the travel directions for going there yet.)

Friends checked up on us by phone or visit and were available even long after the funeral. Our pastor sensed a low time for me and stopped in one day to pray with me and to remind me that "greater is He who is in you than he who is in the world" (I John 4:4 NAS). I had been having an extra heavy bout with depression and remember the haggard and grim face I had seen in the mirror that morning. But as soon as I once again claimed Jesus' words as true, it seemed as if my fallen spirit once again stood up and walked with me.

Others tried to enter our prison of sadness and help us. Nancy, a dear friend and an incurable optimist, had hoped against hope that Sondra would not die because people don't die of pneumonia anymore, and was devastated with the truth that they do. She is a songwriter and so shared her heart in the best way she knew with a song for Walt and me, "There Are Many Mansions," and a song for Kristi, "Angels Are Always Smiling."

The angel song came in response to an incident I had described to her on the phone. One night as I was putting the children to bed, Kristi began to ask questions about angels. What are they like? she wondered. What do they do up there? I made an unwise suggestion—that maybe she would have a dream about angels and find out what she wanted to know. That frightened her even more. When I shared the conversation with Nancy, this song came in response:

ANGELS ARE ALWAYS SMILING

Angels are always smiling, loving and kind,
   gentle of mind.
Why shouldn't they be always smiling?
   They live with the King!
Angels are gladly singing, melody clear,
   sweet to the ear
Why shouldn't they be gladly singing?
   They live with the King!
Angels are with us every day,
   though we may never know
Guarding and guiding all the way,
   watching where'er we go.
Jesus has made His angels lovely and fair
   filling the air,
Oh won't it be just wonderful to see the
   angels up there.

We still don't know all we would like to know about angels or about the state and growth of children in heaven, but this song lifts our spirits. Kristi has enjoyed singing it, as will many others now that it is published. And Kristi is not afraid of angels anymore.

As an added bonus for us, Nancy insisted that we use the check she received for the song to buy something in memory of Sondra. With it and some other unexpected money, we ordered a portrait of Sondra, which now hangs in our living room.

The purpose of these thoughts is not for me to bask in the memory of every casserole or loaf of homemade bread —or any of the one-of-a-kind comforts that cannot be counted on again, either for us or for anyone else. I mention them only as reminders to those of us who would help a friend stricken with grief's upheaval that gifts of love—whether handwritten notes or casseroles or cakes or scrapbooks or songs about angels—all say "I care; I know it won't bring your loved one back, but I want you to know I hurt with you."

And so the long sorting-it-out goes on as we struggle to get it right for the filing away in the brain and for the settling in of the reality and all its related thoughts.

I did not like some of the angel work among us. As Eugenia Price says, there are no pat answers.[19] For me, "pat answers" were statements that were unasked-for truths given in an unfeeling manner. Straight and true answers coming in response to a question are not "pat answers." As anyone in grief can testify, examples of such answers abound. "It was all for the best"; "His death was a mercy." Even predictions for adjustment are most disconcerting: "You'll get over this"; "You'll have more time now"; "It will get harder before it gets easier." One in grief needs the reassurance that his feelings are justified, not to have someone try to talk him out of them.

Even though I did not like them, sometimes such statements were helpful. One came through the mail from a godly lady who said: "Praise God, there are no accidents with Him!"

No accidents? Is God pleased when horrible things happen around the world? Does He spend His time scheduling plane crashes? No, I thought, there are accidents.

But over the months, perhaps from having my head in the Bible so frequently (and whether in grief or not, we need *daily* sustenance from His Word), those "discouraging words" have been reason for a more calm and serene faith than I ever thought of having before. Jeremiah 32:42 and Job 5:17–18, for example, show me that God is not surprised by any of our troubles. He hurts with us and longs for us to grow and respond His way, but there is nothing in our lives that He doesn't permit. Now I think I can say with Paul Tournier, "What I have to do is to put my signature at the foot of a blank page in which I will accept whatever God wishes to write. I cannot predict what He will put on this blank Contract as my life proceeds—but I give my signature today." [20] The God I have met in the Bible and the God who has met my needs is completely sufficient in both love and in power. I believe that there are no accidents with Him, and that all of life is working out according to His plan.

Just last night our ten-year-old Kristi asked me why God did not heal everyone and why even Jesus did not heal everyone when He was here. It did not seem fair to her. That question came in the middle of the night after a windstorm had frightened her into bad dreams. My thinking powers were not sharp, but I think the answer God gave my sleepy brain for her is one that I can also hang on to.

"Honey," I told her, "it is not that big of a thing, sickness isn't. Because we live on through eternity. We outlast our bodies. Our life here is only this long, but eternity is this long. And Jesus knew that. It is what He came here to tell us about. He didn't really come here to heal people, though He did it and many times He still does it, teaching us a lot about faith. But healing people doesn't help that much. They just get something else later and die anyway. The important part is the eternity. Jesus came to give us that. Life forever. Now doesn't that make everything else seem more fair?"

She thought it did; and every time I begin to see the long view of things, I do too.

"There are no accidents with God" became a truth for

me, but for the most part pat answers did not help. "She may have turned to evil in later life, so maybe this is better" or "God picks the best to be with Him." In my humanness, I wanted Sondra, not pat answers. Besides, I had plagued myself with many of them already and did not need anyone else to reinforce my own discomforting thoughts ("You should have prayed more"). Such wisdom is usually not helpful. As Vance Havner has said, "You know too much for me, brother." [21]

Just as there are no easy answers to the enigma of evil in the world, so there are no easy answers in dealing with one who is grief-stricken. It is good for anyone who wants to help the bereaved to remember that the only thing they want is their lost one back. The words, "What can I do to help?" seem pathetic and ludicrous, for there is nothing anyone can do to help. Anyone who comes with "comforting words" must understand this feeling and not expect his "comfort" to work wonders. Comforting words may finally make their inroads, but not until the grieving one lets them in.

A friend who had lost her little five-year-old daughter was deeply hurt by an unfeeling remark. Her daughter had been brain-damaged at seven months from a reaction to a DPT shot. Although the child had required much care, she had been a complete delight to her parents. Now, four years later, she had become ill with flu and had died a very sudden death. Her parents would eventually come to believe that she was better off in heaven, but were not prepared for the "comforting" call that came just the day after their daughter's death.

"You *know* this is for the best," the caller said.

My friend was hurt and tried to calmly show her feelings, but the caller just poured on more salt: "Well, I suppose you *would* get attached to her."

Those unfeeling words put that mother near hysteria. She would be a long time getting over the feeling of loneliness and being misunderstood in her grief—as if she had lost a favorite pet and not the dearest human being she had ever known.

Another friend, whose baby had died at seven months from Reye's syndrome, bristled at a callous remark just after her child's funeral: "They put too much makeup on her, didn't you think?"

One is most fortunate if he has friends who can discern his needs. Sometimes he needs to talk, but other times he needs to be distracted from his grief. Unless one who comes to help knows which is best, silence is probably safest.

All the women that I have met who have lost children have expressed the fact that they have received the greatest human comfort from other mothers who had also lost children. Even members of one's own family cannot help as much as a fellow traveler can, especially when that fellow traveler is one who has *received* the comfort that has come to him and is ready to share it. That sharing of comforts is far more helpful than just sharing of hurts. And those comforts will be far more helpful than the unfeeling easy answers that unfortunately also come during our hard times.

Although the field of mental health is wide in its scope, it is narrow in providing help for the bereaved, and especially for bereaved parents. William Rogers reports that, since three out of four marriages that have experienced the loss of a child fail, counseling for such parents is badly needed.[22] Friends do not often recognize the problem, imagining that the grief is drawing the couple together rather than moving them apart. And parents are usually unable to help each other, estranged as they are in their

own separate stages of grief. The only organization that I
have become aware of whose specific mission is to help
bereaved parents is: The Society of Compassionate Friends,
109 Lillington Road, Leamington Spa, Warwickshire, England. The address of the U.S. headquarters is: Box 3247,
Hialeah, Florida 33013.

There are individuals in the field of psychology and psy-
chiatry who specialize in helping the bereaved. Among
them is Dr. Ronald Ramsey, an associate professor of
clinical psychology at the University of Amsterdam in the
Netherlands. Dr. Ramsey is a pioneer in his own way in
treating unresolved grief (see Chapter 16).

Books are an important source of input for our searching
hearts. I had a difficult time reading anything longer than a
poem for several months, but I was able to get through
the excellent little book *Good Grief*.[23] Westberg's title
jarred me somewhat. I was not in the mood for Charlie
Brown or for thinking that a bad death could be "good
grief." But that book helped me to know that many of my
feelings were natural and that they would pass. I would
have worried otherwise about a depression that seemed
to be frighteningly like a mental illness, about my taste
in music which found rock music acceptable and Manto-
vani irritatingly beautiful and not at all like reality. (Is
that the attraction rock music has—that it more nearly
matches an inner or outer world of turmoil?) "Like vine-
gar on soda is he who sings songs to a troubled heart"
(Proverbs 25:20b NAS). Westberg gives some suggestions
to help a person through the various stages of grief, but to
me the main value was in understanding the normalcy
of the stages themselves.

I read other books that people suggested or provided,
but none of them seemed to move me much. They were a
comfort in making me one among others who bore grief,

but the emotion of it was such a part of my own experience that I saw little that was new.

What I was hoping to find was a book about people's deathbed experiences, perhaps one with a comparison between the Christian's and the non-Christian's experiences. I happened upon just such a book in our pastor's study. *Voices from the Edge of Eternity* [24] was written about people who had lived over a century ago and who had died without the "benefit" of drugs. As I read story after story of last reactions and last words, I saw evidence that seemed to point to a difference: the believer experienced a peace and euphoria and even occasionally a vision at dying that was foreign to the unbeliever, who would often breathe his last breath fighting and in panic.

One piece of information from that book particularly intrigued me. The author offered as theory the belief that an angel comes for the dying and that it comes from the North. I thought back of Sondra, how she had turned to her right as far as she could and had stared out that window with a strange, new calmness. "Honey, what do you see?" I had asked; but she had acted as if she had not heard me, so intent was she in looking out that window. What direction was that window? I wondered. I followed a mental map of the hospital and discovered that it was a north window.

More recently I have read *The View from the Hearse*,[25] one of the best and most practical books available, I think. Joe Bayly does not put much credence in deathbed stories, realizing that pain often changes a person from his true self. He is probably right, but I like to think that, after the pain is gone in that last numbing moment before death, if we could communicate with the dying we would hear about some visions and see a heavenly peace settling in upon those for whom the Lord has prepared a place.

There is a contemporary preoccupation with death that is bringing more and more books to our shelves, more and more studies to popular attention. One such study finds that people who have clinically died and then come back to life, some after several hours, are never again afraid of death. In a study of these "threshold experiences," Karlis Osis describes the patients' feelings as of being dragged back from a place full of light where they had experienced a sense of euphoria. These studies were made from 640 replies from doctors and nurses who reported some 35,000 cases of people who had been to death's door and back.[26] All seemed to share common experiences. (Elisabeth Kübler-Ross is presently involved in a similar study which has convinced her that there is life after death.) All this information must be synthesized with what we already know, if indeed it is true. If it is true, it may prove to some who reject Biblical truth that life after death does exist. One is reminded of Paul's "out-of-body"[27] experience recorded in II Corinthians 12:1–4. Of his trip to Paradise, he says, "Whether in the body, I cannot tell; or whether out of the body, I cannot tell," and then reveals that he heard "unspeakable words, which it is not lawful for a man to utter."

A member of my family once choked on some food and stopped breathing for several seconds. During that time he felt that he had been gone for a long, long time and was finally being dragged back against his will away from a most beautiful place, where he had also experienced a more lovely sound than he ever thought existed. To him, his experience was a trip to a real place, so unlike an experience of "nothing" that simple fainting brings. He and everyone else who has ever been "out" believes that Emily Dickinson was right when she said:

This world is not a conclusion;
A sequel stands beyond,
Invisible as music,
But positive as sound.[28]

Surely these visions are part of that mysterious "dying grace" that we can only guess about. When Corrie ten Boom was a little girl, she asked her father what it was like to die. He answered her with another question: "Honey, when we go on a train trip, when do I give you your ticket?" Then Corrie began to understand about dying and the strength that comes at that last minute.[29] We don't get dying grace until we are dying.

When the Jewish people lived in the desert those forty years before moving into their promised land, they were fed daily from a highly nutritional substance called manna. It apparently fell from the sky; but, however it came, it was supernaturally there—plenty for everyone every morning. It did not come early, it never came late, and it was always sufficient for their day's need.

God, in His providence, gives all of us manna—timely provisions for our every need. We have already appropriated His grace for our living and so we can most assuredly bank on His grace for our dying.

I craved the truth about dying and the afterlife. Books, especially when used along with the touchstone of truth from Scripture, helped me to see God's provisions, still "through a glass darkly," but with the assurance that one day I would see it all "face to face" (I Corinthians 13:12).

How sweet are [His] words to my taste!
Yes, sweeter than honey to my mouth!
From [His] precepts I get understanding...
—Psalm 119:103-104 NAS

For those who grieve, God sends angels of mercy—people who pray, people who help, people who write songs, and people who write books . . . and sometimes even people with harsh words. How beautiful are even the "feet of [them] that bringeth good tidings, that publisheth peace" (Isaiah 52:7 KJV).

16

"Dear Sondra"

HELP ME NOT TO MURMUR

in my small wilderness
disdain the pillar-cloud
the manna and the fire at night
   be ingrate for deliverance
   from Egypt's lords
   from bricks that had no straw
   from furnaces of fire
   in which I am Abednego
unharmed by scorch
and fiery bier.
   Help me to know that Canaan's fruit
   is sweeter far
   than I could beg on quasar-star
and from the vine
my grapes to prune
in sweet content.
   Today has its own manna:
   let me gather it with joy
   despite the pain
   some rattler's head would foster
   —perfect love casts out fear.
There is no room for murmuring—
nor one small tear.
           —Wilma Burton

Most of the hard work of grief must be done alone. All the new information must be sorted and former beliefs must be rearranged or discarded. The mind's messed-up filing cabinet must be straightened out. Such a synthesis takes time and solitude.

> I must withdraw into the cool, dark woods of my mind, rest under tall thoughts that shade the memory-carpeted ground on which my spirit lies. Here there is silence broken only by the falling leaves of comfort, the bird-song of some ecstasy known, the ripple of tears going over the falls of Time. I shall come back soon, my soul serene, my spirit healed.[30]

Some may find the grave site a perfect setting for their solitude. It was not for me. My first visits to Sondra's grave were disturbing. I remember listening to the ground in morbid fear and hope. Faith and doubt sometimes carried on their fiercest battles at the grave site, fighting for control in a sorrowing heart. So I silently prayed to ask God how she was doing and whether or not I should spend more time praying for her and whether or not such praying helped. And the assurance came that, whether I prayed or not, Sondra was receiving excellent care.

So visiting Sondra's grave became neither a ritual nor a compulsion. I wondered why people thought they needed to go to a grave or deliver flowers. If for one minute I could believe that a visit or a flower could matter at all to her, they would never be enough. If attention could help, I would stay there myself. But no attention matters to our lost ones if they are not at the graves. Such attention only tries to prove "how much we loved." When we know that such proof is not needed or possible in that way, we do our thinking wherever we find ourselves alone.

I withdrew to a quiet room, sometimes in the middle of the night, in order to work out concerns, questions, and frustrations on paper or in prayer. One does not really know what he thinks until he forms his thoughts into words. For some, talking the words out loud is best; for others, writing is the most helpful.

Sometimes I imagined that Sondra was the recipient of my writing. Many pages were filled with letters to her. Although they are not especially readable, they represent many hours of a helpful activity. Here are some excerpts:

> Sondra, you are my sunshine. How I miss you. Will I ever get back to wanting to live? Can life be good without you? Tears engulf, but God's peace is very real. Do you know all about that now, too? ... I insulted you sometimes, honey. Was that my job as your mother? I should have been more loving. How I wish for time with you. But then we'd be nervous and not ourselves. Oh honey, I can hardly believe you are not here. If only I could have borne that hurt and fear for you. ...

> I become short with the children sometimes. I hope I don't resent that they are here and you aren't. ... How are you "like an angel" now? Luke 20:36 says you are.

> Your school has a new weather station in your memory. It was a hard night being at that concert where your class sang (the best of all). Tears fell for quite a while (down my cheeks) after Mr. Melody announced the memorial. Janna saw and wiped one away and knowingly, way beyond her four little years, said, "Sondra?" I nodded, yes. Brian and Jon and Kris were there, too. Daddy had to stay home because of water in the basement.

> You never told me all the ways you were helping out at school. Why not? Your teacher said they would need about six people to replace you. And Mr. Melody said he trusted you with jobs he might not

even have trusted an adult with. I wish you had known how loved you were. Did you know?

Some trees and shrubs were planted just outside the all-purpose room at church (where there is a cross on the brick wall). They were from your church memorial fund. You would like the way it looks.

Lots of little children die, don't they? Do you welcome them? Show them around? Or are you still learning things?

I am still glad you came to me to be my new baby, even though it meant this. Remember that day on the love seat? And remember the day on the back porch the night before you went to kindergarten? Now you are gone for good, but we'll see each other again. I love you, dear Sondra. I bet a lot of people do.

I like the pillows you made me for my birthday. I always sleep on the big one. Your birth day and death day are hard. I love you.

One time, after a season of writing and suffering on paper, it seemed that Sondra said to me,

Stop it, Mom; if you knew, really knew this life you would never wish me back. My days there have ended but here it's as if they never began and will never end. Please know the truth of this. I love you and Dad, but loving Jesus is far beyond. You will love Him this way now, too. Don't ache. Don't cry. Just grow. I'll see you soon. I'm sorry I have saddened you, panicked so much. But it all sure turned out, Mom. I love you.

Jon discovered the therapy of writing letters to Sondra all by himself. One day he asked me to type while he said a letter to Sondra. None of my many letters to her said so much in so little space:

> Dear Sondra,
>
> I wish you would have a good time. I wish you came back. I loved you. And I wish you have a happy life.
> Bye,
> Jon.
>
> P.S. I saw you and now I don't. That was a long time since I saw you. First you came down and then you went up. You loved me and now I love you.

Brian worked out his grief on the piano, finding expression for his own words of sorrow or comfort.

The desire to write it down seems to come naturally for those of us in grief. A friend who had lost her baby at birth felt the need to get out of bed one night several weeks later and write her child a letter. It was balm for her hurt. If talking is easier, one should talk to anyone who will listen, or even just to the air. Those who squelch the need to talk it out or write it out may just be prolonging their grief work.

Dr. Ronald Ramsey, a clinical psychologist at the University of Amsterdam, has had a high rate of success in dealing with people who have not naturally faced their grief, but his method is a painful and seemingly cruel one. In sessions that last over a period of two weeks, the patient is forced to face the reality he has hidden from.

Rita, aged forty, had lost her daughter Beverly some two and one half years before coming to Dr. Ramsey. She was extremely depressed and suicidal. During the first session she was forced to make a mental picture of her daughter and then tell herself that Beverly was gone and she would never see her again.

During another session, Rita talked to her daughter's

picture, again telling herself out loud that those eyes, that mouth, those hands were gone from her forever. There were sobs of protest and a few comforting words ("I know it hurts") as the therapist persistently forced his patient to face the enormity of her situation. During a later session she was told to send Beverly away. This was the hardest command of all, for as much pain as Rita felt, that pain was all she had left of her daughter and she hated to let it go. But, finally trusting her therapist, Rita realized that she must send her daughter away. "I don't want to, but I have to," she said with a sigh; and she was finished. Her sigh was one of acceptance, a new sound for Rita. The woman who was so broken and inoperable from grief for so long seemed unmistakably at peace, healed of the damage that refusal to face it had done to her.

This real-life drama was seen by millions of people through the skillful filming and editing of CBS's 60 Minutes.[31] A follow-up report indicated that Rita had no relapse back into her depression as of five months after her therapy.

Jesus said it long ago: "Let the dead bury their dead" (Matthew 8:22 KJV). We must make a break, totally and completely. We must say our good-byes, do all of our thinking, and be done. Even those of us who believe that we will see our loved ones again in heaven must face the reality that we will never see them again in life as we know it here. Most of us feel, and usually obey, the inner urge that tells us to say good-bye, but for those who cannot or will not force themselves away, there must be help from outside, some impetus that forces them to finally let go. And acceptance comes.

Whatever the method—writing letters or talking out loud to a real or mental picture—one must deal with the finality of death and say his good-byes. This final relin-

quishment seldom occurs with the placing of our loved
one in the ground. It takes many hours and many days
of struggling with memories and thoughts. But it must
happen.

Sometimes our dreams help us say our good-byes. In
them we seem to work out some of the anguishes that
never surface during the day. Sometimes we can remember our night wanderings and examine our progress: Aeschylus wrote, "In our sleep, pain which cannot forget falls
drop by drop upon the heart until, in our own despair,
against our will, comes wisdom through the awful grace
of God." I remembered some of my dreams, though I
could not always evaluate my grief progress in them.

One time I dreamed that I was one of several people
who were "dying." We were still there, not gone from our
bodies, and yet we were gradually decaying. I was glad to
wake up from that frightening dream and glad that death
comes as mercifully as it does—all at once.

I had another dream about the decaying process—only
this time there was a reversal. Cells began to grow again,
to reassemble. Even while dreaming I wondered if something similar would happen to dead bodies on resurrection day, reuniting the part of us that lasts with the old,
buried shells.

Sometimes I dream about Sondra, and I enjoy those
dreams in a sad way. The next day there is a lingering
glow of memory about her even when I cannot recall the
dream. Usually it seems that she is in poor health, so upon
wakening I am grateful that she is not saddled with a sick
body in heaven. Sometimes I seem to hold her and the
ache of missing is soothed.

A friend who had recently lost her father dreamed that
she was attending his funeral. She was surprised at how
lifelike her father looked, much better than he had at his

real funeral. After the funeral (in her dream) she went up to the casket and said to him, "You can open your eyes now, Dad. Everyone is gone. But you really had them fooled. You look dead and they all thought you were dead. How in the world did you hold so still?"

Her dream seemed to her to be her own denial about her dad's death, but I think it was her own deep assurance that her dad was actually alive and well in heaven—that he just looked dead to all the people at the funeral.

Recently I dreamed that Jon, now seven and full of independent curiosity, was running toward a window in a high building and then stretching to look down. Panic-stricken, I called out to him from the door of the room, but he paid no attention to my warning. He stretched farther and then fell to the ground below. In my dream I felt again the horror of loss and waste and experienced again the flash of a prayer for an easy death. It was a frightening dream that reminded me again that immediate obedience must become a habit in Jon and I must do all I can to instill it in that curious, impetuous, determined little boy. Perhaps the dream also helped in a way I do not know to more thoroughly work through some unexpressed horror of Sondra's death.

Although I am not always conscious of direct therapy from dreams, I believe that help does come while we sleep and that even our little-understood dreams are evidence that our minds work overtime to get our grief work done.[32]

The heavy work of grief is done alone, but help also comes as we report our progress to someone else, to a friend, or to God himself—or to one's children.

Our three little ones had a round of questions every night for several weeks and then occasionally for several weeks more. They wanted to talk about life and death and they needed to do it for their own healing. So I had a ready supply of listening ears for many of my own thoughts about death.

Some of their questions were disconcerting: "What is she doing there? How did they know she was for sure dead when they put her in the ground? Was the casket standing up or lying down in the ground?" Most of these were Jon's questions. Kristi had been to the funeral; Janna, sick at home, had seen the flutter of people coming in and out; but in his oxygen tent in the hospital, Jon had been away from the action and now felt the need to fill in his gaps. So I talked to all the children individually as I tucked them in at night. Our minds were often in heaven during those early days, and our little talks eased us back to earth. Singing together was helpful to all of us—especially songs using the well-loved Twenty-third Psalm.

The children appear to have worked out their grief quite well. At first Jon was disturbed because he could not picture Sondra, but now he has a clear image of her. Janna often prayed about Sondra in heaven—that she would be having a good time up there—and for more than a year numbered her among the members of our family. Kristi seems to recall more as time goes on, but she especially remembers activities that she and Sondra enjoyed together. She, too, has had the added adjustment of becoming the oldest of the young children and taking responsibility that she never had before. She has decided that it is not easy being the oldest.

The children and I have visited the grave together several times. Janna wanted to dig so she could see Sondra until we reminded her that Sondra wasn't in there—not the real Sondra. She was in heaven. We talked to God about her and then stopped at the park for some playing and went home. They often asked to go to the cemetery, possibly hoping for another trip to the park.

Friends also made themselves available as a sounding

board if I needed them by phone and by visit. Our pastor
and his wife kept in touch with us to check on our coping
and helped us by their availability.

But most of my "talking it out" happened by prayer—
instant help in time of need. Not only is a soul bared,
but direct help—wisdom, guidance, comfort, whatever is
needed—is applied to the problem as needed with no waiting. I could say, along with my dear friend Wilma Burton:

> THINK ON ME TODAY, O LORD
> with the far-fling of universe,
> the stretch of stars,
> and multitudes who pebble earth,
> and vast their human needs,
> I dare to call on You
>   and know that You
>   are God, omnipresent,
>   and all-knowing.
> I can call You, Father-God,
>   and know Your ear
>   is tuned to thunderclap,
>   to baby's cry,
>   or faintest whisper—
>   or even my unspoken sigh.

17
Reentry

He who has a why to live for can bear with almost
any how.

—Nietzsche

Discover a Meaning for Your Existence

Grief propels one into a reexamination of all he has
ever believed. Suddenly, nothing makes sense. His world
has caved in and he is not sure he wants to even rebuild
it. But in working through grief, he has already begun to
rebuild. And when he is finally able to again establish a
reason for living, he may be assured that he is ready to go
on living, with purpose and with confidence.

Even if the only philosophy one can find is one of
despair or meaninglessness, it is a philosophy and it is a
signal that he is ready to begin trying it out in real living.
An acceptance of any philosophy is better than refusing to
think or function and railing out against a God that one
shoutingly proclaims is not even there.

A Jewish psychologist stands out in my mind as one who
found meaning for existence. Out of his suffering in Nazi
concentration camps, Viktor Frankl developed the philosophy contained in his priceless little book *Man's Search
for Meaning*.[33] By harrowing experiences of his own, by
observation of how those around him faced suffering, and
by words from the holy Talmud in his heart, Frankl found
life's meaning. He found that, when normal ways of find-

ing meaning are impossible (such as doing a deed, experiencing a value such as loving or thanking, or finding beauty in nature or culture), there is always one final way to find meaning: to suffer nobly. There is a freedom in such suffering, for one could choose to suffer badly. But in accepting his suffering and giving it his best, one finds meaning. (Is this what Peter meant when he said, "But to the degree that you share the sufferings of Christ, keep on rejoicing" [I Peter 4:13 NAS]?)

Many have found a joyful meaning for existence in Christ. Any of Watchman Nee's books reveal the richness of a life that has drawn on God's strength and suffered well. A *Table in the Wilderness* is full of his ripe wisdom gathered from his many writings. In it he says, "Many Christians are so poor they have not even sufficient to meet their own needs. Alas for one who goes to them for help. Others are so rich you can never assess their wealth. They seem to have resources for all who come to them in need." [34]

Both Frankl and Watchman Nee are men who have come to terms with life by suffering. Each of us who has struggled through the torment of laying a loved one peacefully to rest in our memories must also dip into our suffering and discover new meaning, new motivation, and then move on in new strength. Then we, too, will be anxious to dogmatically declare to all who would ask exactly what that meaning is, sure that it will do for another what it has done for us.

I, too, declare the light of the truth I have experienced. For me the light is Jesus. It is in Him that our lives can discover the deepest meaning of all. It is because of Him that we can get up and go on. What happens to us is not as important as how we respond to what happens. And it is Jesus, who is living in us, who can respond the very best possible way to the very worst possible circumstances—

whenever we let Him do it. In Wilma Burton's "Resurrection Gold," out of her deep and full poetic heart, her own reason for being is beautifully orchestrated; and that reason is Jesus.

> My winter heart is bare and brown. It lies
> inert beneath the mold of some leaf mound,
> reject from last October lullabies,
> beggared, boxcarred upon the earth-cold ground.
> At sudden flick of tail and flip of wing
> earth laughs and joins the golden roundelay
> of bird in lilac-pocket, aproned Spring—
> hitchhiker back from migratory way.
> Rolled from a dormant bed, my heart with earth
> is crocus-crowned and gasps with reverence, awe,
> to see, once more, the miracle of birth
> as April strokes a pussy willow's paw.
> From Arimathea, winter-stone is rolled:
> my risen heart wears Resurrection gold.

Be Thankful

As one finds new meaning for life, new reason for going on, he also finds himself able to be thankful.

Giving thanks leads to good health and happiness. As one is able to be happy again, reentry into the world and recovery of mental health are imminent.

Perhaps one is able to give thanks finally because he has received a measure of peace, but the reverse is also true. Anyone, Christian or not, can receive peace as a direct result of giving thanks. Since there is not room inside us for both resentment and thanks, bitterness makes a fast exit when we start being thankful. With resentment there are despair, hatred, and illness; but with thankfulness there are hope, love, and health. We may take our choice, and all we need to do is start.

Our Jon did not need to be taught this attitude. His Sunday school teacher reported that, on the first Thanksgiving Day after his sister had died, Jon had written a thank-you list to God. Right at the top was, "For Sondra, that we could have her for almost eleven years." Children are good teachers. I thought back and made my list, not for the tragedy itself; that would not come until much later—but for the good things within and preceding the tragedy.

I was thankful for the closeness we had experienced on her last day at home. The night before, I had dreamed about her. She was a little baby in diaper and shirt just learning to sit up. Then all of a sudden she was her own ten-year-old self and was walking out of my dream, disappearing behind a white picket fence.

I remembered the dream when I woke up and went in to tell Sondra how glad I was that she came to be my new baby. She had glowed, sick as she was, in the reminder that she was loved. I am thankful for that dream—that it prompted me to have that special time with her.

I was thankful for the book we read together the night she entered the hospital. It was the story of man's creation and of God's plan for our world. Her eyes had shown her inner responses of happiness to hear the story.

My list grew.

I was thankful that she did not die immediately so that we had those hours in intensive care with her. I was thankful for the times in the weeks before that we had talked and shopped, and even for the trouble we took finding the right winter coat for her.

I was thankful for the letter I had written each one in our family just to thank them for being, and once again for the realization that our times of giving double back on us with their own comfort for the giver.

I was thankful for a song that had come to Nancy just a

few weeks before Sondra had died. The tune was hauntingly beautiful and now it seemed that the words looked ahead to her leaving us:

> Sondra, Sondra, just the sound of her name
> Is like music, like a haunting refrain
> That will linger only for a little while
> And then disappear like the light of her smile.

Not for two more years would I know to be thankful for a kindness from Sondra herself—a book she had brought home from her library for me, a book I had gotten through all my years without ever reading, *The Yearling*. After she died I was not in any mood to read anything, so I sent the book back to the library. My good intentions to read it later were never followed through, but recently *The Yearling* was served up in a way I could not refuse—in a TV special. I watched it and wept. I wept for Jody's mother, who had encased herself in a petrified cocoon of toughness; I wept for Jody; I wept for change and growing up and loss; and I wept with sobs that could not be loud enough with thanks for Sondra's gift. It was as if she were saying to me, even before she died, as Jody's dad had said: "Life sometimes turns back on you, son, but you gotta take it for your share and go on." We can always be thankful for the past, which is, in fact, the only reality. The future may never happen. And, as we look back into that past, we find more reasons than we ever imagined existed to be thankful.

Recently I have seen the results of thankfulness in a woman who is not a believer. She had been in and out of hospitals and doctors' and psychiatrists' offices for the past ten years. No one could find anything major wrong with her. About five months ago she reluctantly agreed to try to be glad about what she had—to concentrate on at least one thing that she could be thankful for every morning.

Only one week later, she was a different woman. She could scarcely remember her vegetablelike existence. She was full of zest and was developing a revived interest in people and things—and she has continued in this miracle for the past five months. I believe that a thankful spirit worked the miracle in her.

Everyone, no matter how bad things have become, should avail himself of the benefits that thanksgiving brings:

THANK YOU, LORD, FOR MELTING SNOW

The beauty of new snow is gone
and the world
crusted with soot
gray as winter skies
would be unbearable
if we could not know
    that tomorrow
    the snow will melt,
    disappear
and the time for the singing of birds
will come to a world green again
with the color of Spring.
    Thank You, too, Lord,
    for melting the snow
    from winter hearts
    that we may know again—
    after the ice of sorrow has gone—
the pussy willow softness
of hope and joy returning.
              —Wilma Burton

Play Ball

There comes a time when we must trade our solitude for activity.

"The sooner you get back into things, the better; the longer you wait, the harder it will be." That was the advice I received and for most of us it is good advice. Just as the doctor insists that his postoperative patient get up the day after an operation, we who grieve must force ourselves up lest we become atrophied in some way. We must "do the next thing." The nature and timing of our activities are individual matters and are dictated by varying circumstances. But as much as possible one should seek a good balance between too much and too little activity. Too much leaves no time for grief work; too little puts us in danger of losing the habit of normal functioning.

There is a sense in which we must mark time and just go through the motions of activities not because we like them but because we need them. These zombielike attempts prepare us for reentry. Perhaps our propensity for tears needs to govern the activities we plan for ourselves. Since most of us prefer privacy for shedding our tears, we can try to avoid encounters that promise to drain us emotionally. For me, tears do not usually attack without warning. I knew that church with sermons about troubled waters and the shadow of death would catapult me back into myself, but I was able to cry on the inside and shed silent tears outside so I did not feel the need to ever avoid church services.

Necessity dictates many activities. For us it was trips to doctors or drugstores or the hospital that propelled us into our new world of grief. I wondered even while doing those things, "How are we *doing* this?" They were our first baby steps up the long road ahead, but without them we would not have been able to make the journey at all.

After the children were well again, activities resumed according to our calendar. For Walt, it was teaching 130 kids a day in school. For me, important steps were helping at a Fun Fair, participating in a panel discussion, attending a Sunday school convention, planning a "Happiness Is" table for a banquet, accompanying soloists, attending a birthday party, and playing volleyball at church on Tuesday mornings. For at least six months there was almost no activity that I looked forward to. I usually felt ripped away, out of my element, and I would have preferred a cloistered atmosphere for thinking and pondering and being sad. But I did not need as much time as I wanted; something in me knew that and pushed me out into the world. There was still time left over which I gratefully hoarded away for working out my grief.

Most activities are unwelcome intruders, but there are some things we feel almost compelled to do. Often these are activities that our loved one would have done if he were alive. Parkes calls these "identification phenomena." [35] One kind of identification phenomenon occurs when the bereaved one develops a physical symptom, either real or imagined, and believes that he, too, may be dying from the same disease that took his loved one. A sore throat for any of us in this house still triggers a reflex fear in me—and maybe it always will. But identification phenomena may also lead to an activity which is much more positive in its effect. A husband takes the long-put-off trip to Hawaii that his late wife had always hoped for; a wife begins to work in her late husband's business and develops a zeal and skill for work she once ignored. Ironically, the very impetus that makes one undertake an activity comes from the one whose loss has for so long made one feel like doing nothing.

Identification for me occurred when I began wearing one of Sondra's pendants, a dove with the inscription "PEACE." I loved wearing something that she had worn, and the symbolism of the dove was a ready reminder that God's Spirit was in me.

Another activity, which was for me an identification phenomenon, was one I did not recognize as such at the time. I joined a baseball team and found it a most satisfying experience. When I realized that Sondra would have joined a baseball team that summer, too, if she had been here, I decided that is what it was.

Another project undone for her was a letter she had wanted to write about her father for a "Father of the Year" contest that our newspapers traditionally sponsored. As it turned out, there was no contest that year; but, not knowing that, I wrote a letter for her and sent it in. Since hers was probably the only entry, the editors noticed it and even published it on the front page that Father's Day. I know that she would have been as thrilled as I was to have her father honored in that way. Luckily he does not have a weak heart or Walt could not have stood the shock of reading the paper on that Father's Day.

Reach Out to Someone Else

"He who does not love abides in death" (I John 3:14b NAS).

KEEP ME FROM BEING OVERCOME TODAY

by all my flaws:
inconsistency, self-pity,
preoccupation when another
needs attention,
or procrastination
(of which I am a master).
   Help me to flee this ego-centered
   thing that blossoms, thrives
   on the four-leaf clover
   of searching for my faults.
Rather, free me from this inverted
pride, this over self-concern

and let me know the joy,
    the sweet delight
    that surfboards
    on the waves of praying for
    and doing things
    for others.
                        —Wilma Burton

Somewhere along the way we begin to see that there are other people in the world, people with problems. As our own needs are met we are able to begin to meet the needs of someone else, to begin to care again. When that happens we are well on our way to recovery and normal living.

One of the first times I sensed that I was any help at all was while delivering Mobile Meals, a community service for delivering hospital meals to the elderly. When I discovered that one of the men on our route had recently lost his wife, I decided he should hear my Vance Havner tape. He was most grateful. He said he listened to it four times and then shared it with several neighbors. Thinking I might have been of some help to him was most satisfying.

Those who have suffered can best help another in need of comfort. I had initially revolted against that idea (found in II Corinthians 1:3-4). I just was not spiritual enough to want my tragedy to be a source of help. I knew that, given the choice, I would never have chosen for Sondra to die, no matter who might have been helped by her death. But when the truth finally entered my head that trouble is bad enough—that we must not completely waste it but use it for good if we can—then I knew that I would gladly comfort others with the comfort that had come to me.

Every effort brought me more and more out of myself, more and more in tune with people again. I felt drawn to those who had suffered a loss and prayed many times daily for them. Sometimes I wrote them letters or notes.

Once we open our eyes to see people with needs, our work is cut out for us, and healing and therapy for our own wounds is fast coming.

Working with a girls' club at church helped me to face head on a bitterness and resentment that had been building against little girls Sondra's age. The first meeting with them was difficult and sad, but the next was easier, and soon I loved them all as if they were my own. That love took care of the bitterness and has usually transferred to other girls in other situations.

At a recent holiday event I was asked to testify to the comfort that is available to us because Jesus came to Bethlehem. It was good for me to look back and to remember what God has done. Normally I would rather hear what God did for a person today than what He did last year; but recalling is sometimes good. As we remember what God has done in our yesterdays, we find ourselves trusting Him more with our todays and tomorrows. When we have tasted and seen that the Lord is good, we are anxious to try Him again. It would be good for all of us who grieve to look back and thankfully remember the help God has given us in our trouble. That talk at Christmas helped me, and the thought that it might have helped someone else has left its own afterglow.

Writing these words is helping me, too. And even though I know that I will keep on learning and revising my own thoughts about life's meaning, and that I will surely wish this writing could contain those changes, I will recognize that these words do reflect the truth that I know right now. Recording God's ways has helped me to trust in His goodness and authority for present troubles and it will be a steady reminder that God can provide for future troubles. If what I have recorded could ever help someone else, too, there is an even deeper advantage.

We can find healing by helping. And there is raw ma-

terial to spare all around us so that we can easily appropriate this means of therapy for our grief—to open our
eyes, our hearts, and our hands to those around us and
help.

As I think back on my few grief ministries and even
review my present ministries, I am saddened by their
paucity. I redden at an accusation made toward many
Christians: that we are more self-centered than other-
centered—that we care more about having God work in
our own lives than in letting Him use us in others' lives.

The accusation is not completely justified. We Christians are extremely busy ministering to each other and to
those whose needs are drawn to our attention. Unselfish
and unsung acts of kindness happen among us all the time,
acts that the outside world cannot know about.

But the truth is that the outside world is not often
enough the recipient of our love. A century ago Christians
were in the front lines righting social wrongs. Why do we
lag so far behind?

Do we back off because social wrongs are being righted
by secular society (using our nineteenth-century counterparts for their models)? Or do we think that the Holy
Spirit has new marching orders for our century, that God's
view of human suffering has changed? Or for some reason
are we not open to the option that He might direct us to
spend more time away from our cloisters and out in the
world of human suffering?

Perhaps we feel that we have enough housecleaning to
do in our own area of interests without going out to clean
other houses. Or perhaps the "God is dead" mentality of
our century has dropped enough leavings of unbelief even
on us to thwart much God-powered action from us. Whatever the reason, not from many of our pulpits and not

from much of our literature are we Christians being challenged to meet the pressing physical needs of the struggling humanity outside our churches. Ignoring the needs is not what God desires. Reading His Word and listening for His direction ought to get us off our knees and into action.

Jesus' life is not our defense. Though He did not "right Rome" or join any organized effort for relieving social injustice, though His ratio of contemplation to action was only 30 : 3, He dealt with both physical and spiritual suffering out in the world. But we dare not compare ourselves to Jesus. Our mission is not to die for the sins of the world. His was. He came—

> To bring good news to the afflicted;
> ... to bind up the brokenhearted,
> To proclaim liberty to captives,
> And freedom to prisoners;
> To comfort all who mourn
> —Isaiah 61:1–2 NAS

—and by dying He accomplished that mission. His death and resurrection have infused the world with the Holy Spirit by Whom we are empowered to do all that Jesus came to do.

What an efficient way to light our world—to use millions of people and not just one. We can be among those people. We can be among those who bind up the wounds of humanity as well as to proclaim the good news of salvation.

The world has had a Gandhi, and a Schweitzer, but as D. L. Moody once said, "The world has yet to see what God can do with one whose life is completely given over to Him." His power is in us, and as we give ourselves over to Him, He will use us in ways we could never dream possible to become instruments of His peace. "The trouble with Christianity is not that it has been tried and found wanting, but that it has never been tried," said E. Stanley Jones.

What a profound challenge to consider. What huge dividends. And what a perfect opportunity we have, even in our grief, to examine our part in that challenge. St. Francis of Assisi wrote:

> Lord, make me an instrument of Thy peace.
> Where there is hatred, let me sow love;
> Where there is injury, pardon;
> Where there is doubt, faith;
> Where there is despair, hope;
> Where there is darkness, light.
>
> O divine Master, grant that I may not
> So much seek to be consoled, as to console;
> To be understood, as to understand;
> To be loved, as to love;
> For it is in giving that we receive;
> It is in pardoning that we are pardoned;
> It is in dying that we are born to eternal life.

18
Out of the Valley at Last

Thou wilt make known to me the path of life.
—Psalm 16:11 NAS

Once, when Sondra was only three, I remember a shopping trip where my mother, two sisters, three children, Christmas packages, and I were squashed into our Cougar, with helium balloons taking what little spare space there was. Sondra expressed her discomfort with characteristic poise: "Oh, I wish it was a long time from now."

That's it. We'll be all right a long time from now. But what about now? Healing takes time, so much time. And, until it happens, the glib words "Time heals" just make us angry. Time will fade out the bad and bring the pleasant into better focus, but time alone cannot work miracles. Rose Kennedy says in *Times to Remember:*

> It is said that time heals all wounds. I don't agree. The wounds remain. The mind, protecting its sanity, covers them with some scar tissue and the pain lessens—but it is never gone. In writing as I have [about her children] I have felt grief and pain, hardly lessened despite all the years.[36]

Thank God for scar tissue. We could not live with open wounds. But as that scar tissue is forming, we must be sure that good grief work is continuing so that no infection of unresolved grief is left to fester later in us or in our children.

A friend who had lost her older brother back in her teenage years tried to help me know that time would help me. She knew I had been writing down my thoughts and hurts for my own therapy and said, "Good; save that and read it later. You are going to be quite surprised in a couple of years to even remember that you ever felt this way."

It is a couple of years later now. I remember balking at her wisdom because I did not want to ever feel differently. Sondra would not ever be any less dead; why should I ever be any less sad? The very idea that time would do some sort of magic disturbed me. Time would not restore her, and that is the only help I could imagine that would be any help at all.

But my friend was quite right. Though I can recall the anguish and even relive it at times, death's shocking finality is somewhat removed by a haze of history viewed through accepting eyes. And I am, in many ways, back to the way I was before Sondra died—silly with the children, laughing and loving, enjoying a walk or my work and the many good things promised by every rising of the sun. Walt is back, too. Though totally saddened by our loss, he was able to come back into normal living more quickly than I was.

And yet neither of us is exactly the same as we were. We are more appreciative, tender, and loving to the other children. Often we are tempted to remember only Sondra's goodness and beauty and almost canonize her. Perhaps the trite saying, "God only takes the best to be with Him," has come from the fact that our memories invariably raise our lost ones to the level of "best." Whether that is a comfort or not I do not know, for it is most devastating to lose one's best.

There are other ways we are different. We hold life—and

especially the life of our children—more dear and count each day with them a gift. We are beginning to see that suffering has its own work to do in us. We enjoy our home more, fear death much less, and stand confident about the future, because now we know the vastness of the power available to all of us, more than sufficient for every difficulty. Healing has happened during these two years. Scar tissue does cover our wounds.

But for one whose wound has just occurred, it does little good for me or anyone else to remind him that someday he will be healed, that someday the shock and horror of his loss will not be such a throbbing part of his life. He is living today and he needs help in just getting through today. He has no desire to even make it through until the tomorrows are better. What can I tell that one?

I wish I could prescribe a pill, a book, a portion of Scripture, a prayer—anything that would lift him once and for all above his grief. I wish, in fact, that I could have made this book much less ponderous, far more sunny and cheerful than it is. But I cannot, not if I am to be real about bereavement. Facing death is not sunny and cheerful.

Not even for a Christian? Shouldn't those of us who know about heaven and know our loved one is there be laughing and dancing and singing for joy at his new condition? Maybe we should, but we aren't. In our humanity, we miss, we wonder, and we sorrow. Of course, by comparison to those who sorrow without hope, our sorrowing may almost look like rejoicing. We *will* see our loved one again. We do believe in that which we cannot see. But that future hope does not cancel out the terrible pain of missing that we suffer now while we are still here and still so very human.

That pain is very real, and I would not mislead anyone by saying it is easy. Nor will I be among those who would judge the Christian in his loss by shaking their heads and saying (inside at least), "What a shame—where is his faith?" We would know about his faith if we could see a comparison of how very much worse he would be without it.

I do not have answers for anyone facing grief. But I know that God does. He will provide help according to our needs. I desperately wish that unbelief would not block the way for anyone. How I wish that everyone would take the comfort available from God's Word and His quiet voice. I wish everyone knew the Presence that can accompany us up that long, lonely road out of the valley. With Him, our loads become so much lighter.

But for all of us, earthly comforts are available for the taking, also from the hand of God—from friends, from books, from our own working, thanking, and helping to lead us toward that long-awaited acceptance.

Time will not heal in itself, but it can form the boundaries for our healing. God heals all of us as day by day we appropriate His help by being honest about our needs. Time proves that we have indeed taken the long, hard journey through all the denial and anger, bargaining and depression; time proves how well we have worked through all the thoughts and the memories; time shows whether we have stopped on our journey, whether we have avoided the journey, or whether we have availed ourselves of the help and gone on.

How much time? There are plateaus of progress. Six months, one year, and two years are common times; but this is no race. Every road is as different from another as the individuals making the journey. Perhaps two years would encompass almost everyone's pace. If after that period one is still not into the sunshine of wanting to live again, he may need to reexamine the road to be sure he is on it, or he may need to ask someone else where he missed the way.

But the sun will shine again. When we reach the top, we recall the trip with a thankful heart. Thankful to be back, thankful for what we learned about death from the wistful look over the valley—certainly heaven never looked more inviting or beautiful than it did from down there—and thankful for the days ahead with new resolve to use them well until it is our turn to make that final trip to the place Jesus is preparing for us.

Before that time comes, each of us will have to make many more trips down into that valley and back up this side. And the travel back up is never easy. The road is never the same, because relationships are never the same. But since we do not ever have to travel alone, since God Himself is with us, we never have to dread the future. Because of Jesus, all who believe qualify for this statement:

> He shall not be afraid of evil tidings: his heart is fixed, trusting in the Lord.
>
> —Psalm 112:7 KJV

Heaven has a new appeal for those of us who have seen a loved one off to that land, but earth has a new appeal too. We have been with God. He was more visible to us in our difficulties than in any of our pleasant times. Now we know something we never knew before, and living on earth has taken on a brand new dimension. One day it will be far, far better—we know because we have had a foretaste of His provision "this side of the valley." But until then, until that day when we all feast together with our loved ones again and with Jesus Himself, there is more than enough help on earth to get us through—in Dr. V. Raymond Edman's words, not just somehow but triumphantly.

SERENITY

Give me a quiet heart, O God,
that leans upon your shepherd-rod
in truth. When whirlwinds gather speed,
let it bring to You alone its need.
O take this throbbing cup of clay,
persuade it with Your deep still way.
Let it not pulse with lesser drum
of some imagined martyrdom,
or tom-tom rife with jungle lore,
or waves that splash a truant shore,
but hear Your quiet thunder's beat—
in Your serenity, complete.

—Wilma Burton

Epilogue:
In a Capsule

I know that peace does not come in capsules, but a friend who read this suggested a summary of helps:

If You Are in Need of Comfort

Learn about heaven and death from God—search the Bible for His answers.

Tell God exactly how you feel—pray the honest prayer and wait for His view.

Talk to God about your guilts and resentments.

Be aware of Satan.

Let your sad memories be spurs to thanking God.

Allow the normal helps of shock, busy-ness, the funeral, tears, etc., to do their work.

Face the reality of death and decide to do your work:

Think through your view of death.

Find out about the end.

Read.

Be alone and think.

Write letters or talk out loud to your loved one.

Say good-bye.

Examine your dreams occasionally.

Talk about your progress with a friend.

Say thank you.

Resume activities as you can.

Find someone who needs your help.
Believe that time is on your side and the sun will shine again.

If You Want to Help the Bereaved

Realize that a warm handshake, a hug, and eye contact are much better than words at first.

When the time is right, talk about heaven.

Avoid unfeeling "pat answers."

Try to sense his stage of grief and immediate need.

If appropriate, help him face the reality.

Pray for him.

Write out the thoughts and Scripture that have helped you in your grief.

Talk to him or write to him about the loved one he has lost.

Be perceptive about household tasks or errands you might help with.

Show your love in your own way—write a song, paint a picture, make a scrapbook.

Give him a short book to read.

Keep on being available to him as time goes by.

Notes

1. Catherine Marshall, *Adventures in Prayer* (Old Tappan, N.J.: Chosen Books, 1976), p. 13.
2. Dr. S. I. McMillen, *None of These Diseases* (Old Tappan, N.J.: Fleming H. Revell Co., 1963), p. 7.
3. C. M. Parkes, *Bereavement: Studies of Grief in Adult Life* (New York: International University Press, Inc., 1972).
4. Vance Havner, tape of Founders' Week Conference at Moody Bible Institute, February 5, 1974.
5. See, for example, Karl Menninger, M.D., *Whatever Became of Sin?* (New York: Hawthorn Books, 1973).
6. Parkes, *op. cit.*
7. Maureen Hay Read, "Walking in His Crunches," *Moody Monthly*, September 1975, pp. 75–77.
8. Catherine Marshall, *Something More* (New York: McGraw-Hill Book Co., 1974).
9. Paul Tournier, *The Meaning of Persons* (New York: Harper & Row, 1957), p. 170.
10. Edgar Jackson, *Concerning Death: A Practical Guide for the Living*, ed. by Earl A. Grollman (Boston: Beacon Press, 1974).
11. *Ibid.*, pp. 4, 6.
12. Elisabeth Kübler-Ross, *On Death and Dying* (New York: Macmillan, 1969).
13. Elisabeth Kübler-Ross, "On the Use of Psychopharmacologic Agents for the Dying Patient and the Bereaved," in Ivan K. Goldberg et al., eds., *Psychopharmacologic Agents for the Terminally Ill and Bereaved* (New York: Columbia University Press, 1973).
14. Parkes, *op. cit.*

15. Granger E. Westberg, *Good Grief* (Philadelphia: Fortress Press, 1962).
16. Parkes, *op. cit.*
17. Paul Patterson, "The Care of the Dying Child and His Family," in Goldberg, et al., eds., *op. cit.*, pp. 291–95.
18. Vance Havner tape.
19. See Eugenia Price, *No Pat Answers* (Grand Rapids, Mich.: Zondervan, 1974).
20. Tournier, *The Adventure of Living* (New York: Harper & Row, Publishers, 1965), p. 195.
21. Vance Havner tape.
22. William F. Rogers, *Ye Shall Be Comforted* (Philadelphia: Westminster Press, 1950).
23. Westberg, *op. cit.*
24. John Myers, compiler, *Voices from the Edge of Eternity* (Old Tappen, N.J.: Fleming H. Revell Co., 1971).
25. Joseph Bayly, *The View from the Hearse* (Moonachie, N.J.: Pyramid Publications, 1972).
26. Karlis Osis, *Deathbed Observations by Doctors and Nurses* (New York: Parapsychology Foundation, 1961), Monograph No. 3.
27. Dr. Charles C. Tart of the Department of Psychology, University of California, has recently done a pilot physiological study of a subject who reported many "out-of-body" experiences, all of which came in a "non-dreaming, non-awake brainwave stage, characterized by . . . slowed activity . . . and no activity of the autonomous nervous system." See *Journal, American Society for Psychical Research*, January 1968.
28. From *Poems by Emily Dickinson*, edited by Martha Dickinson Bianchi and Alfred Leete Hampson (Boston: Little, Brown and Company, 1957).
29. Corrie ten Boom, *The Hiding Place* (Old Tappen, N.J.: Chosen Books, 1961).
30. V. W. Sykes, "In Times of Stress."
31. CBS, "Grief Therapy," on *60 Minutes*, February 29, 1976.
32. Marshall, *Something More*, "To Sleep! Perchance to Dream."

33. Viktor E. Frankl, *Man's Search for Meaning: An Introduction to Logotherapy* (New York: Washington Square Press, 1963).
34. Watchman Nee, *A Table in the Wilderness* (Fort Washington, Pa.: Christian Literature Crusade, 1965).
35. Parkes, *op. cit.*
36. Rose Kennedy, *Times to Remember* (Garden City, N.Y.: Doubleday, 1974).

The
Incompleat
Angler

The
Incompleat
Angler

Fishing Izaak Walton's
Favorite Rivers

ROBERT G. DEINDORFER

Foreword by Nick Lyons

Drawings by Dorothea von Elbe

E. P. DUTTON | NEW YORK

Foreword copyright © 1977 by Nick Lyons

Library of Congress Cataloging in Publication Data

Deindorfer, Robert G
    The incompleat angler.

    1. Fishing—England.   I. Title.
SH606.D44   1977   799.1'2   76-58490

ISBN: 0-525-13292-9

Published simultaneously in Canada by
Clarke, Irwin & Company
Limited, Toronto and Vancouver
Designed by Dorothea von Elbe
10 9 8 7 6 5 4 3 2 1

First Edition

To Ken McElroy, Bob Portner, Brooks Roberts, and Nigel Wheeler, devoted brothers of the angle, in Walton's phrase, who have helped make the long sweet summers such a pleasure.

Foreword

Charm, wit, and warmth are words less and less applicable to current angling literature. Fishermen have become fascinated—even drugged—by the new. New fly patterns, new material for rods, new methods of casting dominate our books, and new frontiers in Argentina, the Arctic, New Zealand, and elsewhere, in our magazines, tease and taunt our imaginations. We want more sophisticated gear, bigger fish, ever new, even exotic, experiences.

The Incompleat Angler is a happy exception. It is a trip backward—to the water Izaak Walton fished, but also to old verities; it is very much a book that embodies, in prose that dances like a bright English brook, charm and wit and warmth.

There are no boasts or radical innovations here, nor any

sought. Bob Deindorfer merely wants to linger awhile with old Walton by the banks of some of his favorite rivers; he wants to catch some of the descendants of the fish the master caught—some of them, like roach and tench and bream, strange fish to American ears; he wants to let many of Walton's words trip off his tongue, to be tested against a current event, to be released from their musty past into the bright light of a very different age; he wants, I think, to bring Walton and Walton's sensibility into an era that may, to its great loss, have forgotten many of the old fisherman's gentle truths.

But Deindorfer is too cunning a writer, too much imbued with a fine practical Midwestern wit, to paint us a wartless Walton. Throughout this book, mingled with hilarious revelations of his own shortcomings, Deindorfer offers a shrewd debunking of Walton himself. "If the old boy occasionally stretched the truth," he says, "it strikes me that makes him an even more appropriate father figure for a cult whose members are often given to hyperbole." And since Walton is a "celebrated old wormslinger," and not above using other lowly baits, to fish Walton's water properly Deindorfer must use the old boy's methods and baits: a facsimile rod for one foray, ground bait, dough, maggots, golden sprats, and even live goldfish. He sprinkles bread on the water with the grace of Leslie P. Thompson, another avid flyfisher who wrote knowledgeably about the canny art of angling for carp.

The marvelous, memorable trip begins on the holy waters of the Test, where Skues, Halford, and Lord Grey also fished, travels to lesser fishing on such rivers as the Trent, the Lee, the Dove, Shawford Brook, the New River, the Manifold, the mighty Thames, the Meon, the Avon, and winds up on the exquisite and haunting Itchen. Along the way we get priceless glimpses of British rurals— "His face was a blotchy red, like a stale salmon, probably because he was a bit late in the season himself"; a telling look at how seriously the British dress for their fishing—there is a friend who ". . . changed *upwards* . . . after a cocktail party before we set off to fish the evening rise"; lovely portraits of back roads and rolling hills, cathedrals and old mills, fishing cottages and delicate rivers, a lady water-bailiff who still talks of Walton and Charles Cotton in the present tense. And there are shrewd perceptions on the sport and on life—"Luck is a measurable factor when men are after roach, just as it is when they are after a corporate vice-presidency, a particular bird, or a seat on the city council." There is even a delicious bit of "match fishing" on the Lee.

The American in England fares well—on *truite au bleu, pomme sable, garre de porc dijonnaise*—at the Sheriff House Hotel in Stockbridge and elsewhere; like Walton, he loves good food and always has time to tell us about it in evocative detail. If he fares somewhat less well on the rivers—blanking out on the Lee, losing big pike, big trout, and an awesome salmon (out of season)—he does so with grace, beyond embarrassment, telling all, to our enormous delight as readers and our instant identification. Deindorfer, like most of us, is as passionate about his fishing as he is prone to disaster. And, like those of us who try long and hard enough, he occasionally hooks and lands some startling fish.

What a delightful book this is, then. Its backward look is revealing and its vignettes are etched with lasting wit and clarity. Deindorfer lives so easily with Walton's words and waters that they come magically alive for us, and his prose is as warm and intimate as Walton's waters.

Nick Lyons

New York
January, 1977

Preface

Between the time I first hit on the notion of fishing Izaak Walton's favorite rivers and the moment when the publisher put his official blessings in writing, an old friend whose judgment generally is more astute than my own filed an objection.

"Sooner or later you'll get bored stiff," he said. "The rivers will begin to look all the same."

In suggesting I back off from the adventure on the grounds there was a genuine sameness to the rivers, my friend exposed an awkward lack of understanding, which wasn't surprising. Despite his other manifold virtues, he didn't and still doesn't fish. If he did, of course, he would know that rivers are no more alike one to another than football players, or people, or even the fish that swim the rivers, for that matter. While streams may seem to bear a superficial resemblance, they vary in terms of pools, depth, color, contour, flow, fly hatch, mood, and such detail as a rock riffling a run up near the far bank, which makes them quite different indeed.

Personally, I only wish that I had had the chance to fish even more of the old boy's assorted waters. Given Walton's perfectly understandable urge to wet a line wherever he went, the supply of target rivers was simply beyond my available time and budget. It would have been fascinating trying my blighted luck on the Ouse, for example, and the Derwent. But since I have angled with Walton more than most people, I have no complaints.

None of this is to suggest that I am any great authority on Izaak Walton. I was introduced to his classic work when I was a fingerling, I have re-read it several times since, I boned up on the book again before my pilgrimage commenced, I even went through a bottle of Murine ransacking English libraries in search of other pertinent background material without ever freighting myself with the knowledge to become an expert. My charter was fishing, not scholarship.

For the purposes of this book, I decided to treat the five editions of *The Compleat Angler*, which Walton wrote and revised, as one. Unlike many contemporary authors who merely correct the spelling and unwind grammatical lapses any time their books go into another printing, he revised quite extensively once he saw he was onto a good thing. While new swatches were added, others were abbreviated or cut entirely, Charles Cotton's section on flyfishing appeared out of thin air. Eventually Walton's original thirteen chapters inflated to a total of twenty-one.

Despite the many changes, I prefer to quote passages without bothering to cite the specific edition. I selectively squeezed the material as suited my purpose, culling some dialogue from one edition, some how-to fishing from another, some background music from yet another. While I jumbled the various editions, I always tried to adhere to the fundamental beat of his work, which doesn't alter from one printing to another.

The fact that I caught fewer fish than I should have, although somewhat more than I honestly expected to, is the fault of the disciple rather than the master. Even the most dutiful application of the detailed directions Walton generously offered up can do only so much in the case of a woefully incompleat angler.

On those few occasions when I actually managed to catch more than my usual ration of fish, which is to say at least one, I may not have demonstrated my usual becoming modesty. The intoxicating experience of catching a fish now and then inevitably produced a certain amount of idle boasting I normally have no cause to exercise. Besides, these infrequent references hew to the stricture laid down in iron not by Walton but by catfish Mark Twain: "Nobody with a full stringer of fish goes home by way of the back alley."

Finally, the traditional acknowledgements are very much in order here. In addition to apologizing to my wife, Joan, and son, Scott, who forgave me my truancy when I might better have stayed home riffling the sports pages or snapping at some baits myself in the kitchen, I am especially indebted to Richard Walker, the splendid British angling writer; to Dermot Wilson, fisher, writer, and businessman; to Pete Thomas of Hardy Brothers; to an assortment of river keepers, water bailiffs, and property owners, who kindly gave me access to some verboten waters posted with "Positively No Fishing" signs; and to Susan Smith and Charles Sopkin of E. P. Dutton, whose patience never faltered.

Most of all, I am indebted to the original who made it all possible. In the softer, more dreamlike parts of my memory I have fished with Izaak Walton on the Trent, on his beloved Dove, on the picturesque Itchen twining through

Hampshire. My only regret ought to come as no surprise. I'm sorry time ran out before both the fish and I had had our fill.

Robert G. Deindorfer

New York City
Closed Season 1977

The
Incompleat
Angler

Up he came, once, twice, three times, pinwheeling, throwing water, fanning a thick tail, glinting in the speckled light, a fish the size of a daydream, an awesome brown trout sullenly trying to shake the number 16 Iron-Blue dry fly hooked in the hinge of its massive jaw.

If that particular trout was not the biggest fish in the river, he was at least ample enough for a date with the local taxidermist, which was exactly what I had in mind. Surely the heaviest trout I ever hooked on a dry fly ought to be hung on the library wall back home, Exhibit A, a conversation piece to be accompanied by a proper deprecating monologue already half unwinding in my mind: "not a bad fish, thanks, a brute when he started to run, had to play him very carefully with such a light leader, size 5x, as I recall, almost lost him in some star weed there."

1

The rod point high, the line taut without straining the leader too much, I worked the fish slowly while my bearded British gillie stood in his waders close by supplying a running pep talk. He was a man well worth listening to. We had been through a good bit together that day, the gillie and I, not the least of it several pints of dark beer he miraculously conjured up to pass the time while a patch he had put in my leaky boots had a chance to set.

Except for the occasional sound of my prize trout thumping the water, the afternoon was peaceful and still. Some ducks lazed below us, cows grazed on a rumpled hillside spilling southward, a willow tree fluttered in the wind near the river's edge. It was a familiar English day, sunshine and shadows, with an edge of chill every time the clouds closed in.

Along the far bank, framed against a roll of green land, the latest production model—green, the wheels polished to a shine, two bucket seats—stood outside a custom-built buggy works. In a garden behind a thatch-roofed stone cottage a withered old man in a deerstalker hat leaned on a fence watching us.

All the sights and sounds of that day remain locked in my mind. After all, I was finally filling in a wistful dream by fishing the River Test in England. Happily for my sake, the old saying "Even God couldn't have a day on the Test" isn't altogether true. As a number of outland anglers have found for themselves, anyone willing to travel a distance and pay the stiff going rate can arrange to fish these waters. It's expensive—with river selling at up to $200,000 * a mile if and when it comes on the market, which is not often, it has to be, of course—but memorable experiences generally are.

* For the sake of my sanity I'm converting dollars and sterling at an easy-does-it rate of $2 the pound throughout this book. During my angling holiday the conversion factor fluctuated some, with an average of around $2, which made prices relatively inexpensive for me, if not the British.

If fishing has its holy waters, they have to include the Test, a river straight out of the gallery, cold and clear, twining through green meadowland dim with distance in the hills of Hampshire. Men whose names are a part of fishing folklore—Skues and Halford, Lord Grey and Hewitt, Ritz and Wulff—have cast, cast, cast their lines on this classic English stream. Better still, Izaak Walton, the original, the one and only, the illustrious old boy himself, not only fished it in his own potluck fashion but also willed an adjoining leased farm to his son.

In the end the vision of the epic trout enshrined on a laquered board went the way of all too many visions. Suddenly he boiled down the river along some bullrushes. As I checked the line only a bit, the leader snapped off; he was gone, captive no longer, free to swim the Test until someone more patient, more skillful, more accustomed than I to walloping big trout brought him safely to the net.

"You lost him." An unmistakable pinch of reproach hardened my gillie's country accents. "You didn't give him time enough, did you, and you lost him."

Later that day, after replaying the wretched scene over again in my mind, it struck me that his brief analysis, while basically sound, was not altogether accurate. Oh, I'd lost the trout all right, lost the trout due to careless fishing, but another Englishman had put such disasters into softer focus.

"Nay, the trout is not lost; for pray take notice, no man can lose what he never had."

Who wrote it? Who else?

Later still, I assuaged some of my grief by ingesting a genuine three-star dinner—*pomme sable, truite au bleu, garre de porc dijonnaise*—at the Sheriff House Hotel in Stockbridge, whose kitchen was the single most impressive I was to encounter in my subsequent have-rod/will-travel tour of England. As I learned on my third or fourth visit, Mr. Fisher, *chef de cuisine*, not only makes his own ice cream but sacrifices any surplus each night and confects a fresh batch again the following morning. If my regard for the cooking at a small-town hotel seems excessive, skeptics need only consider a more significant testimonial. Every summer two Parisian couples reverse life's natural flow by packing off to the Sheriff House for a full week of custom gastronomy they have worked up on a sort of mail-order basis with Fisher ahead of time.

In warming myself on other familiar lines from the standard source after dinner, I realized that it was time to settle an old account. Despite the astonishing fish I had missed, I'd caught seven respectable trout that day, one of them probably four pounds—well, three pounds for sure—along with endless other fish on other waters in other seasons. A vagabond American thankful for years of angling can hardly be blamed for paying proper respects when he gets the chance, can he?

First thing next morning I drove through Nether Wallop and Stockbridge to Winchester, nine miles away, located the magnificent Norman cathedral, parts of which date back to the eleventh century, walked through the massive outer doors. There in the cathedral's south transept, in a small chapel lighted with stained-glass windows, the remains of Izaak Walton lie buried under memorial stone graven with the usual sentiments.

Three hundred years after his death, affable, comfortable Izaak Walton enjoys a special immortality few figures in English literature can match. His name actually has filtered into the language. Throughout the English-speaking world the response to "Fishermen" in word-association games amounts to pure reflex: "Walton."

On the basis of only one book—*The Compleat Angler, or the Contemplative Man's Recreation, Being a Discourse of Fish and Fishing, Not Unworthy the Perusal of Most Anglers*, to spin out the full title—Walton will forever be identified with the leisurely old sport he roved the countryside to pursue. In view of the remarkable popularity of his great hodge podge of fishing techniques, recipes, jokes, verse, ballads, and rural atmosphere, it is no wonder the classic has been a perennial big seller ever since its publication in 1653.

Although Walton was far from infallible—Atlantic salmon do not spawn in April and May, for example, pike don't breed out of pickerel weed, carp grow faster than he realized—his guidance was generally sound.

Hear him: ". . . the crumbs of white bread and honey, made into a paste, is a good bait for a carp." What midwestern farmboy hasn't rolled a piece of bread into a doughball, kneaded it onto a hook, and fished the river bottom in hopes of bagging a scavening carp?

". . . and before you begin to angle, cast to have the wind on your back; and the sun, if it shines, to be before you." What proficient flycaster doesn't go to great effort to approach a promising piece of water with the wind on his back and any sun up ahead where it will not spotlight him for the very trout he wants to bamboozle?

". . . fishing with a dead rod, and laying night-hooks, are like putting money to use; for they both work for the owners when they do nothing but sleep, or eat, or rejoice." Any honest inventory of my own past must include the soft Arkansas night when a dear friend and I ate, slept, and—to the extent it is possible in the village of Mountain Home—rejoiced while a long trotline festooned with I have forgotten just how many baited hooks stretched like a deadfall across the mouth of a bay in Lake Norfork.

". . . broil him on charcoal, or wood-coal, that are free from smoke, and all the time he is a-broiling, baste him with the best sweet butter. . . ." What angler with an IQ equivalent to his body temperature does not much prefer a fresh-caught fish broiled over a woodfire, preferably right

5

along the riverbank, basted with what passes for sweet butter nowadays? The mere suggestion is enough to make the juices run.

Yet contemporary critics fault the litterateur whose remains lay there in Winchester Cathedral on several counts. Among other things, they say he lifted passages from earlier books such as *The Treatyse of Fysshynge Wyth an Angle,* circa 1496, which is perfectly true, although it is only fair to add that Walton specifically credited several sources he selectively poached. And anglers generally have a dim sense of property rights.

Walton undoubtedly would have denied it, I feel sure, but he also stands accused of overstating the facts by way of illustrating various points in his classic. He mentions taking forty trout in an hour on a stream in Kent, never missing fish with a grasshopper, invariably hooking and landing oversized fish any time he set his mind to it. But if the old boy occasionally stretched the truth, it strikes me that it makes him an even more appropriate father figure for a cult whose members are often given to hyperbole.

Besides, Walton frequently gave people as well as fish the best of it. In one extravagant passage he wrote, "most anglers are quiet men, and followers of peace; men that were so simply wise, as not to sell their consciences to buy riches, and with them vexation and a fear to die." Most anglers know that we are no such thing, much as we wish to be, of course, but we like to tell ourselves that this is so.

Almost predictably, the figure whose book has spun down through the centuries has been deprecated by hardshell flycasters for fishing frogs, minnows, grasshoppers, and practically anything else he could lay his hands on. Unless these censors were actually born with Silver Doctors in their mouths and thus didn't undergo an apprenticeship swimming snarls of worms for bullheads—the sweet snapshot of which still lingers in my memory—they presumably once fished in much the same fashion themselves. They also choose to ignore the fact that flyfishing was only in its infancy in the sixteenth and seventeenth centuries that Walton inhabited. He was fishing the status quo.

Along with those and other criticisms, the maestro has been charged with confecting rhetoric a bit rich for the blood. Maybe so. Taste in literary style tends to be highly subjective, like taste in motorcars, political candidates, or, for that matter, live baits. In my own peckish view, many contemporaries who fault Walton on this score are themselves addicted to a lockstep subject-verb-predicate English endemic in all too much business correspondence. "Your check of last week was received with thanks," is perfectly all right provided it is a communiqué from the mail-order house but, for myself, I couldn't read two hundred pages of the stuff without someone holding a gun to my skull.

Literal people who read *The Compleat Angler* strictly for nonskid accuracy, angling technique, and a becoming modesty on the part of the author miss the essential background music reverberating through the work. More than anything else, the book is a lyric hymn to the pastoral life, to leafy trees leaning against dappled skies, to comely milkmaids walking twisted footpaths, to lambs grazing shiny green fields, to good company and good discourse, described as the very sinews of virtue. Every now and then Walton also reminded readers of his own prescription for the good life: "Study to be quiet."

Gazing at the dates (1593–1683) marked on the memorial stone in the south transept, I could not help but realize the formula had worked out well for Walton. Back in an era when most people didn't live much longer than a fruitfly, the angler not only stretched his life to a full ninety seasons but lasted until heavy storms put a dent in the fishing in 1683.

When sightseers began to fill the big cathedral that morning, it was time to heed his advice to "be quiet, and go a-angling." On the road from Winchester to Nether

Wallop—I manfully resisted the impulse to stop by the Sheriff House for an order of whatever they might have on hand—I covered some yeasty territory. Among a host of other misty figures, Dick Turpin the notorious highwayman and Lady Godiva the bareback bareback rider once lived here.

At Dermot Wilson's Old Mill in Wallop, so antique that it is actually cited in the *Domesday Book* (1085), I looked at a dazzling assortment of new rods and reels, lines and lures, boots and jackets in the tackle shop without ever quite breaching a poorboy family budget, but it was touch-and-go there for a moment while I gave a lovely eight-foot cane rod a few sample whips.

In a cubbyhole office in his flourishing shop, I wrote a check to cover the cost of my fishing the day before. Wilson, a brisk, bouncy man whose hairline is disappearing as fast as his native teeth, leases water on both the Test and the Itchen—at least when he isn't fishing it himself, which is frequent, else he might just as well be back in London squeezing advertising copy out of his thumb, as he had for many seasons.

"How about a go on the lake before you leave?" he kindly suggested.

"No, no. I don't think so, thanks very much. I'm running out of time."

"Well, come have a look, anyway."

Behind the old stone millhouse, a large pool shimmered in the sunshine. It looked to measure up to the specifications Walton defined. In a section entitled "Of Fish-Ponds, and How to Order Them," he advises, "And note, that in all pools, it is best to have some retiring-place; as namely, hollow banks, or shelves, or roots of trees, to keep them from danger; and, when they think fit, from the extreme heat of summer, as also from the extremity of cold in winter."

I walked the near side, turned to leave, spun round

8

again. Down in the depths beyond the hollow banks, big dark shadows slowly stirred.

"I don't suppose it would hurt to fish it for a few minutes," I said. A vagrant nerve set my left eyelid to quivering. Fumbling some, I tied a number 10 brown and white marabou streamer—unlike the Test, where only dry flies and upstream nymphs were legal, practically anything goes in Wilson's pond—to a nine-foot 4x leader, flexed the rod back and forth, offered the fish a toothsome bill-of-fare.

For the first few casts I might just as well have been working the Fox River back in Aurora, Illinois, although from what I hear, the old waterway is crusted with so much pollution nowadays it would take a diving bell to submerge a lure. On a fairly long cast a fish followed the retrieve without showing the proper suicidal impulse. The next cast put me into a big boisterous rainbow trout.

The fish rose out of the water, shook hard—"Very pleasant and jolly," to lift a phrase from Walton—and flashed toward a weedbed near the far side. After my galling experience on the Test, I let him run. If I managed to land him safely, I told myself, he might weigh in at close to five pounds. I did. He was. The rainbow measured 21½ inches, scaled four and a half pounds, or about right for two British friends whose access to fresh-caught trout was not what it ought to be, given their prodigious taste for it.

"A nice fish well played," Dermot Wilson remarked.

In the jubilation of finally landing a substantial trout, my normal sense of modesty evaporated. "Remember Walton's line," I said. "Remember, he said that angling 'is an art, and an art worthy the knowledge and practice of a wise man.' Well . . ." Wilson's face went blank.

Once he realized that I was only half serious, however, Wilson did the proper thing by inviting me back into the mill for a memorial drink, although I wasn't sure exactly what the local definition of a drink might be after an offhand remark by my gillie the day before. Apropos of noth-

9

ing at all, unless he was trying to wheedle me into a sponsored tour of some nearby pub, the gillie had admitted to an astonishing capacity. "I take off to the pub and me mates, and I can hold me own with anybody," he had said. "At me best I can do two bottles of an evening." Since this sounded in the nature of a boast, I assumed he meant whisky, not beer, and quarts, not pints, which suggested his best was stupendous.

Over what subsequently turned out to be a total of merely two drinks with me mate Wilson, the two of us traveled a familiar old road together. We talked Izaak Walton. We talked Walton the London ironmonger, Walton the affectionate biographer, Walton the pious churchgoing Anglican, even Walton the instant adventurer.

While the excitement of wrestling big fish up onto the grass was sufficient for our mutual forebear, Walton was caught in a brief flicker of another sort of excitement. After the defeat of the Royalist forces at Worcester in 1651, an officer entrusted him with the "Lesser George" jewels of Charles II, then in exile. Traveling by coach, posing as nobody but himself, brimming with his usual good fellowship, Walton successfully completed the mission by delivering the treasure to the Tower of London.

But mostly Wilson and I talked Walton the angler, whose habits, while otherwise fairly impressive, included maggots and live frogs, which offend the sensibilities of many a modern purist. While Walton was indeed a bait fisherman, which Wilson emphatically was not, the proprietor of Nether Wallop Mill takes a surprisingly tolerant view of the *Compleat Angler*. In his professional opinion— Wilson has several fishing books to his credit—much of the antique masterpiece is surprisingly sound in terms of technique, especially for a report filed more than three hundred years ago, and he considers the mellow flavors effective even by his own former standards. "Walton would have made a splendid advertising copywriter," Wilson said.

With advertising types notorious for privately disparaging their craft en route home to Greenwich, Connecticut, in a new Lamborghini, I was not altogether sure that remark constituted an endorsement, although his occasional exaggeration and plagiarism certainly would not have disqualified Walton from Madison Avenue.

In discussing the celebrated old wormslinger, Wilson and I admitted to regretting the fact that Walton the individual remains a relatively hazy figure. Like a number of other prominent Englishmen who lived at the time, little biographical detail, little anecdotal lore, little in the way of personal belongings survive. One of the very few artifacts still around, in fact, is an heirloom wicker creel he reportedly once carried, which is on display at the Flyfishers' Club on Old Brook Street in London, where both Wilson and I pay annual dues. Except for its somewhat bigger size—perhaps the man who compiled the *Almanach de Gotha* of fishes was not stretching the size of his catch, after all—the basket looks surprisingly like the expensive models displayed in the front window of Abercrombie & Fitch every springtime.

Otherwise Walton did not leave much apart from his classic and the rivers he loved to fish. Nobody knows exactly how many of the abundant English waterways he managed to work in pursuit of a chub, a roach, or a trout. "For the rivers of this nation, there be, as you may note out of Doctor Heylin's *Geography* and others, in number three hundred and twenty-five," he wrote. He did not fish anywhere near Dr. Heylin's arbitrary total, of course, not with public transportation confined to a coach-and-four, but, to read him carefully, he visited a number of rivers, using different baits, killing different species, fishing by day and by night, depending, right around the calendar.

Izaak Walton did time on the waters around his old hometown of Stafford, in the London orbit he inhabited before he became a literary success, in Hampshire where

11

he spun out his last leisurely years. If those rivers were as fascinating as I found the Test a day earlier—well, a whisper of an idea slowly evolved in my mind.

"Wouldn't it be fun to fish Walton's favorite rivers?" I mused.

"Yes, wouldn't it," Wilson mechanically said.

"Seriously now, wouldn't it be fun, really great fun, if I were to fish his favorite rivers for different fish, sometimes in much the same way he did?" It was plain to me, if not to Wilson, that I'd accelerated past the musing limit.

Without in any way trying to let the wind out of my bulging enthusiasm, Wilson felt compelled to offer up a few reference points for the sake of trans-century perspective. While he expected my access to the rivers themselves would be no great problem, not if I was willing to pay whatever the going day-ticket rate happened to be, even an occasional attempt to angle in the authentic style of the original might involve complications, such as line braided out of horsehair. A vision of my wife, Joan, knitting me several yards of the ways and means out behind some stable area was too improbable to conjure up.

In an effort to keep my gathering new project afloat, I couldn't help but recollect Walton's prescription for anyone in search of "those leather-mouthed fishes" he wrote about with such a lyric tone. "You must have a small hook," he said in his book, "a quick eye and a nimble hand or the bait is lost and the fish too." At least small hooks were available at any proper tacklemonger.

If my skills did not measure up to the challenge I was by then plainly prepared to take up, it would not be the first time I had gone into battle relatively unarmed. Twenty-five years earlier, I had agreed to box two rounds with Joe Louis, wrestle reigning world's champion Primo Carnera, and bat against big-league pitcher Bob Feller, all that in return for a magazine check of what seemed splendid dimensions, along with any legitimate expenses to cover medical and hospital costs, which subsequently came to nearly $125. I was no novice at being a novice.

After Dermot Wilson supplied the names of several acquaintances who could help lead me to the sacred rivers, it was time to stop abusing his cheery hospitality. The narrow roadway rose, climbing higher, and when I turned onto a wider, busier track, Stockbridge lay stretched out below me, etched in the soft sunlight, two compulsory waters close by, the Test winding over meadowland to the left, the Itchen a few miles to the right, one of them to be fished again, the other to be worked for the first time, strictly in the interest of research, sort of.

In the rich pudding of a book he wrote, except for those parts he mooched from several earlier works, anyway, Izaak Walton baldly admitted to a happy coincidence. "I have made myself a recreation of a recreation," he said in a long preliminary wind-up entitled "To all Readers of this Discourse, but Especially to the Honest Angler."

Very well. I was about to do the old boy one better. Whatever my deficiencies as a twentieth-century brother of the angle, I was about to make a recreation of *his* making a recreation of a recreation.

In England the natives have a kinky habit of identifying themselves with initials instead of full names—either first or last, depending on rank, Elizabeth R for the Queen, for instance, N.J.G. Wheeler for mere mortals like a brother of the angle—all of which can add a flutter of intrigue to even routine blind communications.

In the case of the water bailiff whose bailiwick happens to include a stretch of the River Dove that I. Walton loved beyond any other, I was given the standard reference, D. Oliver, nothing more. Idly I got to spinning possibilities in my mind while I worked the telephone: Derek, Duncan, David, Douglas, Darwin, Daniel, maybe even Dirk, which had an especially prickly "Be Off—This Is Strictly Private Water" flavor to it.

"Mister Oliver, please," I said once the crapshoot British phone system finally rolled the proper numbers.

"I'm sorry, there is no Mister Oliver here," a pleasant alto voice replied.

So I hadn't got through after all. At least I had better seek some guidance.

"It's Mister D. Oliver the water bailiff I'm trying to get hold of. Could you please help me?"

"I'm D. Oliver the water bailiff." D. Oliver paused, treated me to a gurgling laugh. "D. for Dora."

After arranging to fish the Dove two weeks later, I got to wondering how the cheery immortal whose pet rivers I was working with my usual limited success might have reacted to the situation. As a child of the sixteenth century, Izaak Walton held a view of women that, while essentially tolerant, was not so revolutionary as to see them repairing dams, spearing scavenger fish, and chasing stray poachers through the dead of night. In *The Compleat Angler* and several of the extravagant biographies he wrote, ladies enacted an ornamental and/or traditionally utilitarian role, preferably both, such as his own first wife, a pretty woman who produced a total of seven children, or "three and a half brace," as Walton used to count.

Those women he uses as background to the angling in his masterpiece often are comely milkmaids, serving wenches, young girls playing in leafy glens. While the old boy never once implies that they might be qualified for something more, he does treat them all kindly, as he did in a brief encounter he describes with characteristic relish in a chapter otherwise devoted to a fish called the barbel. "God speed you, good woman," Walton wrote. "I thank you both for our songs last night. I and my companions have had such fortune a-fishing this day, that we resolve to give you and Maudlin a brace of trouts for supper; and we will now taste a draught of your red cow's milk."

Despite his dated assessment of women—and mine, too, come to think of it—Dora Oliver sounded an informed, well-qualified water bailiff. "The river is absolutely crawling with grayling," she told me by phone. "Remember the drill—dry flies and upstream nymphs only, small sizes, if you don't mind the odd suggestion, sixteens, even eighteens, and on fine casts." That last was another example of the English English I was only beginning to adjust to. At my home pool on New York's Neversink River, we say light leaders instead of fine casts.

Up I went, over my wife Joan's dead body once again, a few days before Christmas, my jacket bulging with can't-miss resident flies prescribed by the flimflam man whose tackle shop I practically underwrote there for a few months, a wild old surge of hope rising like sap as I drove the M5 motorway north into the English midlands the night before my date with Ms. Oliver. At Stafford, where Walton was born in 1593, the son of a publican, or saloon-keeper, I spun onto a country road.

After things went a bit hazy I stopped at a welcome wash of light called the Plough—a good honest alehouse, as Walton used to say—for road directions and a healing pint. As things turned out, the healing process ran to two pints before I bothered to ask the proprietor if he could point me toward the Izaak Walton Hotel in Dovedale.

"Best you talk with Spare Time." He reached into a big jar, extracted a pickled egg for another client. "Spare Time knows the way like his bloody face."

"Spare Time?" This was more bewildering than the customary barrage of initials.

"Righty-ho. Spare Time. He has bags of it—and he spends it right here, worse luck. Little raggedy bloke in the corner."

The proprietor had in no way demeaned him. Spare Time resembled many another English rural, small and bent, clad in rumpled corduroys, a tattered jacket and Wellington boots. With a good thatch of white hair and rather less than the normal ration of teeth, his face was a blotchy red, like a stale salmon, probably because he was a

16

bit late in the season himself. The meticulous directions he proceeded to issue in a dry cracked voice were detailed right down to brand names.

"You take a right-hand turning at the next pub, good pub, too, the Three Tons, they serve Joulds Bitters and M and B Mild," he said, "follow on over the rail bridge, take a hard left-hand turning at the T-junction, just past the village store, tobaccos and sweets on sale, closed this time of night, mind you. . ."

Before I had the chance to stop him, Spare Time treated me to an instant replay by reciting the whole monologue all over again, virtually word for commercial word, including a reference to an assortment of potato crisps on sale in the shop shut down for the night, to be certain I didn't miss a mark, as he said.

Given bearings as scrupulous as all that, I drove through a sheeting rain with renewed confidence. Even now I have no way of knowing whether his intricate background detail was sound, although I was briefly tempted by the Joulds Bitters on passing the Three Tons, but S. Time's road directions were what the British call bang-on. In less than an hour I was seated in front of a crackling log fire ingesting a plate of chicken sandwiches at the Izaak Walton, "a dry house over our head," in the words of its illustrious namesake.

Next morning, a bellman felt obliged to justify the big sign lettered over the front door by showing me a slim booklet entitled *An Angler's Days in Dovedale*. "Part of the Izaak Walton is as old, or older than its name," read a section the bellman specifically directed my attention to, "for there is a tradition that in this old farmhouse (since much enlarged) the great Piscator himself used to take up his abode when he had fished down the dales from Beresford Hall with his friend, Charles Cotton." Right: Walton slept here.

Framed in the front window of the hotel, the wrinkled

land spilled down between dry stone walls to the Dove, whispering along a crooked gravel course. Beyond, on the far side, the country climbed into a tumble of rolling hills and limestone bluffs. Sheep and Holstein cattle grazed the distant slopes, remote, immobile, figures off an old canvas.

On a grid of back roads to Ashbourne, where I was to buy my license, I passed through Tissington and Fenny Bently, Milldale and Biggin. Along the way the car radio treated me to what the BBC announcer described as a "gramophone" of B. Crosby singing White Christmas. I paused while a young herdsman drove some cows that were less remote than I originally calculated up the road and into a pasture.

A license to fish for a period of seven days cost me ten pence, or about twenty cents American, a very great bargain, needless to say, even considering a number of prohibitions in fine print on the flip side, such as "the use of explosives," a stricture Walton himself would have applauded, I felt sure, despite his generally elastic definition of baits. The fact that the license was issued in a tackle shop cost me another three pounds, forty-two pence, in various odds and ends I convinced myself I could not possibly do without.

Outside the village of Hartington, I pulled the bell on a stone cottage. A woman appeared in the doorway, a ruddy smiling woman, broad and sturdy, like the cottage. Miss Dora Oliver pumped my hand, waved me inside, invited me to join her for a cup of tea, and introduced a Scottish collie she had found down near the river two years before. In her worn denim trousers, Wellington boots, insulated all-weather jacket, with a kerchief knotted around her brown hair, she looked the very picture of what a woman water bailiff ought to be.

"I have been the bailiff on this piece of the Dove for twenty-seven years now," she told me. "My father was the keeper before me. I was with the British army, a lance corporal, in transports before they gave me a desk job. It nearly broke my heart when they took me off the road. Am I blathering on?"

I assured her she wasn't. "My father, he knew a tremendous lot about fishing, more than most anyone for miles around, fish habits, the flies, a tremendous bit." She paused briefly. "I know enough. You can fish only grayling today. Trout season on the Dove doesn't begin until the eighteenth of March, and that's all we have in the river, grayling and trout, except for the odd predator fish."

That was not true of the Dove back when Walton regularly fished it with any baits he could lay his hands on. It produced a volume of salmon as well as basic trout and grayling. Salmon were once so common hereabouts, in fact, that, according to deeds filed away in the church at nearby Ilam, servants were not required to feed on them more than three times a week, although salmon is a luxury only the rich and the poachers can afford with that frequency nowadays.

"Well, we had best get on down to the river," Miss Oliver said, pulling a heavy mackinaw over her jacket and whistling the dog out front. "Day like this, you never know what might develop."

There was no sun. There was to be no rain, either, but there was no sun. It was one of those tentative, typically English days that couldn't ever quite make up its mind, chill, with some wind to it, the same as Walton must have often experienced. Now that her prewar Austin Seven had gone a bit long in the gearbox, Miss Oliver admitted to normally walking the mile or so down to the river unless some guest angler offered her a lift, as I did.

We parked near a "FISHING STRICTLY PRIVATE" sign nailed to an ash tree, locked the car tight in case any poachers with a taste for something more than fish appeared. Off to our left, the Dove tumbled down over a series of small dams—forty of them in only three and a half

19

miles, Miss Oliver told me—foaming over each dam, slowing in the flats between, piling up before its descent over the next. Once the river reached the floor of the valley, it dramatically changed, widening, losing speed, showing more color, about the size of the Battenkill around Arlington, Vermont, a lovely stream slowly twining across the land.

The solitude, the limestone bluffs rising on the far side, the whisper of the Dove, blotted out melancholy headlines from the morning newspaper; inflation, recession, another PLO raid into Israel, another IRA bombing, in Birmingham, not far away. But the peaceful beat, without intrusion or hurry, made it easy to understand what Walton, whose age was out of joint too, meant when he wrote, "for when the lawyer is swallowed up with business, and the statesman is preventing or contriving plots, then we sit on cowslip banks, hear the birds sing, and possess ourselves in as much quietness as these silent silver streams, which we now see glide so quietly by us."

Quickly I jointed up an eight-and-a-half-foot Hardy Phantom rod, attached a Hardy Perfect reel, knotted a twelve-foot leader to the floating line. Since I would be fishing from the bank rather than wading the river, I had a suspicion that my wayward backcast, which tends to develop some static even in the best of circumstances, might be vulnerable to a row of trees standing not far behind, like an obstacle course. Suspicion confirmed: On my third cast the fly hooked in a dying elm, just out of reach, like old times, which cost me both the fly and tippet.

"Have a go above the next weir," Miss Oliver suggested. "That piece of water holds some nice fish. See, see there, do you see what I mean?"

Near the far bank a fish rose, glinting briefly in the day, rose again. As I fanned the rod back and forth in the prescribed arc, lengthening my cast until there was line enough in play, the fish showed one more time, practically thumbing its nose at me. My response was pure reflex, Kt-KB3, perhaps three feet above the widening circle, almost perfect, except for one thing. Instead of landing with a feathery touch, the fly splashed down and the leader coiled some.

With the game plainly up in that particular precinct, due to my own carelessness, I prudently moved on to fish the tailwater below the next small dam. Casting a fly into a riffle of fast river is akin to boiling an egg: It's hard for even the least proficient among us to go wrong. Sure enough, a trout of two pounds—easily a pound, anyway—took my number-16 Woodcock and Red on the very first cast. So far as I know, the fish has it still, along with a tippet of light leader that snapped when I jerked the rod too hard. In the fell clutch of circumstance I could hardly be blamed for polluting the air with a recuperative barrage of down-home scatology, especially with Dora Oliver out of earshot at the moment.

Unless his language lost something in translation between the riverbank and the printshop, the master invariably exercised a more admirable restraint in the same wretched situations. "Oh me!" Piscator, or Walton, remarked in his classic work. "He has broke off: There's half a line and a good hook lost." In view of the fact that he was forced to pluck, dye, and braid his lines out of horsehair, I personally felt that Walton was entitled to react more emphatically, if he had chosen to.

Although I had yet to take a souvenir from the Dove, I was fishing better by the time I worked up around a turn and came upon the Pike Pool, a stunning sight, so lovely it catches at the throat. The river tumbles under a wooden footbridge, bellying into a broad pool, chutes around a jagged limestone column rising like a chimney stack, classic water, an angler's dream. Along the near side a gray squirrel scuttled up an elm, a flutter of rooks rose from a large horse chestnut.

Standing there on the riverbank in a pair of boots, experimenting with an import Hairwing Coachman fly from the Angler's Roost in New York City, I cast, until a small trout struck short. The fish surged again, "very gamesome at the fly," as Walton would say, connected, spun out of the water. It was a small brown trout, even smaller than I first imagined—so small, in fact, that I refuse to divulge its vital statistics, although not as modest as some of the fish a gray-haired old friend runs through his smoker on the Neversink during hard times.

The absurd sight of that diminutive trout wriggling in the folds of a big, long-handled net dimly reminded me of what amounts to a rhetorical Deindorfer family heirloom. Back when my father was an adolescent he ran mostly to vertical lines, tall and gangly, skinny as a rake, which wasn't unusual for a growing boy, although he was self-conscious about his lack of bulk, same as I was at approximately the same age. My father's bony appearance was in no way flattered by hand-me-down trousers previously occupied by my paternal grandfather, who was built to far more ample German-American specifications.

While my grandfather was a kind man, generous and inordinately proud of his family, he was wonderfully acerbic on any number of subjects, not the least of them his son's embarrassing scarecrow shape. On the occasion, my father used to wryly recall, he was attired in an especially baggy pair of pants which had been taken in not nearly enough. Twirling a cigar in his hand, grandfather rose to even greater lyric heights than usual. "Good God, Red, you've got a gallon of pants and only a pint of ass," he observed with what his son/my father later acknowledged was an altogether accurate interpretation of the situation.

With trout out of season in December and the specimen on hand so small that I was not tempted to breach the rules, I did the proper thing. The hook came out without drawing blood; the fish went back where it had come from.

As I rubbed mucilin onto the fly, Miss Oliver came up the dirt track along the river, stood watching for a few moments, broke some bread into scraps to feed the blue tits— lovely birds, tiny, all soft pastels, which have a hard time of it through the winter. "Mind you take a grayling here in the Pike Pool," she said, moving along, the dog trailing behind.

On my third cast after her departure, I was onto another fish in a heavy crease of water, a grayling, a good grayling, given to quicksilver runs, its telltale dorsal fin opened like a fan, using the current, drumming downriver, straining the 5x leader, running hard, a marvelous fish, fourteen inches by the tape, slim and perfect.

In *The Compleat Angler*, where seldom is heard a discouraging word about any particular species, not even the wretched ruffe, Walton reached an extravagant peak in cataloguing the virtues of the grayling. "For he will rise twenty times at a fly, if you miss him, and yet rise again," he observed, which, if true, strikes me as a great virtue indeed, especially in terms of the angler. "He has been taken with a fly made of the red feathers of the paroquet, a strange outlandish bird; and he will rise at a fly not unlike a gnat, or a small moth, or, indeed, at most flies that are not too big. He is a fish that lurks close all winter, but is very pleasant and jolly after mid-April, and in May, and in the hot months. He is of a very fine shape, his flesh is white; his teeth, those little ones that he has, are in his throat, yet he has so tender a mouth that he is oftener lost after an angler has hooked him than any other fish. Though there be many of these fishes in the delicate river Dove, and in Trent, and some other small rivers, as that which runs by Salisbury, yet he is not so general a fish as the trout, nor to me so good to eat or to angle for."

On the basis of my first and only grayling to date, those were my sentiments exactly. After the stirring experience with the fish in the Pike Pool, I worked on up the Dove at no particular profit except for an eerie sense of detachment. All round me the slack day lay peaceful and still. I lost a grayling in a swirl of fast water, undoubtedly the fault of that tender mouth, I gently reminded myself, and while I never saw a fish so avaricious, or fatuous, as to rise twenty times, another actually did make four passes at a small nymph without ever quite committing itself.

Later, I caught up with Dora Oliver as she was picking fallen kindling off the footpath along the river. To accomplish what she calls keepering the Dove for the family whose good fortune it is to own it, she mends any of the dams in need of repair, cleans the river with grappling irons, mounts a guard against any and all natural predators, including poachers. "I'm always on the lookout for poachers," she told me. "I vet the cars I don't know, stroll the lane near the river straight through the year. Every so often they really have me on the run, I can tell you that." Hemmed in by alien forces, stretched by long nights of patrol, Miss Oliver has developed a paranoia that seems fairly endemic among water bailiffs in England. "They keep trying, they always keep trying," she said, an edge to her voice, a suffering expression pinching her ruddy face.

After she managed to get a grip on her cheery disposition again, she led me on upstream to the special place she obviously considered the feature of any outlander's visit. Beyond a clump of willows, the river gently curled behind it, stood the fishing temple that Walton's brother of the angle and adopted son Charles Cotton—who himself contributed Part Two of the standard reference commencing with its fifth edition—had built for the two of them despite his chronic financial problems. It was a cubical gritstone retreat with leaded windows and a tall chimney, and an ornamental weathervane for which my friend Brooks Roberts would give what is left of his soul set over the steep slate roof.

"Come along inside," Miss Oliver said, unlocking the

double oak door. We passed under a heraldic-looking crest: Piscatoribus Sacrum, the initials CC and IW entwined in a cipher. Miss Oliver offered me a chair, a sandwich she extracted from a canvas bag strapped round her worn mackinaw. She offered everything except a log fire in the ample hearth behind me, which would have been nice on that chill December day. Even a shrew that squirted across the floor while we talked looked cold.

"Sometimes I sit in here by the hour," she said. I must have registered surprise. "Oh, I read some, the papers, a magazine, a paperback, and I think a lot. I often think of the two of them."

Miss Oliver unwrapped a sandwich for herself but made no signs of piling wood onto the fireplace. "I am fond of Charles, you know, of both of them, as a matter of fact, Charles and Izaak Walton. It warms me just to think of them. Charles is a nice man, a very nice man—kind, generous—a proper gentleman for all his financial problems."

All of a sudden I experienced a spooky feeling. All of a sudden I realized that she occasionally used the present tense in discussing two men who had been dead and gone for nearly three centuries. But I didn't even consider editing her lapse. Given the mood, the sweet music of the Dove washing outside, and the fact that this had once been their most favorite water, time was beginning to blur for me, too.

Surely it was easy to picture the two of them still, yarning, reciting remnants of verse, fishing what the old boy described as "the strongest swifts of the river," Walton soaking a few lobworms or a penk, Cotton casting an antique fly with a fourteen-foot greenheart rod, fishing until they killed enough not only for themselves but also for some resident milkmaid who forever seemed the beneficiary of Walton's kindness.

"They say poor Charles used to hide from his creditors in a cave up there." Miss Oliver pointed vaguely toward a steep limestone bluff. In view of my own hairline solvency in general and a forthcoming American Express statement covering a profligate pay-later shopping spree in London— what a dear English friend might describe as "a jolly good spend-up"—in particular, I idly wondered whether the cave would accommodate a size-46 extra long.

On our way back down the river after Miss Oliver locked the fishing temple tight, we paused beside a pool so clear I couldn't help but think of a pinch of Vermouth and a twist of lemon. Not ten yards away a grayling, a trout, something, dimpled the surface. Down I went. Face to the ground, elbows spread, my stomach flat as I could make it, I levered forward and to the left. From a crouch I cast a tiny Coachman, connected with another double-jeopardy small brown trout, undersized as well as out of season.

At the Pike Pool where I had earlier scored twice, sort of, I offered the water bailiff my rod if she wanted to have a fling. "No thank you," she said. "I was taught to flyfish when I was very, very young, but I don't fish anymore." With classic water like that available to her the year round, I expressed some surprise. "Well, you're living with nature, and when you live with nature, you don't kill things," she said. "Or at least I don't."

By swearing off angling completely, although nourishing no prejudice against those who enjoy it, Miss Oliver amounts to an ever greater conservative than the source who brought us together. While Walton never pretended to be a purist—far from it—he admitted to an aversion to all other forms of bloodshed. "For I am not of a cruel nature, I love to kill nothing but fish," he wrote.

Later, I left Dora Oliver in the cold afternoon, a hardy woman filled with buoyant spirit, her pickup dog on a leash, a walking stick in her hand, a scarf pulled tight over her brown hair, the rocky land rising behind her, the river chuting under a narrow footbridge, happy, contented with her lot, caught up in the spell of a mellow area, as I was, a good strong individual who has come to terms with modern times despite an occasional dip into the past.

"Mind you don't forget to mention Charles Cotton if you write anything about the Dove," she called as I waved through the car window. "People don't know so much about him, but he is a very nice man."

On my return trip twenty-four hours after Spare Time had given me such detailed road directions at the Plough, I could not resist the temptation. Inevitably, I suppose, he was right in position, same corner table, same rumpled attire, same empty pint, and a diminishing stack of potato chips within easy reach.

"Remember me?" I asked.

"Um, you are the Yank was looking for, um—" He blinked as his memory caught hold. "—looking for the Izaak Walton in Dovedale, that's it."

"Still looking."

"*Still* looking?"

His toneless old voice rose. It looked like I might take him on the very first cast.

"Yes, it must be two or three hours now since you were kind enough to issue me directions, but I'm still looking. I keep missing at the roundabout beyond the village store."

"Whee-crikey. It wasn't two-three hours ago. It was yesterday evening. Mean you been potting over the near roads ever since yesterday evening? Whee-crikey!" The pensioner's rubicund face drained white. I did not even have to change flies.

"You've been pecking away at that malt for too long, Spare Time. It can't possibly be more than two or three hours—well, four, at the most."

The rod tip high, the line tight, I was in no great hurry to wind the reel. A fellow who has traveled a distance to walk Izaak Walton's bootsteps on the River Dove can not really be blamed for playing a stray fish even out of season some, can he?

THE fish jumped, a foot of gleaming silver, arched for a long moment in the soft, summery air, hit the surface hard in an effort to shake the feathered Judas lodged in its jaw. Quickly it drummed upstream, reaching for the fast water washing below a stone dam, where it jumped again, slim and perfect, a brown trout with an I-say-there English accent.

The brownie stunting in the picture river was not the biggest I have ever hooked, precise specifications of which I refuse to divulge for fear my career trophy might not sound as epic as it ought to, but it was not the smallest, either, especially after several seasons on the Battenkill in Vermont. Besides, the game was far from up. After all, I was fishing fairly fine, with a number-16 Cockwing Dun knotted to a twelve-foot 5x leader, which can add a shiver of suspense playing even small fish due to my boyish tendency to overreact before things have reached a proper boil.

For a change I managed to resist my customary manic impatience and let the trout gradually wear down, although there was an experience near a flat rock when it looked like more of the same old thing. In the end the fish slipped obediently into the net, quivering in the folds, went slack after a ritual blow with a staghorn priest, mine own, to lift a phrase from Izaak Walton, who was known to have lifted a few himself, the patron saint of angling, whose favorite waters I was sampling—something more than mine own, in fact, because that fourteen-inch brown trout happened to be the very first return in an inter-century challenge match I was personally conducting there on the Manifold River in Derbyshire.

The idea for such a match had evolved several weeks before during a long, hazy night with a British friend at a rural pleasure-dome entitled Lords of the Manor. We talked motorcars, politics, literature, women, racehorses, the parlous state of the world, opening the catalogue of our mutual interests, but mostly we talked fishing, which has both of us in its iron thrall.

"Of course you should fish at least one river exactly the way Walton used to fish, shouldn't you?" my friend Nigel said.

"What do you mean?"

"You know what I mean. I mean you should use kit straight out of the old fanatic's book—a rod six yards long, a line braided out of horsehair, genuine seventeenth-century kit."

Before a tolerant publican finally called Time, the two of us had improvised on that basic theme to a point where it sounded almost sane. According to the informal regulations we adopted, I was to work the Manifold with a good modern rod, reel, and flyline for an hour and a half, work the same stretch all over again with antique tackle, a close-up confrontation between now and then. The only slight cheat involved the choice of lures. Instead of fishing dry flies and nymphs with the flyrod and basic garden hackle with the blunderbuss rod, it seemed more equitable to use artificials with both rigs, despite Walton's chronic preference for live bait.

That fondness for back-to-nature lures shows through the pages of his classic work. "The trout is usually caught with a worm, or a minnow, which some call a penk, or with a fly, *viz.*, either a natural or an artificial fly," he wrote in *The Compleat Angler*. After tipping readers to the fact that trout feed by night as well as by day, Walton went into specific detail: "And the manner of taking them is, on the top of the water, with a great lob or garden worm, or rather two, which you are to fish with in a place where the waters run somewhat quietly." The amiable Royalist, while a wildly enthusiastic all-round fisherman, could by no stretch of the imagination be described as an expert with the fly, else he wouldn't have had to poach from others, as he did in the case of Thomas Barker, a retired cook, humorist, and outdoorsman, or fold in a long addendum specifically devoted to flyfishing by his dear friend and adopted son Charles Cotton, beginning with the fifth edition of his dialogue.

If he amounted to no more than a recording secretary when it came to the fly, however, Walton cannot be faulted on his assessment of trout, including the demonstration model I had just landed. "The trout is a fish highly valued in this and foreign nations," Piscator-Walton advised his disciple during the course of their book-length rambles. "He is a fish that feeds cleanly and purely, in the swiftest streams, and on the hardest gravel; and . . . he may justly contend with all fresh-water fish, as the mullet may with all sea-fish, for precedency and daintiness of taste; and . . . being in right season, the most dainty palates have allowed precedency to him." In my own opinion, Walton, a didactic man who seldom had anything but the most lavish praise for particular fish, particular rivers, and attendant brothers of the angle, was putting it far too mildly in the case of trout. In my opinion, trout rank right up there with my wife and son, who need to be gently played on occasion, too.

After landing that inaugural trout on hard gravel in a swift stream, I continued on up the Manifold, fishing the likely spots with contemporary tackle that anglers more proficient than I could be proud of. I was using an eight-foot Leonard cane rod, a three-and-three-eighths-inch Hardy Perfect reel I uncovered with the help of an English town crier whose whirlwind lungs I hired to spread the word, and a double-taper floating Cortland line, which together had run me more than our hair-trigger family budget could stand, if only we were prudent enough to formulate one.

The dry flies and nymphs I was fishing, most of them, anyway, came from the Foster Sporting Services in nearby Ashbourne, established in 1763, as management generally reminds prospects in its literature, although the building on John Street, into which the firm had moved since my last visit six months before, was emphatically pre-Walton, the beamed front section where an assortment of flies was on display dating back to the ninth century. The fact that the flies were not only beautifully tied but came to merely twenty-five cents American, or half a bus token to the deadfall I generally patronize at home in New York City, put me in a mood so euphoric that I ordered far more than my usual ration.

A cheery man at Foster also sold me a cheap Severn-Trent Water Authority license good for seven days. The flip side of the ticket reminded everyone of the realities: "This license does not entitle the holder to fish in any private waters without permission of the owner." Since virtually all trout and salmon water in Britain is privately held, this meant I had to make some personal arrangements, which Foster Sporting Services completed on my behalf with its usual efficiency.

The blessings the proprietor had bestowed on me as I left the shop earlier that morning could hardly have been improved upon. "Tight lines," he said, "and if they're not as tight as you wish, you will have a memorable time of it all the same." A small trout boisterously rose, struck short, scudded away. I was fishing at no numerical profit now, but the whisper of the river, the soft green hills latticed with dry stone walls, some of them six feet high, and the cattle practically painted on the land already imprinted the gathering young day on what passes for my memory.

In a glossy run of water another small trout rose to the fly, a colorful blur in the sunshine. This one actually touched the fly, its jaws unhinged, reacting far faster than I, as frequently happens, the silence positively deafening. A galling amount of slack—"cumbered with too long a line," Piscator would probably have diagnosed it—allowed the fish to correct its tactical error before I could turn on some whiplash. It seemed almost blasphemous to expose my penny-ante reflexes there on one of the sainted rivers.

According to dated maps filed away in a local library, the Manifold follows much the same course it followed back in Walton's time, but the resident fish supply—like so much else—undoubtedly isn't what it used to be. More than three hundred years ago, for example, the abundance in England generally was so great that the maestro could admit to taking as many as twenty to forty trout at a standing. Several oak trees on adjoining fields go back to Walton or before, while the vicar swears that one public footpath pointed mostly east to west has been tramped ever since the fifteenth century.

Over a roll of many years, sights and sounds of modern times have intruded on the blissful old scene until, nowadays, the area in and around the village of Hartington looks much like any other part of rural England. But if cars drum up the narrow roadways, huge combine harvesters pick the fields clean of grain, and rude struts of television aerials rise like nightmares over the antique stone cottages, some of the pastoral scenes Walton portrayed with his normal relish still endure. Not the least of these are sheep, which graze the landscape in numbers so excessive that I literally found myself inundated in undergraduate lamb chops as I approached the Manifold by car. An alarming flow of sheep, patches of wool on their flanks stamped a proprietary red, driven by two small collies and a lank shepherd, covered the two-lane track.

"How many in this flock?" I asked.

"Approximately four hundred just now," the shepherd replied, his mouth a vacant wind tunnel suggesting that the state of British dentistry had not changed much since Walton's time, either.

The two-mile stretch of the Manifold assigned me for the day must have pleased the old boy beyond any singing of it. Like any river with real character to it, it varies considerably as it twines through the countryside, tumbling over stone dams, flattening in long slick runs, deepening in lovely pools, bending left and right, straightening briefly again, parts of it humped with rock, other parts shaded by beech or willow or oak.

Cursed with drought conditions, the water itself was not what it had been the season before, or the season before that. The blight had sunk the Manifold to vexing levels, thin and only ankle-deep in spots, and I do not suppose any of the stretch I fished ran to more than thirty feet across. What water there was was what Walton would have called silver and contemporary angling writers with a more jaded frame of reference invariably would describe as gin clear.

Despite the dry spell, however, which carried on for another few months, one long pool beyond a right turn in the river was four or five feet deep. Unfortunately, willow branches spread ominously close to the surface. After several tentative casts with a low sidearm motion, like Eldon Auker, who pitched for the Detroit Tigers in the 1930s, I climbed a ladder leaning against a steep bank, portaged through yellow musk around the frustrating pool, climbed back down into the Manifold a few yards upstream, where both the water level and the foliage along the bank were more to my taste, although I had no further success with my space-age rod and reel until I reached the tail of a more modest pool covered with nothing more than open sky.

A small trout was dimpling fairly close to the far bank, feeding on something I could not see, working a very small beat, sociable enough but never moving more than a rod-length. The fish did not show the proper suicidal impulse when I cast over it first with an Upcher's Fancy and then with the Cockwing Dun, both in an eyesore size 16. But the first time I cast a British Oakden's Claret, the light sparse fly with the long tail was taken. There was a surge in the river, followed by a tantalizing pull. The trout had hooked itself, which was probably just as well, and from the feel it was no bigger than it had looked.

Whatever the actual size, I played the fish carefully on the light leader, mindful of the jangling warning Walton cast upon the centuries. "You may, if you stand close, be sure of a bite," he wrote of trout, a bit optimistically, I thought, "but not sure to catch him, for he is not a leather-mouthed fish." The soft gum tissues held while I slowly worked it in, a respectable brownie, eleven inches on the nose, a second vote for the status quo, no potential land-slide, to be sure, but perhaps sufficient.

As things turned out, that was the sum of my experience with the Leonard rod: two trout, neither one especially big, not even for me. So much for modern times. In an hour and a half I had missed two other fish, cast to several more rising in the river, hooked a fly in the crotch of an oak

34

tree, which water bailiff John Bonsall, who, at the age of eighty-five, followed me from along the bank, sort of, extricated with the crook of his walking stick.

Moments earlier, Bonsall had screwed his ruddy old face into a critical expression when I fished some open water without any cover. He didn't edit me by shouting across the Manifold, but it was perfectly clear that he didn't approve of my casting from a half crouch. If he had ever bothered to read the masterwork, of course, he must have covered the long swatch Walton's friend Cotton contributed, in which he specifically addressed himself to the plight of any brother of the angle fishing a shiny river on a sunny day. "And if you are pretty well out of sight, either by kneeling or the interposition of a bank or bush, you may almost be sure to raise, and take him too, if it be presently done," Cotton wrote. "The fish will otherwise, peradventure, be removed to some other place, if it be in the still deeps, where he is always in motion. . . ."

Since I was fishing a special Walton river for the first and only time, an eventual backache seemed a minimal price to pay. After all, whether Bonsall realized it or not, I conceivably might have gone to more elaborate lengths than a rheumatic crouch by way of camouflage. Among a number of artful ruses developed over the centuries, Dr. Thomas Birch, the Oxford scholar with the wonderfully telltale name, hit on what many anglers consider to be the most enterprising. Any time Birch set out to bamboozle the fish, he dressed as a tree—he would have been a smash at the Fancy Dress competitions that are such an integral part of British church and village fêtes—right down to an outer-coating of branches, leaves, and even pine cones.

By the time Bonsall and I toddled back to the official starting point alongside a stone bridge and I assembled my blunderbuss rig, it was almost twelve of the clock, as Walton told time, which made me wonder whether the odds were not stacked against phase two of the competition between now and then. Fewer fish were rising in the river, the fly hatch had diminished, the speckled sunshine had given way to a bright cone beaming down from clear blue skies. In conditions like that, the long rod might cast a shadow roughly the dimensions of the Black Forest. Besides, I wasn't sure that I was up to doing the dated tackle justice, either, especially after the previous tour up the river had taken a bite out of my tired blood.

For a gaffer with so many years on him, John Bonsall expressed a bouncy curiosity in my tackle. Like a couple of strangers I encountered along the river later, he specifically wanted to know whether I had made the rod and line from scratch myself, which, mercifully, as I explained, I hadn't had to, thanks to a prominent British angling writer name of Dick Walker, who, when I phoned for advice on how to start braiding horsehair, kindly offered me the complete Walton kit he had concocted as a lark several years before. While the butt section of the three-piece, eighteen-foot rod was thick as the handle of a snow shovel, the tip thinned to a sporting size, live and supple, as I had learned on experimentally casting to, hooking, and landing an experimental trout on a reservoir in the Cotswolds the week before.

I have no way of knowing whether Walker laid on a troupe of Bavarian elves to help with the horsehair line or not, but, if he didn't, he probably should have, at least if he followed the meticulous stricture Walton outlined in his dialogue. "First let your hair be clean washed ere you go about to twist it; and then choose not only the clearest hair for it, but hairs that be of an equal bigness, for such do usually stretch all together, and break all together, which hairs of an unequal bigness never do, but break singly, and so deceive the angler that trusts to them," Walton wrote without coming up for air. "When you have twisted your links, lay them in water for a quarter of an hour at least, and then twist them over again, before you tie them into a line: for those that do not so shall usually find their line to have a hair or two shrink, and be shorter than the rest, at the first fishing with it, which is so much the strength of the line lost for want of first watering it, and then re-twisting it." As a friend remarked on reading those stalwart directions, Walton could easily have moonlighted turning out catch-as-catch-can bindings for pioneer bondage fetishists.

However Dick Walker had managed it, the line he sent me seemed more than adequate for my purposes, strong, loose, brunette in tone, free of the frets, unevenness, and scabs the father of us all had warned about. I knotted it directly to the tip of the rod in the seventeenth-century tradition—and, indeed, the tradition of my own faded youth, when modern engines such as reels were regarded as sissy stuff. In view of prohibitions up and down the Manifold, not to mention my own chronic sloth, certain modifications were in order in completing the kit I was to fish for the next hour and a half. Since the worms or penks Walton regularly fished were illegal despite my special pleading, I looped on a Cockwing Dun, a tiny number 16, with wings, a yellow body, and not much hackle. Instead of using the classic single strand of hair as a leader, or cast, I tied a length of 5x nylon to the braided horsehair line.

If my first few casts in a nice run where the river turned right were not an absolute disaster, they were enough to move Bonsall the water bailiff away from the bank where he had been leaning on his cane in a thicket of margeurite. A stand of birch trees close behind me rather restricted the movement of the epic tackle, but my own defective casting contributed to the basic problem too. Twelve feet of line tied to an eighteen-foot rod isn't my normal distance.

Still, the day thrummed with promise when a treeless stretch widened across to a steep rocky bank. Several fish—"a leash of trouts," as Walton would have said—fed in the sunshine, the rings of their rises enlarging, along with my hopes. Briefly, very briefly, I was fishing according to the code of British purists: I was casting only to rising fish.

37

Swinging the rod with both hands, I dropped the Cockwing Dun lightly in the middle of a gathering ring, felt a slight but definite touch, pulled up too late, alas, an undeniable error I attributed to the long-range tackle. By the time the belated message finally reached me through a circuit of that total length, the fish undoubtedly had had time to read the fly-tier's signature.

After breaking the point of one hook on a flat rock, entangling another in a nest of stinging nettles behind me, and putting down more fish then I care to admit, I finally made what was, for me, a bullseye cast, three or four feet above a rising trout, in exactly the right longitude, in quiet water with no drag to it. The fish rose to the fly as if it had not eaten all day long. Once it engorged the lure, the trout showed no signs of being undernourished, however, running, running hard, stunting out of the water, abruptly doubling back, while I kept a bit of pressure on and wondered how to land anything with all that distance between us.

Eventually I was reduced to pulling in the rod, running it through my hands, foot by foot, trying to keep the tip elevated and giving no slack, until, with no more than five or six feet of it still before me, I reached far out and scooped my captive into the net. It was a reasonably good brown trout except for a slightly deformed right pectoral fin, nicely colored, fairly deep, breakfast size, all of eleven and three-quarters inches long, or more than enough to prove a point. Mark one up for old time's sake.

Given an open piece of water and an encouraging supply-demand factor, I saw no reason not to work the same arena after the remaining fish commenced feeding again. I humped down on the riverside, coating the walls of my lungs with the waste of another cigarette, pleased that Bonsall, who probably considered my antique fishing an American novelty item, had witnessed the encounter from the far side. It was pleasant sitting there smoking, making notes, confiding to a small tape recorder I packed along.

Yet it was even more pleasant when I started fishing that quiet flat water all over again. I took another trout, and another, ten inches and twelve and a half inches by my pocket measure, good fish, both of them, especially the biggest, far brighter than the usual brown, which would have looked magnificent hanging on my library wall if only it stretched a few more inches, three trout in thirty-five minutes of fishing with neo-Walton gear. Maybe the amiable old Royalist's primitive rig wasn't as quixotic as contemporary split-cane-and-floating-line anglers bluntly assume.

As I waded upstream toward the stone dam, a rumpled rustic walking a dirt track across the river paused to make some friendly noises. "If it's a few pounds of fish for dinner you want, I can nip back to the cottage for my spinning kit," he said, his voice stiff with a country accent. It was apparent that he didn't realize—perhaps because of my own formidable, no-nonsense tackle—that I was fishing for the sake of my soul instead of my stomach, the one being in greater need of sustenance than the other, and I declined his offer with appropriate thanks. Treating me to an encouraging thumbs-up signal I no longer felt any need for, he continued on up the river, a dwindling figure lighted in the sunshine, before he was finally lost to sight in a shelter of trees.

The brief encounter put me in mind of the touching misunderstanding an artist friend named John Groth experienced many years ago on a trip to Asia—Nepal or Afghanistan, I forget which. During a hike through the countryside, Groth came upon a river so inviting that he could not resist the urge to joint up the Orvis Rocky Mountain Special rod he often packed along on trips in case he made a good connection. When several natives who spoke no more English than he spoke Urdu, or whatever, saw that Groth was having little or no success, they proceeded to rip limbs from nearby trees, string lines to them, bait primitive hooks, and start piling fish onto the bank. Smiling and pointing to the growing heap, they emphatically indicated that the fish were all for Groth, who, although he kept shaking his head, never quite managed to breach his sponsors' bedrock sense of pragmatism. In the evolving world out beyond God's back, as in Derbyshire, at least in the case of the countryman who had just passed by, anyone with a rod in his hands is regarded as a man in fundamental pursuit of fish to fry.

Up the river another few turns I missed a nice fish, the best of the day, no doubt about it, if only I had succeeded in landing it, which I did not when my leader snapped. But I took a small trout in the same run, nine inches, on an Oakden's Claret, fishing close against the leafy bank under a spread of willow. This latest captive, while it didn't make the competition a runaway, did make it fairly decisive, four fish to two, seventeenth century.

Swinging the triumphant long rod for a cast into some pocket water, I was transfixed by a cry from somewhere below me, a high, half-strangled sound, like the noise of an infant screaming for help. I peered back, searching for a stray child in trouble, and the cry rose again, not once but several times. Alarmed by the phantom noise, I looked quizzically over at Bonsall, whose broad face creased in a smile. "River hen, down under the trees, sounds like a tad of a boy, doesn't it?" he said.

At the deep pool that had given me such trouble on my previous tour with the Leonard rod, I sat in the grass pondering how to drift a fly onto the most likely part of it without hanging up on the foliage overhead. In the midst of my market research, I abruptly stiffened with excitement. There in the top of the pool lay an enormous fish, deep, husky as a fullback, occasionally twitching its tail. If it didn't quite measure up to Walton's extravagant description of "a trout that will feed six reasonable bellies," it was certainly big enough for a British family of four, to whom I was very much indebted for a splendid dinner party in my honor not long before.

Even Walton might have acknowledged that a prize so great as that called for extra precautionary measures, although he took a fairly stiff view of these matters. "And let not your line exceed—especially for three or four links next to the hook—I say, not exceed three or four hairs at the most, though you may fish a little stronger above, in the upper part of your line," Walton counseled with his normal bravado, "but if you can attain to angle with one hair, you shall have more rises, and catch more fish." In his hitch-hike section of *The Compleat Angler*, Charles Cotton was no less rigid on the subject of horsehair leader. ". . . he that cannot kill a trout of twenty inches with two, in a river clear of woods and weeds, as this and some others of ours are, deserves not the name of an angler," Cotton wrote. Not quite certain of my own name in these challenging circumstances, I replaced the 5x leader with stronger 4x, attached a size-14 Cockwing Dun, with which I had had most of my fish, and, almost magically, dropped the fly precisely where I hoped.

While a cast like that deserved something more, the big bull trout expressed no particular interest in my deceitful offering. It turned slightly in the water, regarded the fly as it passed over, fanned its fins, straightened out again, a demonstration of idle curiosity, nothing more. For fifteen minutes that ran my blood pressure up, I cast into the pool, as intended, or into the overhung foilage, as wasn't, changing flies every so often, revising the Blue Plate Special, trying Upcher's Fancy, Oakden's Claret, an import Hairwing Coachmen and Quill Gordon in size 14, all this without a flicker of genuine interest from my prospect out in the Manifold. Desperately I even tried an indigenous novelty nymph called the Derbyshire Belle, dark, bushy,

41

and winged, two tiny red beads for eyes, ugly as sin, with the same response as I had been experiencing, meaning not much at all.

On my final cast of the intriguing day, from a few feet closer to the prize that had obviously resisted temptations far greater than mine during its long life, I slipped on a mossy stone. A perfectly good pair of patched corduroy pants and a sweater worn through at both elbows promptly flooded, which reminds me that American anglers are generally more informal in their dress, as well as their profanity.

On the better streams, our English brethren look like a full-page advertisement for Pickering and Hill, Ltd., of Old Bond Street, attired in tweed jackets and slacks, club neckties knotted against fresh shirts, under a grouse helmet, a deerstalker, or a twill cap, plus rainwear, of course, just in case. A friend with whom I fished some actually went so far as to change—he changed *upwards*, mind you—after a cocktail party before we set off to fish the evening rise. Along with other differentials previously adumbrated herein, resident angling garb amounts to further culture shock for an outlander long accustomed to the easy informality of my home waters, the Neversink in New York, where participants dressed in anything more than denim shirts and rummage cords are suspected of putting on airs.

Despite the stiff upper British dress code, anglers are apt to belittle one another's general concept of fashion, especially in the matter of even more formal wear such as black ties. According to an especially sniffish member of the Flyfishers Club of London, whose roll abounds with hyphenated names and pennywhistle titles, "Most of my fellow fishermen look as though they habitually catch fish in their dinner jackets." On the basis of two appearances at annual club dinners, I'm inclined to agree. Gentlemen anglers who invariably strike me as full-blown popinjays out on the riverbank gave off a rumpled, wrinkled, ill-fitting image of the South End Social Club in Aurora, Illinois, when they gathered for a hazy night of good company and good discourse, which Izaak Walton once identified as "the very sinews of virtue."

If the old prints are to be believed, Walton himself couldn't be charged with violating the local ordinance. A celebrated oil shows him seated against a tree along the Itchen, his rod, net, and wicker creel beside him, unmistakably a fop, wearing a vest, a waistcoat, a clean white bib and white roll-back cuffs, looking for all the world as if he happened to be bound for a matins service at the nearest village church—which might well have been the case a bit later, after he flogged the river some, because Walton was an all-rounder who took his religion every bit as seriously as the proper mix of groundbait.

I skinned down to nothing and wrung out my own wet down-home clothes before coiling the horsehair line and unjointing the eighteen-foot rod. John Bonsall hobbled over, turning his hearing aid on full throttle, for a last remnant of conversation.

"You did old Walton jolly proud, taking those fish on stroppy kit like his," he said.

Modesty prohibited me from responding in quite the boastful tone I felt entitled to employ.

The trip to a day of fishing is invariably a great pleasure, but in some ways the trip back after some successful sport is greater still. I was using a form of horsepower not known to Walton and those honest anglers he wrote of, six cylinders signed by Rolls-Royce instead of a live bay, but our sense of contentment teetered in a similar range. Six trout lay in the trunk of the car, memories, every one of them, moments to relive through the dark winter yet to come.

At the edge of a small stone village in Staffordshire, I heard the peal of church bells, just as Walton might have heard them, a lovely chord in the still day as some vagabond bell-ringers took their turn, perhaps a complicated

Cambridge Two or a Triple Bob Major, a sound reverberating through the centuries. The peal faded, I covered the narrow two-gauge road feeding on the memories I had scooped into the net, mourning the loss of that prize I hadn't.

After a number of reflective miles unwound, I decided that the bittersweet aspect of angling probably hadn't altered over the years, either. No matter how seldom he admitted in print to even a mild setback, the one and only Piscator, another of whose rivers I had just fished in his fashion, as well as my own, must have returned home every so often wondering why he had been repeatedly snubbed by a true beast of a trout, too.

DURING a series of impromptu background briefings
shortly before I set out to wet an alien line in several of
Walton's favorite rivers, a friend whom the old boy undoubtedly would have described as a brother of the angle
ran up a list of native deadfalls to be approached with extreme caution, if indeed they had to be approached at all.
Along with eel fishing, automatic fly reels, and live mice as
bait, the roll specifically included British match fishing,
about which my friend nourished some stiff incidental reservations despite a basically tolerant view.

"Match fishing lifts the classic man-against-nature conflict
onto another plane," my knowledgeable source observed.
"You compete not only against the fish, which is challenge
enough, or at least it is for me, but also against a collection
of flaming five-star cranks you simply would not believe."

As he depicted them, match fishermen are so consumed by their sport that they often ignore the conventional realities, such as the time of day. In good times as well as bad they brood on how to improve their competitive position, endlessly concocting prescriptions for miraculous new ground bait, developing featherweight floats to register the slightest twitch, turning over rocks in the dark of the night in search of grubs, slugs and other exotic live baits. They are driven men forever dreaming extravagant dreams of fish, fish, fish—the fish they will catch next time they troop down to some crowded riverbank for another competition.

On exploring the possibilities of participating myself if the proper arrangements could be made, I learned that competitive matches crowded right through the coarse fishing season, to put it mildly. The schedule on any given weekend is so formidable, in fact, that an alphabetical listing fills two pages in the *Angling Times,* a lively weekly that practicing match fishermen look upon as the Judgment Book. For one raw Saturday in January of 1976, the lineup in various parts of Britain consisted of no less than 173 of these sweepstakes, not to mention a number of others not enshrined in the publication for one reason or another.

Nobody, not even pop anglers who win as much as £1,500 a season, is quite certain when the craze for match fishing first evolved, although several hazy theories are in circulation. Undoubtedly the most popular, if not necessarily the most accurate, of these suggests that formal tournaments first began on the Thames near Windsor in 1846 with a pot of two shillings for whoever weighed in the most fish. Whenever they actually commenced, however, matches amounted to a natural refinement of the traditional casual wagers among anglers as unalike as Walton and this particular contemporary disciple.

On the basis of several references in what he invariably described as his Discourse, Walton was not above a slight flutter himself every now and then. "If I had had the luck

46

to have taken up that rod, then 'tis twenty to one he should not have broken my line by running to the rod's end, as you suffered him," the old boy, in the guise of Piscator, remarked at one point before launching into a critique. "I would have held him within the bent of my rod (unless he had been fellow to the great trout that is near an ell long, which was of such a length and depth that he had his picture drawn, and is to be seen at mine host Rickabie's, at the George, in Ware); and it may be, by giving that very great trout the rod, that is, by casting it to him into the water, I might have caught him"—Walton appears to be reconsidering that twenty-to-one price downward here—"at the long run; for so I use always to do when I meet with an overgrown fish, and you will learn to do so too, hereafter; for I tell you, Scholar, fishing is an art—or, at least, it is an art to catch fish."

In my own case, despite a prickly aversion to long odds, I have indulged in the sort of potluck wagers that led to match fishing for almost as long as I can recall. Back in the mists of my boyhood, Kenny McElroy and I used to feel like genuine hellbenders by betting Great Depression-type money, sometimes as much as two cents, winner-take-all, on who would catch the first bullhead on our frequent trips to Blackberry Creek outside Aurora, Illinois.

Exactly how Walton would have reacted to match fishing if it had existed when he was roving seventeenth-century England in pursuit of anything wearing fins is a matter of conjecture. Apart from its speculative aspect, which no doubt would have appealed to his crapshoot instincts, the competitions strike me as far too highly structured for his rambling, eclectic tastes. While Walton enjoyed angling beyond anything else, it remained part of a bigger picture that also consisted of tuning in birdsong, lazing under a honeysuckle hedge, and pausing at some honest alehouse where he would—in his own phrase—"wet his whistle."

No matter how the master might have felt about it,

match fishing in Old Blighty is as endemic as bad teeth and beef-and-kidney pie nowadays. While no other competition is as rewarding as the Woodbine Challenge, which awards a gusher of £2,000 to the winner, or as prestigious as the international matches against picked fishermen from France, Germany, and other European countries, English riverbanks are stiff with sweepstake loonies right up to the end of the season in early March. As might be expected, the traffic is especially dense on major waterways like the Severn, Trent, Thames, Humber, and the Warwick Avon.

But for a river its size, the Lee a few miles to the north of London is the site of a disproportionate number of these match tournaments, which struck me as a happy coincidence. After all, Walton considered the Lee a particular favorite. Until he finally left London at the age of fifty, "judging it dangerous for honest men to be there," Walton regularly traveled by horse, coach, or shank's mare up to flog the Lee for the rich variety of fish it produced. In the very first paragraph of *The Compleat Angler*, in fact, he sets out on the familiar track: "I have stretched my legs up Tottenham Hill to overtake you, hoping your business may occasion you towards Ware, whither I am going this fine fresh May morning."

In arranging to enter a midwinter competition on the Lee, I spoke with a number of resident authorities, not the least of them Richard Carr, a likable long-haired young truckdriver who not only volunteered to enroll me but also to supply some personal coaching on the day of the match. His generous offer sounded wildly promising. As the most successful tournament angler up and down the Lee Valley, Carr is a fisherman of such lofty stripe that officials who choose the English team for international tournaments already had scouted him on three separate occasions, and his renown extends to the pages of the angling magazines. I couldn't do much better than that.

"Mind you bring a couple of tins of cooked lunch meat for bait," he advised me.

Early on the prescribed Sunday morning in February, I went tailing along one of those lovely British motorways, burning up more than my share of the earth's resources, determined to reach the Fishers Green stretch of the Lee beyond Ware by "eight of the clock," as Walton would have put it. It was a fairly typical English day, raw and windy, without any sunshine showing through the dirty skies.

As I abruptly learned on another bitter February morning, Walton was not the only luminary who had fished some bewitching river before I had. During one of several trips to the Test, down near where it joins the sea, I casually inquired of stalwart Vic Foot, who was my mentor that particular day, if he had any idea where our former Ambassador to Great Britain, Lewis Douglas, had worked the sainted river.

Foot stopped still in his gumboots. "Funnily enough"— not the most appropriate locution in the circumstances, as I was to learn—"it was right here, on this loop of the river, just at the fishing bench there, where Mr. Douglas lost his eye," he said. "It was a very windy day, with some frost too, and I was gillieing for him. Never forget it, I won't. I cut the cast off after he hooked his eye. His friend and I took him to the hospital."

A shoal of competitors bundled in thick turtleneck sweaters, heavy coats, and assorted headdress stood near a registration table stamping their feet on the ground, pouring hot tea, coffee, or soup from thermos jugs, indulging in the lighthearted banter that passes for conversation among coarse fishermen in general and match anglers in particular.

"Told me to keep me maggots out of the fridge, she did, ruddy cheek, I call it, because it was me paid for the fridge

49

in the first place, same as everything else, wasn't it," an owlish-looking man encased in an enormous military great-coat told a sympathetic audience as I joined up.

The small talk, which had been skittering some, instantly took on real definition, the boys competing with one another in describing the lack of tolerance they encountered around the house. A pinch-faced Londoner sporting a full beard admitted to buying a second fridge—strictly out of his match winnings, he went to some pains to make clear—in the interest of restoring a greater degree of domestic harmony. Another boasted of resolving a similar crisis by trading his peckish wife in for a more agreeable new model whom he described as having splendid pectoral fins besides, although a skeptical member of the panel rolled his eyeballs in disbelief at such an abundance of assets.

At the registration table I signed my name and address on an official entry form, paid my entry fee of £3. In theory this investment could roll into the top prize of £55, if I was so lucky as to weigh in the most fish, which was a possibility so remote as to not even register in my skull. The organizer invited me to dip into a wooden box and pull out a small bright orange card—I assumed the commercial for P & B Hall Fishing Tackle of Waltham Abbey stamped on the front and back meant they had been wheedled into paying printing costs—to determine which peg I would fish.

In British match competitions, the river is divided into numbered ten-yard pegs, or swims, marked along the bank, some of them better than others, of course, just like the fishermen. While tournament anglers generally are fatalistic about the draw, a particular peg known to be especially barren provides legitimate trappings for the if-only post-mortem diagnosis virtually everyone is addicted to. Every so often a match fisherman will even pack up and return home if he pulls what he regards as a doomed stretch.

"Mister Beinsorfen"—the registrar was plainly having

trouble deciphering my penmanship—"has peg number one hundred and thirty-three."

On hearing the announcement, a lank contestant rolling a cigarette sounded a two-note whistle, which I regarded as being favorable, a suspicion that was confirmed by accompanying remnants of talk.

"Big Yank drew one-thirty-three," someone said.

"Good as any, one-thirty-three, isn't it?"

"Sure enough. But he probably won't do nothing much with it."

I hoped his gift for prophecy was no better than his grammar. In fraternizing with the opposition there in the chill of the morning, I learned that they worked at jobs as assorted as hotel bellman, engineer, and doctor, came from as far away as forty miles, and averaged at least one match a weekend, whatever the repercussions around the house. To a man they agreed that Richard Carr, who had yet to arrive, ought to be the match favorite, on the basis of his current form, which an electrician from Maidenhead extolled as "quick, very quick," unless Carr happened to draw a bad peg.

Moments later, the celebrity angler arrived and promptly drew what everyone, including Carr, considered one of the least promising of the fifty-five swims to be fished that day, "I'll have to really chug a stack of bait in the water to do much at that blinking peg," he grumped. Up the riverbank we went, with Carr carrying enough gear on a two-wheel trolley to stock the Neversink Valley Sports Center in Liberty, New York—nine rods from ten to eighteen feet long, eleven reels, a folding chair, an umbrella, a keepnet, a long-handled landing net, boxes of floats, tins of hooks and weights, cans of maggots, casters, and meat, three loaves of bread—until we reached the stretch he had drawn.

Down a fairly steep grassy bank, the Lee looked no more promising than the overcast weather. It was a wide river,

51

probably twenty yards across to the wooden pilings on the far bank, up to twenty feet deep in the channel, according to Carr, with a good vigorous flow, but the whole of the Lee at Fishers Green was the color of rust. "Once I get sorted out here I'll set up proper," he said, opening rod cases, unfolding the chair, spreading boxes and cases on the turf. We stretched our legs to the very last peg, number one-thirty-three, which meant that while a rival was squeezed up on my left side, I had nothing but open water to my right.

In his incidental role as my sponsor and coach, Richard Carr quickly assembled the kit he judged would be suitable for me. He jointed a stiff ten-foot glass rod, mounted an open-faced spinning reel wound with five-pound monofilament line. "You can cover the whole swim with this, you can," he said. At the end of the rod he attached what he called a quivertip, an eight-inch extension spun out of fine fiberglass, sensitive to even the slightest touch. "You will be ledgering instead of using a float," he explained. After running the line through the quivertip and pinching on three split shots, Carr cut a tin of Plumrose Pork and Beef luncheon meat into half-inch cubes, one of which he impaled on an eyeless size-14 hook. "On a day like this, luncheon meat is good as anything else, probably better," he said, sinking a metal rod rest into the ground for me.

Once those preliminaries were over and done with, Carr abandoned me to return to his peg and set up his own tackle. I fell to brooding about the borrowed rig I would be fishing. At the risk of sounding fairly long in the tooth—my situation exactly, come to think of it, as a recent $950 periodontal bill might confirm—I did my apprentice angling back before spinning reels had been developed. Eventually I graduated from a bait-casting reel, a Pflueger Supreme, the moment I could afford one, to flycasting, with only limited experience, to put it mildly, handling spinning tackle since then.

The contestant on my left, a sparse little fisher in a stocking cap whose National Health Service teeth didn't fit him very well, balanced a revolving lazy susan on top of a support stake, carefully filled its fitted trays with maggots, casters, bits of meat, bloodworms, and crusts of bread. His fingers kneaded some paste, stroking, pulling, rolling gently. In addition to his regular rod already assembled, he unlimbered two auxiliary rods, one on either side of his canvas chair, and then stood two packs of Rothman cigarettes on another stand laden with sandwiches, potato chips, and a thermos.

"I think I'd better take a practice cast or two." With the match scheduled to last for five hours, a conversational gambit seemed eminently sensible. "I'm not at my best with spinning gear."

My neighbor rummaged through a metal tackle box until he found a pair of long forceps, tied them to a bit of string, looped the string to the arm of his chair without so much as acknowledging my overture. Gambit declined. If he had ever read his Izaak Walton it was plain he'd either skipped over or vetoed the observation that "good company and good discourse are the very sinews of virtue."

"I say, I think I'd better take a practice cast or two." Five hours can be a long time.

While he at least did me the courtesy of responding, his words were brief and right to the point: "No, can't break the water before the whistle at ten o'clock, can you," he said, giving the lazy susan a test spin, reorganizing the tray of baits for the third time.

Shortly before ten, Carr returned, running hard, his frosted breath showing in the cold, filled with a barrage of last-minute guidance, which I felt sorely in need of. "Pitch it to the far side, mind, close to the pilings, just above the two gulls riding the river there," he said. "Then you keep your eye skinned watching the quivertip. First time it jiggles, pick up a little but don't lean into the rod. Take some

53

line in your fingers and strike when it feels proper. Everything you catch, bung them straight in your net and sort them out later." He blew in his hands, shook them, invited me to offer up any final questions. Idly I wondered whether any contestant in my area might be worth watching for the sake of technique.

"Oh yes, that chap three pegs up, he's a good one," Carr replied.

"Who is he?"

"Butcher chappie, in blue overalls, fishes maggots, mostly, won two matches last month. He has a soft touch, one of the softest. He could take a few quick on a day like this."

Carr gave me a ritual handshake, asked me to come see him if I needed anything, pelted up the riverbank, diminishing in the gray, presumably dreaming his dreams of a bonanza, just as I was. What put my own dreams into orbit were sundry match results listed in the angling press, such as a recent competition where twenty-one anglers had landed a total of 837 pounds of fish on the Humber. The match commenced when a shrill whistle sounded. Along one of Walton's favorite old rivers, rods flicked, lines uncoiled, assorted baits splashed into the muddy water. Surprisingly, my own first cast carried almost to the far bank, or about where I wanted it. That initial barrage was followed by a cloudburst of groundbait as contestants peppered their individual swims with maggots, bread, meat chips and other *hors d'oeuvres* in hopes of stirring things up.

If the churl fishing the adjoining peg had shown signs of strain earlier, he turned into an absolute manic with the competition officially underway. Lighting one cigarette from another, muttering to himself, audibly grinding his misfit teeth, he reeled his line in a few feet, shifted the rod rest, shook out the landing net, dipped into a canvas bag for another tin of meat, which he opened and proceeded to cut into small cubes. Then he picked up a slingshot about which I had been wondering and arched a spray of maggots out around his slender striped float.

"Bullseye!" I said. "That was a lovely shot."

He didn't even bother looking up. As I was considering an abusive comment on this latest slight, the quivertip extension on my rod twitched, twitched again. Heeding Carr's basic instruction, I picked up some line without jerking the rod, ran a bit through my fingers, waited, pulled up when the tip got to thrashing, late, too late, no fish, no bait, nothing but a bare hook. Easy come, easy go. Quickly I skewered another piece of the local version of Spam, cast my rod in a majestic parabola, up over the river, up over the far bank, up over the top of a ten-foot fence sternly posted KEEP OUT—MINISTRY OF DEFENSE, where the hook and weights twined round the top strand of wire and broke off. The nervous wreck fishing beside me paused—he was stirring another dark pudding of a groundbait in a plastic bowl now—to drink in the poignant scene.

Up the line five or six pegs an old man wrapped in a tartan blanket swung a small fish onto the bank, measured it with a wooden ruler, sadly slid it into the river. In matches on the River Lee, dace have to measure seven inches, roach and rudd eight, perch nine, chub, bream, carp and tench twelve, barbel sixteen, and pike a full two feet. Legal fish go into keep nets for the official weigh-in at the end of the competition; anything smaller goes straight back into the river. Whatever it was the senior citizen had caught, it hadn't measured up to legal specifications, although as the first fish taken in our general area, it did generate some interest.

"What is he fishing, Trevor?" In addressing the competitor to his left, my neighbor demonstrated a loquacious nature he surely had not bestowed on me. "Bread? Bread?

Bread in a cold wind? That was balls-up luck. He won't do much with bread day like this." Moments later, I noticed he was furtively kneading a crust of bread on his hook.

The fact that several anglers focused on the old man to see if he was employing any other wiles came as no surprise. As Carr had explained to me before the match began, competitors sometimes go to extremes in an effort to uncover techniques they might put to their own advantage. In one match Carr won with an especially impressive total catchweight, a rival skinned down to his underwear despite the January weather and swam across the Lee to retrieve a copyright new float Carr had made out of a drinking straw and snagged on a branch on the far side.

"They watch you like hawks, they do, other match anglers," he'd told me. "When I was going well another weekend I got a bottle of water, plain water, added some orange dye to it, just for a laugh, mind, mysteriously poured some of it into the river at my peg every so often, like I didn't want anyone else to notice. At the end of the day I left the bottle there with the name and address of a chemist friend and a potty formula number I scratched on it. Well. Next week, two match anglers popped by the chemist asking for the same number prescription. Watch you like hawks, they do."

While contestants emphatically do keep an eye on one another, judges, or scrutineers, in English English, maintain an official watch of their own, which is just as well, rectitude among British fishermen being no greater than it is among their American counterparts. Three years earlier, a fairly well-known match fisherman was banned for the season when scrutineers discovered that the voluminous baggage he transported to his assigned peg one morning included more than five pounds of live fish, still squirming some, which he planned to slip surreptitiously into his keepnet by way of a head start.

At the end of the first hour of competition the morning I

fished the Lee, nine anglers on my end of the line had caught a total of just two legal fish. While my neighbor kept at his frantic rain dance, bouncing up and down, action on my peg was so dormant that I embarked on an inventory of resident birdlife to file away for my wife, who has a mild interest in such things. Seagulls wheeled over the river, a lone swan flew on a line overhead, its wings producing a whistling noise, some blue tits and a finch worried in a pussy-willow tree close by, a coot black as coal drifted in the water near my line. Clearly, the day was better suited to ornithology than to ichthyology.

At the suggestion of a spectator who stopped by for a brief visit, I reeled in, chunked another cube of meat on the hook, scattered several pieces in the red sector on casting again, with results no greater than I had experienced to date. It was time for some basic market research. Ignoring my neighbor, whose good fellowship I had finally abandoned, I walked the bank to solicit the comments of other competitors, leaving my angle rod behind to "fish for itself," as Walton expressed it in his standard reference.

"Never was a good piece of water," a rotund taxi driver from London remarked.

"Too roily, much too roily," another suggested.

"The wrong wind, isn't it, east wind, which always makes the fish a bit stroppy." The old man who had caught the undersized fish earlier kindly offered me a beer. "I only had the one roach—and that was a tiddler."

I passed up the track behind a red-faced sack of muscle who looked as if he might be a splendid rugby forward if he could only remember the signals, just as he was flicking his spinning rod. Suddenly aware of another figure close by, he spooked some, losing his regular rhythm, tangling his hook in a tuft of grass on the rolling bank.

"You fouled me rig, mate," he said in a threatening tone.

"Wrong, you fouled it all by yourself," I said with a bravado I didn't feel, hurrying on.

At the end of two hours, the first seventeen anglers up the line from me had taken a total of only three legal fish, which suggested I wasn't doing so badly in the melancholy circumstances. In the face of these hard times, most of them were experimenting by changing baits, leads, floats, lines, even rods, and shoveling various groundbaits into the water. Personally, I wondered whether the target fish were not overgorged by all that high living. Eventually I arrived at the unfortunate swim Richard Carr had drawn to find the match favorite wonderfully cheery in the face of adversity. He shrugged and pointed to a keepnet as empty as most of the others.

We sat talking maggots versus meat, ledgering versus float fishing. One of Carr's cases was so bulging with assorted floats that I felt compelled to comment on the abundance. "More than a hundred in the box, I reckon, different types, many of them, made from drinking straws or peacock feathers, beautiful floats too, if I do say so, even if they aren't flagging much of anything this morning." Carr admitted to changing over from live maggots to casters, which are maggots in a somewhat further stage of development, and switching to a lighter rod. Then he pointed to a bulky figure fishing not on the Lee but in a gravel pit a long cast behind us. "Ade Scutt, a blinking great character in match fishing, who works as a debt collector," he said. "We call him the Bleak Machine."

As Carr explained it, Scutt has perfected an assembly-line approach to catching prodigious numbers of bleak, a tiny shoal fish about the size of a minnow which most anglers use only as live bait for something bigger. But by skinning literally hundreds of bleak off the top of the water—"I've sat next to Scutt when he took eighteen pounds of bleak in five hours, and they don't weigh more than half an ounce, do they?"—Carr told me the quantitative specialist wins an occasional match with the biggest total catchweight. Unfortunately for Scutt, if not for the official contestants, rules for the competition on this particular day prohibited any fish measuring less than seven inches long, which explained why, although physically present, he was merely doing calisthenics for the next match his metier qualified him to enter. "I try to practice an hour a day, straight through the week, so I don't lose me touch," Scutt said when I walked over and watched him whip a few silvery little fish out of the pit. "Took over seven hundred one competition, you know."

There was little need to wonder how Walton would have felt about so proficient a supplier. Three centuries earlier, the maestro wrote "I will tell you, Scholar, I once heard one say, 'I envy not him that eats better meat than I do, nor him that is richer, or that wears better clothes than I do; I envy nobody but him, and him only, that catches more fish than I do.' " Aside from the aesthetic factor, which seldom appeared to bother him much, anyway, Walton would have envied the Bleak Machine beyond any singing of it.

On my return to the peg that several rivals had suggested was especially fortunate, I found my rod had fished no more successfully by itself than it had while I was right there standing guard. But a look at the empty net next door showed I was not alone, except perhaps in maintaining the status quo. The mute little crank was ledgering instead of float fishing by now, working fairly short range, only a few yards off the bank, showering even more groundbait into the river when he wasn't otherwise engaged in moving his umbrella, repositioning his chair, sorting through trays of bait, boxes of hooks, and weights like the seven furies.

Despite a rising flutter of futility, it was relatively pleasant on the riverbank. The day grew progressively better. It never turned into what might be described as warm, or even moderate, but at least it became less cold, less gray, less windy. I fed on some sandwiches I had packed along, two down-home Mounds bars from the American Food

Centre in London, a thermos of hot chocolate a nearby inn-keeper had kindly provided before I had set off early that morning. Up the line a few pegs, a young contestant, whose hair was so long I initially suspected he might be wearing a fur cap, ingested several bits of meat he had originally cubed for the fish.

My quivertip jiggled seriously a little later, but by the time I got hold of the rod and reeled in, the intruder had fled, along with my bait, worse luck, although I had an ample supply on hand, having no particular taste for the stuff myself. I had another strike later, quite a strong one too, if the quivertip accurately reflected the size of the fish, tentatively in my thrall before it let go, apparently not one of Walton's "leather-mouthed fishes of which a hook does ever scarce lose its hold." With things picking up some and the clock running down, I chugged a few handfuls of bait into the Lee myself.

"Any luck?" A leathery old man walking a dog put the Big Question.

"No fish, no luck, not even any stimulating company close by," I said in a voice loud enough to reach the adjoining peg. "But two or three fish have taken potluck on my hook."

"Not to worry," he assured me. "Very few fish have been taken up the line. East wind, I expect, east wind, the weather too fresh, as well. You may tie into a big carp, never know, do you."

But such was not to be. There was no need for the water bailiff trundling a scale with a basket swinging underneath to stop at my swim at three of the clock when the match came to an end. A bearded maintenance worker named Mick Hood was declared the winner with a total catchweight of three pounds, twelve drams, or precisely the weight of his one and only legal fish, a hippy chub, taken ledgering with two casters on a size-14 hook. Together, the fifty-five contestants caught a total of merely fifteen legal fish during the five-hour match, "bad, a very bad competition, one of the worst of the season," as the bailiff told me.

So I'd been blanked on the River Lee, as I've been blanked on all too many other waters elsewhere. Still, my total catchweight on one of Walton's pet rivers came to exactly the same as the aggregate run up by my sponsor Richard Carr, match favorite, frequent tournament winner, likely prospect for the British all-star team next time the wacky diversion goes international, who also produced what the locals describe as nil.

Izaak Walton, the amiable old Royalist who, while he didn't actually invent what he described as the gentle art of angling, as so many people seem to think, at least cast the most renowned single book ever written about it afloat onto the centuries, took an agreeably tolerant view of all manner of fishes. In his extravagant opinion there was much to be said for even the least inviting species swimming the lower depths.

Whatever his merits as a writer and an angler—both of them matters of some dispute among contemporaries who admit to being one or the other—Walton was never especially discriminating. Ruffe, tench, penk, eel, loach, bleak—he found something favorable to write about the sorriest fish wearing fins. As a critic, he was no more abusive than my mother, a sweet, incredibly tolerant lady who once, put to what struck me as the ultimate challenge, gently suggested that, well, Adolf Hitler did have nice eyes.

Surprisingly, Walton failed to rise to his customary melodic heights in enumerating the virtues of the roach, a hippy, coarse fish quite popular among anglers who ply his favorite old rivers, as I myself was doing. "He is a fish of no great reputation for his dainty taste; and his spawn is accounted much better than any other part of him," Walton wrote by way of introducing the roach in *The Compleat Angler.* "And you may take notice, that as the carp is accounted the water-fox for his cunning, so the roach is accounted the water-sheep for his simplicity or foolishness. . . . The roach is a leather-mouthed fish, and has a kind of saw-like teeth in his throat." Perhaps aware that he hadn't awarded the species typically high marks, he did manage to gush a bit before launching into a windy passage on relevant baits: "And lastly, let me tell you, the roach makes an angler capital sport, especially the great roaches around London, where I think there be the best roach-anglers." So, two cheers for the roach.

Despite what was, for Walton, a fairly modest assessment, I was specifically fishing for roach in the synthetic New River to the north of London one wet March afternoon. In case my quarry failed to demonstrate quite the simplicity or foolishness Walton reproached the species for, I was accompanied by a big, bluff auxiliary force, who was reported to be nothing less than one of the most gifted roach fishers in the whole London megalopolis. My companion went to some pains not to quarrel with that estimate.

"If there are roach to be had, I expect that I can pull them up on the grass as well as anyone," he allowed as we drove through Ware and spun onto the A10. "Roach are a speciality of mine. I have been fishing them for more than twenty-five years now—and, frankly, there isn't much I don't know about roach."

Beyond Ware, suburban bedroom communities blotted out the last of the urban flavors except for the traffic, which piled along the road in both directions, big articulated lorries swaying under loads of whatever the stricken British economy had been able to produce during a period of reverberating labor unrest. Two days of intermittent rain stood in green fields on either side of the road. The expert kept talking roach without giving himself any the worst of it.

"I haven't had much experience fishing roach," I said, which was to put it mildly. "Fishing with a man like you, a genuine London-area roach expert, I really don't have much chance. I suppose you'll be the one who catches the really big fish today."

His moustache quivered agreeably. "Uh-huh." It was clear that the beefy man from nearby did not regard me as any transatlantic threat to his lofty reputation.

"Well, I've had some very nice roach out of the water, dozens and dozens of them—hundreds, actually, with the biggest a two-pound, six-ounce fish, which is quite a large roach for a river of this sort, as anyone will tell you."

Down a slope on the far side of the road, past a sprawl of modern semidetached commuter homes, the New River ran over the wet land. It is a narrow river with few bends to it, close to the Lee, four or five feet deep, not over twenty feet across, originating at an abundant spring in Amwell, running for twenty-seven miles, although it was longer when it was first dug in 1613, in the reign of James I, as the source of badly needed fresh water for London during the plague. " 'Tis a match, Sir, I'll not fail you, God willing, to be at Amwell Hill tomorrow morning before sunrising," Piscator said in dating up his discipline Venator at the very end of the first chapter of his Discourse. Since Walton's seven children by his first wife all died at an early age—several of them reportedly of the plague, although the evidence is hazy—Hapwell and other biographers assume the old boy was especially pleased with an instant new river that promised both food and drink.

"This was always one of Walton's favorite rivers, you know." My guide abandoned the first person singular to sketch in some pertinent background. "He hiked out here many a time from London, twenty miles or so, a tidy ramble, packing the heavy kit they used in olden days. Where we will be fishing presently was the old Manifold Ditch he so loved. You can see the original shape of it up on the other side of that weir."

As a member of a fishing club officially entitled to fish that particular piece of the New River, he stopped outside an old brick pumping station, eased his car onto a cinder track. We watched two laborers in bib overalls on the far side use pike poles to pull a work barge up toward a narrow concrete dam. At first glance the New River was no more impressive than the east branch of the DuPage near Lisle, Illinois, which, while undeniably diminutive, was scaled to roughly the size of a small boy who fishes it still in my memory. Perhaps Izaak Walton's appraisal of the many individual waters he fished was as excessive as his view of their contents.

Pelted by the thin rain, whipsawed by the sound of traffic drumming on the motorway on the far side and the whoosh of commuter trains shuttling in and out of London behind us, the two of us started fishing on a turn in the river just above the dam. He was using a flat wooden float, like a popsickle stick, while I was ledgering with a quiver-tip extension on a twelve-foot glass rod, as I had in that doomed match competition on the neighboring River Lee a few weeks earlier. For bait we were both of us using crusts of bread, from a cottage loaf he had brought along, which we pinched on size-14 hooks and lightly cast in hopes they would not fall off or dissolve before descending to the proper depth. In casting bread upon the water, we were fishing for roach in the grand tradition, of course. "You may fish for them with a paste made only of the crumbs of bread, which should be of pure fine manchet; and that paste must be so tempered betwixt your hands, till it be both soft and tough too," Walton had written in ticking off a list of likely baits. I had boned up on his roach chapter before this latest venture onto his pet rivers and accordingly had laid on a selection of bread myself, although none so exotic as the pure manchet loaf he prescribed.

"I expect it won't be long before I show you what a live roach looks like." Squeezing another crust of bread on his hook, my accomplice spoke with a breezy certitude. "It won't be long before I show you exactly how it's done. The conditions are spot-on, you know."

As it happened, I didn't. "What conditions—rain, water level, temperature, barometer, time of day?" I inquired.

"Well, they are in order too, but it's the wind I like, the wind, a rattle of a south wind. Takes some beating, a wind like this."

Three centuries before, Walton had arrived at a similar opinion, which may have been no more original then than it is now: "You are to take notice, that of the winds, the south wind is said to be the best. One observes that when the wind blows south, it blows your bait into a fish's mouth."

The big Englishman flicked his rod, the hook and popsickle stick landing exactly where he seemed to want them, judging by the contented smile on his broad face.

"Besides, the roach have been fishing very well hereabouts lately, have for me, anyway, I mean to say," he told me without so much as a blush.

On the basis of my scrambled experiences flogging waters half the world over, although never before specifically for roach with English accents, I suspected it was time for my mentor to define his terms. "How well?" I asked. "How well have the roach been fishing lately?"

"On a good afternoon I've—" Yet another train shooting

along the track behind us obliterated the answer just as he got around to his favorite subject. He backed up and started again. "On a good afternoon I've been taking three or four fish, roach, lovely fish, beautiful fish."

At the risk of sounding something or other, I said that three or four coarse fish through an afternoon did not constitute what would be defined as especially good sport back where I came from, unless the fish happened to be muskie or catfish. Visions of sweet-tasting cat, skinned, cleaned, rolled in flour, sputtering in a pan of deep fat, rose in my mind. Almost immediately I regretted the jingoistic reference. Despite the fact that he was fitted with an ego the size of a watermelon, which would supplement fresh-fried catfish beautifully, come to think of it, he was a kind and decent man who graciously had invited me to fish roach with him in some club water I wouldn't otherwise have had access to. I amended my observation to say that three or four fish amounted to a bonanza for me personally, which was and is perfectly true.

After an hour neither the reigning champ nor I had taken a fish, but both of us had felt an occasional twitch and lost bait. We moved on down below the dam, where the river ran straight as a string, unfolding canvas chairs on the grassy bank, feeling the wet day through our slickers. Once we resettled I peppered the river with bits of bread, in the proper Walton tradition, but with no profitable results.

Far up a rolling hill beyond the busy motorway on the far side of the New River, a solitary golfer playing through the rain took several practice swings, pulled his club around in a malevolent arc and hit the ball, which was not visible at such a distance on a gray day, not nearly as far or as accurately as he had hoped, judging from the angry war dance he promptly went into. "Strange birds, golfers, playing a game in the wet, not much to show for it," my friend remarked.

In time I found that our new locale was no more successful than the old. Half a loaf of the bread he had given me was better than none, I suppose, but I had gone through the last of mine without so much as a knock, as British anglers call it, below the dam. For all his earlier bombast, my brother of the angle, seated under a deerstalker hat twenty yards away, was suffering the same hard times too.

With the last of the gift bread gone, it was time for some market research involving a miscellaneous supply I had brought along myself. For no particular reason I started with a package bread named Elms Farm, medium sliced, for what it's worth, with a thin tentative crust, fifteen pence the loaf. The scraps I pitched out as groundbait after working a bit of the end crust onto my hook floated down the river instead of dissolving and sinking right where I was fishing. Whatever its nutritional value, which I guessed to be exceedingly dim, Elms Farm bread was not notably tempting for roach during the ten minutes or so I fished it.

"How is the package bread going?" the expert hailed from the swim he was fishing.

"Same as the last—not at all. I might just as well make this into a sandwich for myself, although I probably wouldn't have greater appetite for it than the fish."

"Try fishing shorter range, about the distance I'm fishing." His popsickle float lay on the muddy water only ten or twelve feet out. "I'll have a roach on the bank fairly soon. Most days it doesn't take me nearly this long, knowing the water and knowing roach as I do."

"Oh."

Blanked with the bread he had contributed, no more successful with the Elms Farm brand of my own, I next ripped open a loaf of Mother's Pride, sandwich sliced, a pale, spongy assembly-line brand especially popular among the British, to judge by all the striped company trucks seen on the roadways, which does not say much for resident taste. Any roach in my sector of the New River were, alas, more discriminating. Except for what might possibly have been a sample knock, quickly abandoned, Mother's Pride did not look any more like the staff of life to fish than it did to me. As I flung a last handful into the river, my collaborator let out a disgruntled whoop.

"Missed one, missed a very nice one, too." He screwed his face into an angry mask. "I don't miss many, you know."

If I took a perverse satisfaction in that fleeting failure, it was not because I nourished any hostility toward the generous Englishman who had taken me under his wing. Personally, I found it reassuring that the most gifted, most knowledgeable, and most celebrated angler among us missed an occasional fish, too.

Still, in the bleak circumstances, he felt obliged to offer up what was, except for his clenched British accent, exactly the same maddening commentary I have been hearing for most of my life. Whether I endanger the hairline state of our family solvency by investing in a trip to Center Hill Reservoir in Tennessee, Wisconsin's Flambeau, or Bull Shoals in Arkansas, the message never seems to vary much.

"It seems a bit slow, doesn't it," he said. "Too bad you weren't here Saturday. I can't remember it fishing any better than it did on Saturday."

At four o'clock it was plainly time to unlimber what conceivably could amount to my secret weapon, another brand of bread, Hovis, a tin loaf of Hovis, dark, the color of the river, straight that morning from the A. C. Collett Mill Bake shop in a Cotswold village called Lower Slaughter where we temporarily were living. Support your local merchants—and especially at eleven pence the oven-warm fresh loaf. Alf Collett's bread even seemed to have a better grip to it as I pressed a stiff-crusted piece onto the hook and softly swung it into the river.

"Dark bread doesn't attract the fish much," my guide, who had been watching me change baits again, remarked

69

from his wet seat downriver. "Plain white bread is what you want for roach." Nodding agreeably, I nevertheless tore into the loaf, scattered brown scraps of Hovis reasonably close to my hook, line, and sinker.

For five minutes, his downbeat forecast proved to be distressingly accurate. But then the quivertip extension on the rod twanged, bending, arching, springing up and down, a clear indication that I had a rapping bite. A jerk on the long heavy rod and it was well hooked, scudding in the roily water, thrashing, finally showing on the surface about the time my mentor rushed over for a play-by-play commentary.

"Yes, yes, yes, yes, he's on, a lovely fish, just look at him, a roach, a lovely roach," he said, sweeping the net out, lifting a fork-tailed light fish showing some red where the fins joined the fuselage onto the bank. "Well, we have our first roach." Unless I had gone deaf from all the commuter trains hurtling past behind us, he had switched from the first person singular to the first person plural without so much as pausing to make any "you" sounds.

"How much will my roach weigh?" I pointedly inquired.

"About three-quarters of a pound, I'd guess, lovely fish."

"Is this one a representative sample?"

"Oh, my. Yes, he is, large scales, fairly small mouth, color in the fins, the notched tail, the beautiful shape. Yes, he is."

Before we chucked the roach back into the river where it might enjoy the good life a bit longer, provided one of the voracious incumbent pike didn't have other plans, I photographed it with an understandable glow of pride. In Izaak Walton's back-number locution, "the fish joyed me to look on him."

Another crust of Collett's Hovis bread skewered on the hook, another scatter of dough in the immediate vicinity, and I was fishing again, my aspirations rather more substantial now after that initial success.

"Let's see if we can get a brother to that one," he said. While a bit more subtle, his message still had a whisper of the plural to it. Moments later, I struck too late for a fish, which meant rebaiting and casting out again, but then I was into another fish, a better one too, I hoped, although if it was indeed a brother to my earlier fish, it happened to be an identical twin, the same coloring, the same size, even the same mark across the tail, less than a pound. If I felt a bit exhilarated there in the wet, it's because a man doesn't expect to fill out the miracle of loaves and fishes much these days.

With the game score two-nil now despite my companion's boisterous confidence earlier, he lurched into exactly the sort of bombast I myself would have employed by way of suggesting that this was merely an off-day.

"A funny river, this, never know what will come out of it," he said. "Over the years I've had a seventeen-pound pike, a nine-pound barbel, a fourteen-pound carp, five-pound trout, a four-pound, fourteen-ounce bream, quite a biggish bream for a water of this sort, and roach, dozens and dozens of roach, of course, my very favorite coarse fish, up to two pounds, six ounces." He paused, reflected on that last item. "Roach that size calls for some sure fishing."

While I did not exactly tune him out then—I have a fuzzy recollection that he included a thirty-seven-pound salmon from the Hampshire Avon by way of citing his credentials beyond the New River area—I had a more immediate problem of my own. My bladder nearly runneth over. But given the exposure of a treeless riverbank with traffic humming past on the road beyond and British Rails seldom out of sight to the rear, I didn't quite know where to relieve myself until, finally, I toddled to the old brick pumping station behind which stood an antique *pissoir* so venerable that Walton himself might have wet a line in it, for all I knew.

No further roach expressed a proper taste for Alf Collett's Hovis bread, or so the quivertip told me, but I fished on through the rain in hopes of something more. My mate tried several other swims in the river with no more success than he had experienced to date, although I could see from the way he handled the rod, gently cast and gummed bread on the small hook that he was indeed a superior angler, no doubt of it, despite the score. Luck is a measurable factor when men go after roach, just as it is when they're after a corporate vice-presidency, a particular bird, or a seat on the city council.

Two men trooped up the river, a big strapping sort in a slicker and a companion half a head shorter, bent and lean as a stick, squishing in their boots as they approached with a greeting for my companion, who introduced the two of them, the water bailiff and his workman. They talked fish, fishing, and fishermen in a leisurely manner before I mentioned the fact that I was working the New River because it happened to, be one of Walton's regular old waterways. Brooding on what he regarded as the dramatic background differences between now and then, the bailiff went into a gloomy, increasingly testy commentary on the current state of England, which he found ominous.

"Trade union people mucking up the economy, too many layabouts on the dole, politicians don't care about anything but being elected, youngsters with all that hair spend their nights in pubs, the thick Irish blowing up our soldiers, makes you right angry, doesn't it," he said. "It's not nearly as peaceful and, um, pleasing, yes, pleasing, as it was in Walton's days, is it."

Whatever his merits as a water bailiff, which undoubtedly were substantial, if only because his physical bulk must have been intimidating to prospective poachers, he could not be given particularly high marks as a historian. In Walton's day England was afflicted with blights even more serious than the plague and the casual criminal violence—highwaymen, footpads, throat-cuttings—of equally epidemic proportions. Shortly before *The Compleat Angler* was first published, the suffering country experienced a bloody and extended civil war that lasted for nine years before the Roundheads replaced the monarchy with a rump parliament. Angry mobs walked the streets of London crying "No Popery, no Bishops"; major battles raged in Nottingham and Oxford, Bristol and Preston; Walton's father-in-law by his second marriage, the Bishop of Bath and Wells, was imprisoned in the Tower of London and stripped of his office.

"We will cut off the king's head with the crown on it," Oliver Cromwell reportedly told his commissioners on the eve of a High Court of Justice organized to try the monarch on various charges they had drummed up. Cromwell was a man of his word. On January 30, 1649, in an era the water bailiff seemed to find so peaceful and, um, pleasing, King Charles I stepped onto a scaffold at Whitehall and laid his head on the block. The King is dead, long live the Roundheads.

The two of us carried on fishing after the bailiff, his rage subsided, walked on up the riverbank with his workman. I did not add to my total of two roach any more than the expert added to his total of none at all, although he did miss a fish he guessed might be up to his customary standards.

"I prefer to fish for quality fish rather than for the numbers," he informed me. "I say the roach is a fascinating fish, fascinating, not overly strong, mind you, like the trout, which I also fish with some success, but fascinating. There's a real mystique about taking large roach—oh, over a pound and a half." There's a real mystique about taking large Americans, over 220 pounds, too. He knew neither of my roach had weighed as much as a pound.

The last of my Hovis bread had gone and I was back fishing a package brand without much hope when he hurriedly reeled in his line. "A fish just broke over there, near the far bank, a roach, probably, a good one, with any luck." His hook and bobber plinked down near the far bank. "I've got him, not a very large one, after all, a carp, it's a young carp." He was audibly disappointed, needless to say, but he promptly interpreted the situation in a favorable light. "That isn't bad, a crucian carp, fairly hard to come by, round, a very round fish, with no barbels, a rather pretty fish, isn't it. See for yourself." In my opinion the carp, bigheaded, heavily scaled, flopping in the folds of his net, was no prettier than innumerable members of the same basic tribe I used to see come out of the Fox River in Illinois, and this was smaller than most of them, besides.

At the water's edge he extracted the hook, returned the fish, and washed the slime off his hands. "Well, we've had two species from the New River now," he said, emphasizing the first person plural again. "But the day is dying and I expect it's time to muck off, before we lose the last light."

We spun through late commuter traffic, along a bewildering maze of roadways, back to a motel where I'd parked my car earlier, both of us "hungry as hawks," in the phrase of the immortal angler who once covered the same area afoot or by horse during his London phase. Our conversation never veered much. When we weren't talking roach, we talked bream, or tench, or barbel, or pike, or trout and salmon, which he hoped to fish the following week down in Hampshire, in another river Walton had angled in his sunset years.

"Walton, I don't think he was a very scientific angler, not even for his day and age, but he's a fascinating person, fascinating," my companion said. "And his conversation between various people en route to the fishing was lovely. That's another thing I love about angling—the lovely conversation."

Later, I drove off into the wet night soaked with a sense of accomplishment I experience not nearly as often as I would like. Perhaps I had not fished particularly well, because bread cast upon the waters was not my normal technique, but I'd fished at a profit, to the tune of two fish, exactly the fish we'd set out for too, which is the next best thing, so far as Walton and every other angler is concerned. Almost every other angler, anyway.

A last remnant of that lovely conversation my brother of the angle had extolled as being such a pleasurable aspect of fishing still remained, warped, partisan, the proper credits badly blurred. "Well, I told you we would catch some roach on the New River, didn't I?" he said as we parted. One man's fish are two men's fish, in the keepnet of the imagination.

Uɴᴛɪʟ I finally managed to kick the habit, I had always contributed more than my proper quota to the conjure men who extravagantly peddle can't-miss new fishing flies, lures, and baits. No matter how preposterous the anonymous accompanying testimonials—" 'Wore my arm down just a-pulling them into the boat,' says lifelong angler A. F. of Eureka, Arkansas"—might sound, I slavishly tore out the coupon, slavishly scratched a check, slavishly added the latest variation to a tackle box already abrim with such things. Over a period of all too many years I've invested in upside-down trout flies, bass lures trailing a trickle of what looks like blood, jointed pike plugs emitting a battery-fed squawk as they twitch through the water, top-secret-formula catfish bait so foul that my blissful marriage almost came unglued when I once insisted on storing a jar in the family refrigerator theoretically planned for better things. In my case, at least, the cornucopia of magical *objets d'art* that litter the back pages of any otherwise respectable outdoor magazine invariably catches more fishermen than fish, by a score of one-to-nothing.

In an especially infirm instance a good friend never lets me forget, I even went so far as to respond, at a cost of $3.95 plus mailing charges, to a typically hypnotic wheedle for a jimdandy lure rigged with both a small light and a pellet said to give off a scent no practicing cock fish could resist. Yet the inbound traffic in the water where I tested it was desolate as ever.

In view of my old role as the sod that tackle manufacturers ought to have enshrined as Customer-of-the-Year, at least in terms of novelty items, I was naturally warmed to discover, on carefully rereading his sprawling masterwork, that Izaak Walton also believed in bamboozling fish by offering them a genuine smorgasboard, which, by the way, unless I misread him badly, is what the old boy personally relished any time he seated himself in one of those rustic country inns he described right down to the table line. Allowing for the relatively limited technology available back before the Industrial Revolution, the father of us all fished nearly as many different lures and baits as I have.

The fact that his bountiful bill-of-fare invariably turned out to be far more successful than my own—"I'll catch only one, and that shall be the biggest of all," Piscator told his disciple Venator during a field course on the chub, and promptly did—undoubtedly relates to his superior skills as an angler. Not the least of these was a fussy attention to pre-launch detail. Whatever bait he chose to dangle at the end of his braided horsehair line, wherever he fished it, Walton was as meticulous as a cordon-bleu chef.

Hear him:

". . . I say, put your hook, I mean the arming-wire, through his mouth, and out at his gills; and then with a fine needle and silk sew the upper part of his leg, with only one stitch, to the arming-wire of your hook; or the frog's legs, above the upper joint, to the arming-wire; and, in so doing, use him as though you loved him, that is, harm him as little as you may possibly, that he may live the longer."

With an author so scrupulous as that, it isn't surprising that *The Compleat Angler* positively glistens with specific baits. Depending on the target fish and other variables, Walton recommended artificial minnows, live minnows, lob worms, red worms, marsh worms, dock worms, oak worms, flag worms, grubs, maggots, tag tails, caterpillars, twachels, and beetles. He recommended cheese, snails, shrimp, bread crusts, barley, bees, wasps, grasshoppers, ant flies, Mayflies, caddis, penk, and brandling. If and when circumstances struck him as appropriate, Walton also fished cockroaches, special pastes he mixed himself, and congealed sheep's blood.

Weeks before my scheduled trip to a stretch of the Trent not far from the maestro's birthplace in Stafford, an English friend, whose sources of information are invariably more accurate than mine, reported that the river had been producing a number of bream, which is what I assumed I would be catching too, if, for the sake of novelty, I managed to catch anything at all, of course. Instinctively I thumbed my tattered reference book until I reached what seemed the pertinent section. Halfway through Chapter X, which is entitled "Observations of the Bream, and Directions to Catch Him," I uncovered exactly the sort of juju I'd been hoping to find.

"You shall take a peck, or a peck and a half, according to the greatness of the stream and deepness of the water where you mean to angle, of sweet gross-ground barley-malt, and boil it in a kettle," Walton advised. "One or two warms is enough, then strain it through a bag into a tub, the liquor whereof hath often done my horse much good, and when the bag and malt is near cold. . . ."

Righty-ho. So there I was, a brother of the angle several centuries removed, in need of a connection who could supply barley malt, gross-ground barley malt, sweet gross-ground barley malt, a peck and a half of the stuff, due to the water I was to fish, whose greatness and deepness, which I had yet to see for myself, were nonetheless a matter of public record. For obvious reasons the local feed store in Bourton-on-the-Water, a mile from our small forwarding address cottage in England, seemed the likeliest place to commence.

"Yes, sir," a weathered tradesman in bib overalls acknowledged my presence.

"I'll have a peck and a half of sweet gross-ground barley malt, please." My voice thrummed with synthetic bravado.

"Barley malt? Sweet barley malt?" The old boy's eyeballs visibly bulged. "If you wait, no bother, I hope, I will call me manager."

In a brief conversation with management, during which, despite his curiosity, I could not quite bring myself to explain the misty reasons for my request, I learned that West Midland Farmers neither stocked barley malt nor measured the produce it did sell in pecks. But I learned something else too. The Donnington Brewery might be worth a try.

The brewhouse sits in a fold of green hills near Upper Swell, small, soaking in the sunshine, built of honey-colored Cotswold stone, with stocked trout in an adjoining private pond from which water is drawn for the brewing process. ("They say it needs a good thunderstorm to stir up the mud in the pond to get a good pint out of Donnington," a local mechanic regarded as an authority on such things told me later.) After tuning in my story, the brewery owner, a cheery countryman and an occasional basic angler himself in rare moments when his family develops a taste for trout, not only produced the required malt but invited me to come fish his water sometime—dry flies only, barbless hooks, he quickly added, so the fish, which he feeds with pellets, could safely be returned to the pond.

Once I finally got hold of the basic ingredient, the rest was a breeze. I boiled it in a large pot, two warms, straight out of the book, strained it through cheesecloth, let the residue stiffen while I considered offering the run-off liquor to a neighbor who owned a peckish horse. But with our relationship already tattered, I decided against it on the off-chance that Walton the jiffy veterinarian was no more qualified than Walton the salmon-spawning-cycle mahatma.

The boiled malt was bagged and shipped to Archie Braddock on the River Trent, on whom I had to rely for this and other preliminaries, if only because I was not scheduled to arrive there until the day we'd arranged to fish together, when we would be meeting closeup for the first time. In an effort to guard against anything being lost in translation, accompanying directions amounted to a photocopy from page 260 of my edition:

". . . take it down to the water-side about eight or nine of the clock in the evening, and not before; cast in two parts of your groundbait, squeezed hard between both your hands: it will sink presently to the bottom; and be sure it may rest in the very place where you mean to angle: if the stream run hard, or move a little, cast your malt in handfuls a little the higher, upwards the stream. You may, between your hands, close the malt so fast in handfuls, that the water will hardly part it with the fall."

By English standards the Trent is an enormous river, wide and deep, almost two hundred miles long, the main channel surging with water, washing through the industrial Midlands whose factories it helps keep spinning with power from a series of hydroelectric dams. Inevitably, the dams and industrial wastes pumped into the river have put an alarming dent in the abundance of fish found in Izaak Walton's time. "I have this morning on the River Trent, where I pursued my contemplative recreation, hooked a fine trout," he wrote. While this is troubled water still, the Trent, like English rivers generally, has shown dramatic improvement in recent years, to a point where it produces some trout and even an occasional salmon, fourteen of them between Nottingham and Newark the season I visited, along with a mixed grill of coarse fish, specimen copies of which I hoped to see for myself.

On a cold afternoon in late February not long before the coarse fishing season was due to end, Archie Braddock and I humped an alarming pile of gear across a slanting field slick with cow dung near Long Eaton. Beyond a stand of hawthorn trees, we could see the Trent foam down over a laddered power dam. Even after flattening into a right-hand turn far below, the water had such a surge that I could not help but wonder whether the Walton special formula Braddock swore he cast in the previous night had not washed on down.

But when we reached the area we were to fish, I suspected it had not. We unfolded chairs, furled a canvas to ward off the wind, uncoiled a long keepnet, and drove rod rests in the ground not by the dam but in a small cove, a jigsaw cutting, a backwater with little or no ripple to it. To a potty import item eager to get on with it, the secluded bay off the main channel looked wonderfully promising.

As he locked an open-faced spinning reel onto a twelve-foot fiberglass rod, Braddock, a big moustached theater agent in his late thirties, felt called upon to express a mild apology. Despite some special pleading, the angling club he belonged to and on whose contract waters we were fishing, would allow only one rod between us. In my case, at least, Britannia did not waive the rules.

Quickly Braddock assembled our joint-venture rod, looping on a six-inch porcupine quill float in three living colors, skewering four maggots on an eyed number-12 hook, pinching three split shot what looked like the proper distance—"let there be about a foot or ten inches between the lead and the hook," wrote Walton—up the four-pound monofilament line. Gently, gently he cast perhaps twenty-five feet out, halfway across the bay, the float standing on the surface, the doomed maggots presumably on the bottom. "Spot on." My host was audibly pleased. "Spot on. Just where I laid a carpet of your barley malt yesterday evening."

"Good-oh," I said. Two could play the English English game.

Soon the last of the sun faded over a roll of hills off to our right, two other anglers below us packed up and left. Whatever it might yield in the way of fish, the gathering night was not altogether a blessing. An abrupt chill set us to stomping our boot-shod feet on the riverbank while we sat passing the rod back and forth in hopes of some instant abracadabra.

Somehow I felt caught in a centuries gap, a beneficiary or victim—I wasn't sure which—of the whole bittersweet shape of modern times, packaged Cadbury chocolate bars, monofilament, fiberglass, great pylons strung with power lines all round us, diesel-fed lorries drumming along the M1 motorway a mile away, a blighted river, slowly recovering, an evening newspaper with shock headlines of Ireland, Ethiopia, Bangladesh, Angola, my own land, modern times, the twentieth century, the good and bad, yet with the antique star of Izaak Walton to steer by on this particular night.

At Braddock's suggestion I heaved the few remaining pieces of barley malt into the bay, as close to the float as possible, one lump so close it actually hit the quill. "Pinpoint groundbaiting, that's the secret, if there is a secret," he remarked.

Within a matter of five minutes the float twitched slightly, disappeared, and we had our first fish, or Braddock, who was handling the rod at the time, had our first fish, sort of. He whipped the rod, spooling line, before a pathetic fish no bigger than my finger, which he identified as gudgeon, squirmed in his hand.

Moments later, we had another fish, all mine, this one, almost identical, same size, same species, normal measurements for a gudgeon. After shucking the fish off, Braddock replaced two maggots plainly the worse for wear. With the small colorless worms selling at thirty-five English pence the pint, the price/earnings ratio wasn't what it ought to be on a basis of those two early dividends.

"Pests, these gudgeon, blinking pests." If Archie Braddock never once lapsed into profanity, not even later, when he had sufficient cause, it was because he's a better man than I. "We're rigged for bream—and these pests keep hammering the bait."

Three centuries earlier, Walton took a more tolerant view: "The gudgeon is reputed a fish of excellent taste, and to be very wholesome. He is of a fine shape, of a silver colour, and beautified with black spots both on his body and tail. He breeds two or three times in the year, and always in summer. He is commended for a fish of excellent nourishment. The Germans call him groundling, by reason of his feeding on the ground; and he there feasts himself in sharp streams, and on the gravel."

Braddock and I sat in the twilight, yarning, eating chocolate, passing the rod back and forth, waiting. Every so often he strung on another fresh maggot or two. But most of the time we hypnotically focused on the porcupine quill softly riding the darkening sheet of water.

All of a sudden a cloudburst of bleak, twenty or thirty of them, tiny fish, roughly the size of the gudgeon, rippled the surface on the far side of the bay. "Some big predator fish is chasing them," Braddock observed. "I wonder if it's a pike." Personally, I wondered how long it would take another type of predator, Ade Scutt, generally known as the Bleak Machine along the River Lee, where he catches as many as 900 in fishing matches, to clean out a school like that. Not very long, I decided.

Shortly before six o'clock, the float disappeared. It didn't flutter tentatively or glide sideways. Instead, it dropped straight out of sight, gone, now you see it, now you don't. Whooping some, Braddock tightened the line until he felt the fish, jerked the rod tip, spun the reel, slowly at first, then faster and faster.

"I think it's a roach," he said. "Bream just never give you a bite as strong as that. Strange. Usually roach like a little streamier water than this. Yes, a roach, it's a roach, a small-ish one, mind you. We probably won't be needing the net."

As things turned out, we didn't. My sponsor whipped the roach up onto the riverbank where it lay quivering, a hump-backed fish with a small mouth, brassy sides, and lower fins colored a bright orange, a small roach—only six ounces according to the balance, in fact, about the size of a respectable muskie bait around Hayward, Wisconsin. Still, it was a whisper of better things to come.

We promptly collaborated on two more roach, good fish, both of them, bigger than the first, although nothing to threaten the British record of three pounds, fourteen ounces. It was so dark by then that Braddock mounted a flashlight on a rod rest, focused the beam on the float. Patches of mist rolled in off the river, woolly and spectral, and the night grew colder.

Braddock was treating me to a whimsical story about three artists, "two strippers and a naughty comic" he had booked for a club several nights before, or thought he had, when Walton's River Trent swallowed the porcupine quill in one great gulp. Something substantial—a carp, a big bar-bel, perhaps a pike—shook the rod, shook it again. With a fish like that I had no choice: I let it run. The line sawed through the water. Sullenly it switched directions, right, left, right, out of the bay, into the main river, and broke off, hook, line, and sinker, which caused me to reflect on the vagaries of life, most of them negative.

But Braddock, a bouncy, buoyant party teetering up in the manic range as he undoubtedly had to for the sake of his nerve ends, with showbiz—although it currently sustained him to the tune of matching His and Her 4.2-liter Jags—essentially as big a crapshoot as angling, put the calamity in cheery perspective even as he went about assembling a new rig in a pale wash of torchlight.

"It is fishing well." He pinched a Swan weight, two 3A shots on the line. "I can't recall this slack water fishing much better, not even year before last, when it was very good indeed. It must be the special barley malt."

So much for whatever it was that broke off the line. After threading on a new hook, choosing a replacement quill from a supply so abundant the porcupine must surely be an endangered species, he impaled on the hook only three live maggots in the larva stage instead of the usual four, because, as he explained, not altogether to my satisfaction, fewer might offer better visibility in the dark water. Like most other brothers of the angle it was my good fortune to encounter along Izaak Walton's favorite rivers, Braddock was as fussy as the founding father himself.

Before he gently cast the new rig—it was obvious my error had cost me our shared rod, at least for a while—the big countryman checked the water temperature again. It read fifty degrees, or a good bit warmer than it was on dry land, the result of the hydroelectric power plant pumping warm water back into the Trent not far upstream. He aimed a handful of maggots at the float in an attempt to draw fish to our bait, which wasn't so extravagant as it might seem with the clock beginning to run out on our evening's fishing.

"If we can stick it out, particularly for another half hour, the bream will come on." Braddock was wearing three sweaters and a canvas hat. "Bream like a soft bottom. They're sort of a rooting fish. If we can stick it out in the cold, we'll be into the bream, sure as Harold Wilson is Prime Minister, blast him."

Archie Braddock is a fisherman right down to his nail-bitten fingertips. He fishes regularly two or three times a week right through the long coarse season, and while he isn't listed in the Guinness Book of Records, he admits to seldom getting blanked. If the fish are running well, or even if they aren't, he often tends to lose track of the conventional realities, like the time of day.

"Oh sometimes I used to pack out here about now and fish straight through till twelve or so," he said, moving the float into the cone of flashlight.

"That's fairly late at night," I said.

"No, no. Till twelve the following day, I mean, fishing carp."

"That was before you were married, I suppose."

"Well, yes. Mostly."

Along with everything else, Braddock is an angler in the classic hyperbolic tradition as well. During a flutter of correspondence before we met, he had added a postscript about a walloping twelve-pound carp. As we sat there in the night he mentioned the fish again, a carp, taken in the very cove we were fishing, biggest carp of the season, twelve pounds level. Later, in a dialogue on the bounty to be had close at hand, one of his fishing mates who had come out to join us felt obliged to cite a specific instance.

"Yes, Archie got hold of a nice eleven-pound, two-ounce carp right here the other evening," he innocently said.

In the darkness I couldn't see whether Braddock blushed fourteen ounces' worth or not. Probably not, mild exaggeration being a congenital part of the leisurely old diversion, just like lost fish and cold feet.

We fished on after his friend left to return home to a

86

television show he did not want to miss, which illustrated some dramatic differences between now and then. Back in the seventeenth century, a sportsman returned to "a cleanly room, lavender in the windows and twenty ballads stuck about the wall." From what I had seen of British telly, the ballads sounded a positively pleasant evening.

But bream hadn't changed much over the ages. The first one landed was exactly as Walton described it, "very broad, with a forked tail, and his scales set in excellent order; he hath large eyes, and a narrow sucking mouth." Braddock slipped it in the long keepnet coiled in the water below us, where he was soon joined by two more bream and another roach, all of them taken at fairly short range.

We subsequently hit on a series of minor misfortunes. Something picked the hook clean, the float came loose and drifted into the night, the whole rig snagged badly on the bottom and snapped off. Arming the line with another float, another hook, and new leads, Braddock testily observed that these essentials were not producing much up there in the grass.

Similar sentiments have been expressed by one of my favorite ichthyologists, Lee Humphrey, who also raises hogs. "If you want to catch trout, keep your slop in the water," he once told me as we drifted the White River in Arkansas. Humphrey's slop—live worms, plastic worms, Mepps spinners, Daredevil spoons, a generous antipasto—was confined mostly to the river, while mine strayed some, such as up a tree on the bank, which probably accounted for the fact he outfished me seven-to-three.

After Braddock pitched the new rig into the night he eased back in his chair, the rod guyed in the metal rest between us, the quill caught in the beam of light. Slowly, slowly, it stirred. Just when I got to thinking it was a hallucination, the quill float jiggled again and submerged. It was no hallucination to the man who grabbed for the rod.

"It's a barbel, I think, or a tench, and a big one." There was an exciting lift to Braddock's voice. "Careful with that net when it comes time."

Barbel or tench, the fish put a twanging bow in the heavy rod. It stripped line, running hard, off on a tour of the bay, and when I finally scooped it in with the long-handled net, it bulged in the folds, a bream as big as a carving platter, its notched tail thumping. Archie Braddock used a big pair of forceps to extract the hook from its incompatibly small mouth, wiped the slime off his hands.

He hooked his spring scale to a loop at the top of the net. "Three pounds, eleven ounces," he said admiringly. In view of the earlier exposure involving the carp, I peered over his shoulder for an official audit of my own. In this instance Braddock hadn't stretched the actual weight by so much as an ounce—three pounds, eleven ounces, an honest count which could cost him his license in New York's Neversink Valley.

"Better than average bream, that," he said. "Better than any bream I have had all season, actually. And it was a lovely pull."

Walton had put it much better than that: "They will make noble sport, and are very shy to be landed."

After a fish like that one, it seemed an appropriate time to pack off. Besides, heavier mists were rolling in and the flashlight had lost much of its juice. We took down the rod and rests, released the fish from the keepnet, and walked the dark field toward a far bridge, transatlantic brothers of the angle, another few fish notched up in the memory.

In an hour and forty-eight minutes by the clock we had caught eight fish in the Trent, not counting the gudgeon, which amounted to pre-game calisthentics. If the total wasn't beyond my wildest dreams, it certainly had exceeded my realistic expectations. Braddock felt the same. In the warmth of the Jag that strippers and naughty comics helped to sustain, he asked me exactly how I had gone about stirring up the witches' brew he scattered in the slack water the previous night.

"I want to get it right, can't blame me for that," he said, piling the car through the dark. "Evening like this, on a river he used to fish, we've got old Walton to thank for the fish, Walton and his special barley malt."

Old Walton—and the Donnington Brewery near Upper Swell, I told myself. I swore to lift a long grateful pint of Big D next time I got within range of one of its few rural retail outlets. Done and done.

Anyone who embarks on an angling tour of Izaak Walton's favorite rivers, as I did once a big-hearted publisher finally agreed to underwrite me on a cost-plus basis, can honestly prolong the experience almost indefinitely, which isn't and wasn't a bad idea. This is so because Walton was constitutionally unable to pass a river without jointing his long rod together, uncoiling some braided horsehair line, and baiting an antique hook with whatever delicatessen struck him as the most appropriate. He liked some of them more than others, same as contemporary brothers of the angle, of course, but Walton never actively disliked any stream provided it assayed a few fish of one kind or another.

During the long ninety years of his life, angling's original father figure covered enough water to float the whole prewar British fleet. We know for a fact that he fished the New River, Dove, Manifold, Derwent, Lea, Wye, Test, Itchen, Thames, Kennett, Severn, Ouse, and Shawcross Brook, for example, right around the calendar, in winter as well as summer, depending on a number of variables, such as the condition of the fish.

Long before fish-and-game officials began fixing rigid seasons for various species, he hit on a typically pragmatic approach, as readers of *The Compleat Angler* can see from the following extract on trout. "Till the sun gets to such a height as to warm the earth and the water," Piscator tells his pupil Venator, "the trout is sick and lean, and lousy, and unwholesome; for you shall, in winter, find him to have a big head, and then to be lank, and thin, and lean." Here endeth the lesson.

Whenever he chose to fish them, however, the identity of nobody knows how many other rivers he flogged is strictly a matter of conjecture, precise biographical data being no more abundant in the case of Walton than most other antique British luminaries. Still, by seventeenth-century standards he was as itinerant as the salmon, about which Walton said "he stops not long in one place." His travels included frequent extended stops with ecclesiastical figures in various parts of the country, a pioneer Man Who Came to Dinner, especially if dinner happened to consist of fresh fish from quite close by.

But until almost two hundred fifty years after his death, nobody knew for certain that he also had worked the shiny little Meon near Winchester, although anyone with an IQ no higher than the water temperature could have guessed at it. After all, he spent considerable time in the general area and gave territorial rivers impressive marks. "And you be to know, that in Hampshire, which I think excells all England for swift, shallow, clear, pleasant brooks and store of trouts . . . ," Walton wrote with what strikes me as perfectly legitimate superlatives, for a change. On the basis of some diligent research gathered and published by a cleric named John Vaughn in 1904, even normally skeptical anglephiles were persuaded that in the last few years of his life at Droxford rectory, Walton indeed regularly fished the Meon, where I found myself one feathery day in late June.

As it happened, it was measurably the single longest day of the year, which was probably just as well, because according to the ambitious itinerary arranged by a big, bluff man named Richard Seymour—who has, in his own words, "been keepering a nine-mile stretch of the river for many years, poured my soul into it too, since it's one of old Walton's waters"—we were to fish standard trout by day and sea trout by the dark of night, if and when. Seymour admitted to crossing his nerve ends for a wash of sea trout we could shoot at later. When he learned I had not ever been formally introduced to the species, the extroverted former Royal Navy lieutenant went to some pains to paint in the essential background.

In his partisan opinion, the sea trout amounts to the world's ultimate game fish, a spectacular fight on fairly heavy tackle, an equally spectacular meal next evening. The fish is variously known as sewin in Wales, white trout in Ireland, finnock in Scotland, and salmon trout, jack salmon, or the more common sea trout in different parts of England. By whatever name, it is, quite simply, a brown trout that has gone to sea, as steelhead found in our own Pacific Northwest are rainbows with a seasonal itch for salt water.

"The Meon doesn't produce the sea trout it used to, mind you." An expression of infinite sadness creased Seymour's meaty face. "It used to hold a tremendous head, a really tremendous head, of sea trout. Why, I've caught as many as two hundred in a season myself, nothing under three pounds, up to eighteen pounds, a thrill, man against fish, every one of them, pound the stuffing right out of you. A chap has to be fairly strong fishing sea trout."

Fortunately I had consumed a British breakfast in the grand tradition on the run down to Hampshire, fruit juice and a pitcher of milk, home fries and a round of toast, kippered herring—a suspect sirloin at the next table looked to be high-risk steak—and a grilled tomato. Individual taste is subjective by definition, but I much preferred my menu to one Piscator mentioned in the Discourse: "We will make a brave breakfast"—brave might be exactly the right word to describe the following—"with a piece of powdered beef, and a radish or two that I have in my fish bag." If a feeding such as kipper and home fries failed to fortify me for the challenge Seymour so eloquently depicted, at least it seemed sufficient for our preliminary quest for brown trout, which run to more modest sizes. Besides, the sheer bulk of my keeper companion clearly indicated an eventual stop at some pub featuring food as well as drink prior to the evening phase of our double-header on the Meon.

On a rutted road twisting toward the river we passed a big truck lettered with the perfect name for its sponsoring mattress company: REST ASSURED. "This is Anjou Bridge," Seymour said as we eased over an old stone crossing, "third oldest bridge in all England, so old Walton used it too, in fact, quite fascinating, really." As my guide explained, the bridge was built from scratch in less than a week back in the fourteen hundreds for the royal coach carrying King Henry VI and Mary Margaret of Anjou to Titchfield Abbey, only a brief turn up the road, where they were to be married. The sequential sighting of the mattress truck and the royal matrimonial bridge couldn't help but strike a basic midwesterner as wonderfully appropriate.

After we parked the car alongside the road at Holywell, climbed a stile, and walked a field of honeysuckle, I abruptly realized that, win or lose, another empty creel or not, this particular trip was definitely necessary. Beyond us the Meon bubbled over a stone dam under some willows, three or four feet deep on the far side, not over twenty feet across, a fish briefly flashing out of a patch of starwort, the water clear as a bell. Given a giddy view like that, I could hardly be blamed for fumbling a box of English Greenwell's Glory flies when I hurriedly assembled the ways and means.

Standing in hip waders, the left boot slowly filling with wet from a slow leak I had forgotten about, I cast a light leader into a twirl of water just under the dam. It started as a day like relatively few other days for me, a fish rising to the fly almost at once, rising short of it, sad to say, rising again on my next cast, fatally, this time. It boiled the water, spun into the sunshine, and obediently came to the net after a last twanging run, a precedent brown trout thirteen inches on the nose, pretty as a picture. The beauty of a fish much like this moved Walton to say "the very shape and the enamelled colour of him hath been such as have joyed me to look on him."

Almost immediately I was joyed to look on another trout similar to the first, also by the dam site, a second victim for the American-tied Hairwing Coachman I was fishing for tactical rather than patriotic reasons. A third fish rose at the edge of the rapids, thought better of it, refused to come again despite several further casts, apparently a proper English trout willing to buy only local merchandise. But I was ahead of the game, two fish ahead, by actual count, and it was time to work on up the river.

A turn above the dam I paused where a growth of water buttercup fluttered in the current. A fair-haired lady raking hay up the bank on the far shore turned, dropped the old wooden fork, smiled, and waved. So far, at least, it was a smiling sort of a day.

As anyone with a grasp of the dramatic unities might guess, however, my luck subsequently went slack as my floating line. I missed a lovely fish along the buttercups, snagged and lost the good-luck Hairwing on a truant backcast, missed another trout, which I judged to run easily two pounds, up under a high bank. Just as I hung a second fly too high in the willows to retrieve, Richard Seymour, who had been fishing several bends behind me, walked up a footpath to see how I was acclimating to a strange new river. Under friendly cross-examination, he himself admitted to catching and releasing a total of four fish in the brief time we had been flipping our rigs.

Although Seymour suggested I knot on one of the English flies he had been kind enough to lend me, I kept right on fishing the Coachman after he left for some further sport. Normally I am not mulish about these things, especially when the trout show a diminishing taste for my fly, but the identical pattern had netted me a bonanza of seven trout on the non-Walton Coln at Bibury two weeks before, which indicated I ought to give it more time. Quite apart from those two nice trout already in the bag, I start with a Hairwing Coachman on new pools and new runs, as a pro quarterback often hammers his fullback up the middle on the first play of the game to sample the defense.

Further up the river, a good deep fish kept rising to a mysterious light hatch too fine for me to identify. I persisted with my favorite fly, casting no more accurately than I do on the Neversink, my leader fatally coiled on the clear water in what was otherwise a promising cast, until it was obvious that I had better heed Walton's judicious advice. "And lastly, note that you are to repair upon any occasion to your magazine-bag, and upon any occasion vary and make them lighter or sadder, according to your fancy, or the day," Walton, or some earlier authority he had plagiarized, wrote. My fancy turned out to be the same as a dead English brother of the angle named Wickham, in an eyesore size 18, which meant I had to put on my reading glasses during the substitution, but the biggish trout in the small pool expressed little or no interest in the Wickham's Fancy even when I hit the occasional bullseye cast.

Almost miraculously, the long volley of casts never quite

spooked the fish. It moved in a short range, still snapping at the real thing, whatever that was, descending, rising to the surface for another legitimate fly, a maddening sight after my experience back below the dam. Given so visible a target still locked in a holding pattern, I went right through my flybook—an American Quill Gordon, an English Tup's Indispensable, an American Light Cahill, an English Greenwell's Glory, a fly I did not recognize, bushy, with a gray body, twin tails, and brown and gold ribbing, nationality unknown—in an effort to find something more to the trout's selective taste. After a while I decided—"I will meddle no more with that," Piscator told his stooge in rather similar circumstances—it was loony to stay marooned there with another mile of legal water still before me.

The pastoral sights all round me would have moved the master right up the scale to the rapture key. Two magpie fluttered over an oak tree, heavy and gnarled, rooted in a field of mustard. The river went twirling into a long swift run, sound without fury, the water foaming past a heavy boulder. Three speckled moorhen eggs nesting on top of a cupped nest of weed up against the left bank were enshrined with my Minox.

On top of the run I took a small trout—by my modest standards, a small trout is anything under ten inches—with the mystery fly I have yet to identify. Moments later, I got hold of a bigger brother, a streak of silver bowing my eight-foot rod, which did its best to win before it finally lost, just over fourteen inches, also on the size 18. I revised my humble previous forecast upwards, kept spraying the Meon with casts.

Before Richard Seymour came to collect me, I saw a fish so awesome it could only have been a sea trout. It came riding the main channel, big, far bigger than any trout to my rod, ever, a fish scaled to the size of those fanciful stories at the Anglers' Club on New York's Broad Street, leaving a wake as it piled up the river. Despite my laudable success with small flies earlier, I quickly knotted a number-12 Coachman to 4x leader in case that particular fish happened to be leading a parade. After taking a few stiff casts while x-raying the water through polaroid shades, I mournfully decided it was not.

"Best you leave some fish in the Meon for later on." My new chum the river keeper stood near a clump of holly smoking a thin cigar. "It's time we push on."

However mistaken several other assessments turned out, my guess that big, comfortable Richard Seymour wouldn't miss a meal was what the British call spot-on. At a basic pub called the Bold Forester, in Soberton Heath, where Seymour was plainly no stranger, we talked an hour away over long pints of lager, generous servings of chicken and chips.

Once he got warmed up, Seymour almost bowled me over with an explanatory monologue depicting his burdens as river keeper, a responsibility he transacts on what amounts to a moonlight basis, some thirty hours per week, quite apart from his more gainful role as assistant secretary at a university in nearby Portsmouth. According to him, the job trapping trout, stripping hen fish of their eggs in a bowl, fertilizing the eggs with milt from cock fish, and then submerging the eggs in perforated boxes every autumn is only a part of the whole. He also mends timbers supporting the walls of pools, clears the stream of assorted debris, such as a submerged baby carriage he once found, trims and cuts water weed, keeps mud banks from building up too high, and stands guard against poachers, who pose an artful, sometimes ominous threat summer and winter.

"Poacher blokes can be very nasty, you know." Seymour signaled for a last round of lager. "I've known them to use nets, spears, bows and arrows, air rifles, even shotguns, especially when we have a head of sea trout tailing through. One evening in July of 1962 a poacher bloke I finally caught up with pointed his gun at me and said he would let go if I took another step. It gave me pause, I can tell you. But I lunged and seized the gun all the same, not very smart, as my wife told me later. He had time to work the trigger before I got hold of it, but the steel dart went wide of the mark."

There at the Bold Forester in Soberton Heath, Seymour worked himself into a minor rage brooding on the current status of morality, which in his opinion is sinking fast. "Long hair, young people living on the dole, night after night in the pubs, layabouts, really, kids aren't what they were when I was a boy-oh," he said. "It leads to more poaching, this attitude. Last year alone I took rods away from thirty-one people on the water I keeper." His dudgeon did not evaporate when he lifted a fresh pint, far from it, in point of fact, but easily half the suds did.

That afternoon we wound through villages like Lower Upham and Wickham on our way to fish two other patches of water, both of them on Walton's Meon. Although the glaring sunshine seemed to have no effect on Seymour, who regularly caught and released small trout, the hard times I have experienced elsewhere came over me again, despite his attentive private coaching. "Drop it on the near side of that riffle," he advised on a breathtaking run washing between high stone banks. I cast exactly where he directed, cast again without any agreeable return. On a last hopeful fling at the riffle, the fly looped completely across the river and up into an oak tree where it broke off when I tentatively twitched the rod, which for reasons I still cannot fathom set the two of us to laughing—"an accidental piece of merriment," to borrow from Walton again.

On our return to his home waters at Holywell, the scene of my four (4) conquests earlier in the day, Seymour went into an old routine by feeding resident brown trout he had been spoiling ever since they were in the egg phase. We heaved out scraps of bread and cooked meat, scattering them from along the shore, watching an astonishing number of fish, including several quite heavy ones, boil out from protective weed cover, rocks, and undercut banks. "There's a trout here has a taste for curry," he told me. "One day I tipped a bowl of leftover curry in the river; he came to like it. Any time I bring curry along now he chases the others away—he's a biggish fish, mind you—to feed on it himself. I call him Charlie." In view of Walton's idiosyncracies regarding baits, I wondered if he would have altered the procedure by impaling any such potluck on a hook beforehand.

Slowly we worked our way down the river pitching bread and meat to the needy. It was a pleasant experience, green countryside all round us, the bright sun still high in the sky. My only reservation was that we might be stuffing the trout too full before the traditional evening rise I looked forward to fishing.

My original first-look estimate of Richard Seymour the practicing consumer proved to be overly modest. A large sack of sandwiches, roast beef and ham, on good country bread, came out of the trunk of his car around seven of the clock. Seymour rose to the bait as voraciously as those trout he keepered. "I suppose I prefer the simple life, first light of day, the river, angling, a day out of doors," he said, ingesting another simple round of the roast beef. Elemental good manners demanded that I match him sandwich for sandwich.

Fortified for the challenge ahead of us, we fished brown trout on light tackle waiting for the long day to die. Seymour disappeared for a few minutes, returned with the blunt news that he hadn't been able to spot a single sea trout riding the carrier stream up from the ocean. Now that the nocturnal drill we had planned looked downright bearish, my companion set after the consolation trout like the seven furies.

Personally, I'd grown accustomed to being outfished by the experts, although seldom by the shameful margin I was that particular evening. While feeding fish rose to many a cast, I had trouble hooking and landing even one in three, while Seymour, who worked pools I'd just covered, soon lost count of all the trout he brought to the net. Pitching his small fly precisely where he wanted, hooking virtually everything that rose to him, playing the trout with a sure tight skill, he took fish immediately below me, immediately above me and, once, at my insistence—by then things were so embarrassing I no longer cared—right alongside me. The result of our unspoken match was enough to deflate an ego even more overdeveloped than mine.

One last humiliation awaited me after Seymour came back from a survey trip around a left turn in the Meon, all smiles and good fellowship, absolutely aquiver with the good thing he wanted to put me onto. "He'll go three pounds, four pounds by a thieving butcher's scale, lovely fish, right along the bank, your name written on the tail," he said, hurrying me up the path toward this gift trout. A brief look at the fish rising in clear water convinced me that Seymour was in no way exaggerating. It couldn't possibly weigh in at less than five pounds.

Blessed with a confirmed sighting of these heroic dimensions, I was completely in the river keeper's thrall. Obediently I tied on a number-14 Greenwell's Glory, obediently I eased up the river another few steps, obediently I cast slantwise across the river, feathering the fly to a landing about right, if the trout's reactions were more polished than my own. They were. It surged in the water, sizzling for the counterfeit, struck a tick too late, a shade after I jerked the tip to set the hook in that absentee oldtimer's bulging jaw. Allowing for the differential between artificials and live baits, I had failed to heed a dictum—"Let him have time to gorge the hook"—every syllable of which is as valid today as it was when Walton penned or poached it more than three centuries ago. An extended sorrowful sigh, like the sound of air escaping from a toy balloon, rose from where Seymour leaned against a tree.

"Well, time to have a go at the sea trout, real fish, these," he said, a kind man trying to help me blot out the immediate past. "It's dicey, fishing sea trout, but you won't forget it if you set the steel once."

When it came time to change gear I shifted up from an eight-foot Hardy Phantom to a hand-me-down nine-foot salmon rod, stiffer, stronger, fitted with an extended butt in case two hands seemed better than one. In gathering twilight I fastened a heavier leader, twisted the end of it to an alien juju called the Teel and Silver. The rod cast better than I, covering a surprising amount of water, if no fish. Still, it was exhilarating pitching into the Meon, and Seymour and I had a good time of it for nearly an hour. In the end even the buoyant river keeper agreed that we had better call it a day, or a night, a slitted moon ascending the skies, because he saw no signs of any sea trout thudding up the river.

"A pity, a great pity, the fish ought to be running on a night like this," he said after I sought to offer up the excessive thanks to which he was entitled. "Great pity, isn't it?"

Well, yes and no. Despite our joint venture failure to tie into one of those sea trout Richard Seymour praised beyond any singing, despite my individual botch with that three-, four-, or five-pound brown trout, I had taken far more than my usual ration, eight more than I had taken on many another day, come to think of it, which, together with the drumming answer to what endured as a controversial question for far too long, made it a day to pin away in the memory.

Did the long list of rivers Izaak Walton used to fish include the little Meon in Hampshire? The answer need never have awaited John Vaughn's belated and impressive research findings in 1904. Given water as sweet as that, given a shot at both sea trout and down-home brownies in a fold of England he knew like the back of his maggot-encrusted hand, the question is blitheringly rhetorical: Of course he did.

THE boy had been fishing for almost an hour without so much as a teasing bite. He sat on a grassy bank, hopeful, still hopeful, a small boy lighted with sunshine, fishing as many fundamentalists have fished through the centuries, swimming some live maggots under a light cork float.

All round him lay soft countryside, the glazed fields rolling off into the distance, the dry stone walls and farms showing against the sky, the scene so peaceful that a jaded American visitor felt a rare catch in his throat. The background might well have been painted by the British Tourist Authority. Cattle grazed a slow hillside, a sway-backed old gray mare who positively was not what she used to be stood under a dying elm, yellow roses bloomed in the garden behind a half-timbered Elizabethan cottage.

The stream itself was scaled to the size of the small boy.

It wound through the green pastureland, slender and shallow, washed under a stone bridge. Even where it bellied out some, the stream wasn't any bigger than the Hinkson outside Columbia, Missouri, and, so far, at least, it had produced even fewer fish, if possible, but it was very special water all the same.

The boy was something special too, being my own. On a junior-partnership basis, Scott had killed trout with a flyrod in America and England, cast for salmon in Wales and Scotland at no profit, without even once pausing to sample the assorted flavors of coarse fishing. While the full significance eluded him, it struck me as altogether appropriate that he should be introduced into the mystic order there on Shawford Brook, which was cherished by the immortal Izaak Walton, whose favorite rivers an older Deindorfer happened to be fishing with what could only be described as mixed results. Beginning with the third edition of *The Compleat Angler,* brought out in 1661, in fact, the old boy obviously felt compelled to cast up a typically ornamental testimonial: "Or, with my Bryan and a book, loiter long days near Shawford Brook."

On the grassy slope, Scott jiggled his rod tip some. Every so often he reached into a sack of potato chips, poured himself another cup of milk, or broke off a bit of milk chocolate, while the dormant cork float lay slighted on the slack water. At the age of seven, a boy's attention span isn't any greater than it ought to be.

"Seven trains," he said, his voice muffled by the sound of a goods train whooshing over a rail bridge off to our right, "We've seen seven trains already."

"Seven trains—and no fish," I said. "I'm sorry it isn't the other way around."

"So am I. When will I catch one?"

"It won't be long now." We both of us desperately wanted to believe me.

When I impaled two more live maggots on his hook, a similar laying-on-of-hands flickered in my memory. There we were, my redheaded father and I, back an age that seemed wonderfully quiet and uncomplicated, setting off in the family Reo Flying Cloud, a picnic chest lashed to one running board, bound for Turtle Rock on the Fox River or the east branch of the DuPage, fishing with an old cane pole, my father forever stringing worms, reminding me to keep an eye on the float, unhooking an occasional tiny bullhead or sunfish, after which we would skin or scale the fish, depending, and I would proudly hand them over to my gentle mother, who dutifully fried them with a great show of enthusiasm while my father tried to keep a straight face, snapshots straight out of my lost boyhood.

But a rising whoop of excitement put an end to my wistful recollections. On a turn in Shawford Brook, Scott's float twitched, twitched again. Before I had the chance to suggest a precautionary measure of patience, which I myself seldom manage to demonstrate in such wildly promising circumstances, Scott leaned into the rod and spun the reel. Up it came, the whole rig, first the float, then the weights pinched onto the line, and finally the small hook itself, bare, tragically bare, without as much as even a shred of maggot still clinging to it.

"Drat!" His choice of words was properly decorous, of course, but the emphasis, the sense of rage and the faint self-pitying look suggested he might have the makings of a first-rate fisherman. "He was a whopper too, I think." There was no doubt of it.

For what it was worth, I thumbed the tattered copy of Walton I had specifically carried along in search of some appropriate background music, which runs throughout the book like those cowslips and comely milkmaids. "Listen to what Walton wrote," I said. "He wrote—and I'm quoting him now—'he that hopes to be a good angler, must not only bring an inquiring, searching, observing wit, but he must bring a large measure of hope and patience, and a love and propensity to the art itself.' "

The boy paused for a long moment, reflecting on the spirit of the quote, I hoped, especially that brief reference to the Biblical virtue of patience, I hoped.

"What does pro—pro—propens mean?" he inquired. "Here comes another—eight trains now."

In view of what sounded an alarming lack of respect for his elders, Walton and me, I went into a mild scolding before Joan, relaxing on a slope of land behind us, reminded me that Scott may have had his fill of the father of us all. Perhaps he had. Earlier, before we commenced fishing the small stream, the three of us had toured that half-timbered Elizabethan cottage past the garden in the manner of pilgrims finally arriving at some holy place. Certainly it struck me as a holy place.

The cottage is small, worn, oblong, a place without any particular visible appeal, yet it thrums with meaning. Built of wattle, brick, and plaster, the original thatched roof replaced with slate, bulking along the roadside near Shallowford, the flat-sided, two-story cottage was once the private residence of Walton himself.

Like many another man who forsook the town where he was born and raised to seek his fortune in a bigger city a dream away, Walton abandoned Stafford without ever really letting go of it. During his years as an ironmonger, sempster, or draper in London, during the years he gradually turned more and more to writing, he returned home many times, first to the family residence on Eastgate Street, later to Halfhead Farm at Shallowford, where he and his second wife used the old cottage and he fished the adjoining stream my son was so hopefully working.

A year after *The Compleat Angler* first appeared and Walton presumably had the means to indulge his chronic whim, he decided to forsake the mean, crime-shaded streets of London. Walton always had a split-level attitude about money. While he frequently belittled fiscal over-achievers who managed to accumulate more than their share of the world's goods—"for these poor rich men, we anglers pity them perfectly, and stand in no need to borrow their thoughts to think ourselves so happy"—he knew ex-actly what to do with the stuff when he got hold of a potful himself. What he did in the spring of 1654 was to buy Halfhead Farm with its built-in fishing.

During a guided tour of the premises conducted by Mrs. Ada Popple before Scott started fishing and inventorying British Rail traffic, I could see that the cottage amounted to an ideal haven for anyone interested in filling the larder with fish. Through a rear window it was easy to focus on the stream and judge its height and color. An abundant spread of land behind the cottage undoubtedly supplied all the worms, maggots, grubs, slugs, grasshoppers, bees, wasps, gnats, moths, and other baits the master habitually fished.

To Walton's credit, and as he implies in his book, he was a generous man, especially when it didn't matter much anymore. Specifically, he willed the Halfhead property to his old hometown of Stafford for what he described as "the good and benefit of some of the said towne," in the event his only son hadn't married on arriving at the age of forty-one, which he hadn't despite what must have seemed an impressive inheritance back then. In the elaborate will he drafted himself, perhaps because of a generally peckish view of professionals who normally drafted such docu-ments—"as lived in those times when there were fewer lawyers"—Walton got right down to a precise distribution of any rentals once he was dead and gone.

"And I would have and do give ten pound of the said rent to bind out yearly two boys, the sons of poor but honest parents"—it struck me that Scott had all the neces-sary qualifications here—"to be apprenticed to some tradesman or handycraftman"—maybe he could be a rail-wayman—"to the intent the said boys may the better afterward get their own living," he wrote in the presence of two official witnesses only four months before his death in 1683. "And I do also give five pounds yearly out of the said rent, to be given to some maid-servant that hath attained the age of twenty and one years, not less, and dwelt long in one service, or to some honest poor man's daughter that hath attained to that age, to be paid to her at or on the day of her marriage."

In view of the alarming sterling/dollar conversion rate, which had come to grief, at least for the British, we didn't even consider casting around for a future Stafford heiress who might be a match for our son. Walton, having staked the younger generation to what was then a generous bounty, in no way ignored the plight of less fortunate elders, whom he included in his bequest with a characteristic flair for detail: "And that what money or rent shall remain undisposed of, shall be imployed to buy coals for some poor people, that shall most need them, in the said towne; the said coals to be delivered the last weike in Janewary, or in every first weike in Febrewery; I say then, because I take that time to be the hardest and most pinching times with poor people; and God reward those that shall do this without partiality, and with honesty and a good conscience."

Any things-aren't-what-they-used-to-be soreheads who suspect that political corruption is of recent manufacture can gain some useful historical perspective by pondering the skeptical drumroll with which Izaak Walton concludes the meticulous section improving the lot of the disadvantaged. "And if the said maior and others of the said towne of Stafford shall prove so negligent, or dishonest, as not to imploy the rent by me given as intended and exprest in this my will, which God forbid," he ominously wrote, "then I give the said rents and profits of the said farme or land to the towne and chief magistrates or governors of Eccleshall. . . ."

Eccleshall is a nearby village whose chief magistrates or governors never laid a hand on the property, which is still under the jurisdiction of the Stafford Borough Council. The adjoining farmland was sold off years ago, but the gift cottage and garden the three of us explored earlier on the day Scott fed the fish a pint of maggots remains a public landmark.

As Mrs. Popple explained over the customary cup of tea, she inherited the job of live-in curator on the death of her husband James, a hearty countryman who often used to boast that he would live even longer than Walton, which in fact he did. By surviving for ninety-one years he outlasted the old boy by a full season. At eighty-seven, the widow Popple, a brisk, bouncy woman—she had just finished the washing and ironing, was about to tidy up the back garden for a family wedding reception of thirty people scheduled for the next morning—with no physical infirmities and a surprising musical lift to her voice, struck me as a fairly good bet to beat the both of them.

Judging by our subsequent conversation, it's just as well that Mrs. Popple hasn't yet been fitted with orthopedic shoes. During the summer months, the museum attracts up to a hundred visitors a day, most of them fishermen, of course, along with a trickle of teachers and other bookish types interested in Walton the literary eminence rather than Walton the angler. "People come visiting Mr. Walton's cottage from miles and miles away," Mrs. Popple said, her voice running up and down the scale. "They come from all over England, from Germany, France, Italy, Spain, Switzerland, Poland, Sweden, South Africa, Australia and New Zealand, Canada, the United States, quite a number from the United States, actually. Why, only a fortnight ago, two students from Tokyo popped by with a Japanese edition of Mr. Walton's book."

Wherever they come from and whatever their particular interest, visitors are treated to the same standard tour once they pay the modest admission fee of five pence, which helps cover incidental expenses such as the tea Mrs. Popple offers anyone she takes a shine to. With a reverent hush they peer into the beamed living room warmed by an inglenook fireplace on the far side, climb a warped twist of steps for a look into two comfortable bedrooms, track specimen samples of Walton's small, crabbed orthography amidst the miscellaneous profusion of artifacts on display in a kitchen area built round an antique oven in which his beloved Kenna presumably baked the all-purpose loaves Walton ingested and used for bait.

In our case we lingered in the open kitchenway studying photographs and old prints, heraldic crests and framed testimonials. Except in a casual generic sense, not all the oddments in the small exhibition happened to be authentic Walton heirlooms, as we discovered on reading the fine print describing the various items. The stuffed head of a thirty-four-pound pike, for example, its teeth so malevolent I had no trouble comprehending the recent newspaper story of an Englishman whose normal ration of five toes abruptly diminished to merely two after he dipped a foot in the Norfolk Broads, was identified only as an impressive hometown Stafford pike. But those teeth were nothing compared with the formidable tusk of a narwhale mounted on the wall near a rear window, which struck me as profane in a shrine celebrating the most illustrious fresh-water angler who ever lived. If Mrs. Popple hadn't treated us with such unfailing kindness, I would have asked her to pass a prickly objection along to the decorator. Anyone who confuses fish and seafood ought to have his license revoked.

I couldn't be sure how much of our tour lingered in Scott's mind as he hopefully fished Shawford Brook in the sunshine behind the cottage. If more detail lingered in my own mind, it's because I tend to look backward instead of forward, the one being painfully bigger than the other at my declining age.

"Why don't we try a crust of bread as bait instead of the

maggots?" I inquired with a bravado based on my long years of catching not nearly enough fish.

"No, the man said to use maggots." Scott paused to add another train to his inventory. "The man who wouldn't take any money said to use maggots."

It was perfectly true that the proprietor of a tackle shop in downtown Stafford, a long, angular man with a forbidding underslung jaw, like an old cock trout's had refused to accept any money for the pint of live maggots he prescribed.

"Compliments of Izaak Walton," he said. "Either fish them on the bottom or drift them in the current. Roach, rudd, chub come out of that water, some jolly nice fish too, small piece of water like that." It's also perfectly true that I had already invested two pounds, twenty-five pence, for an assortment of split shot, hooks, floats, and plastic worms, which he was only too glad to ring up without making any philanthropic noises. "Tight lines, lad," he said, his underbite giving the words a gritty sound, as we left for an equally essential stop at a bakeshop two doors up the high street.

Our son the apprentice coarse fisherman reeled in, invited me to replace his dead bait with two of the maggots, and swung the rod across the stream, where the whole thing snagged on a branch of a willow tree. It was just as well I'd laid on a supply of spare parts. Once he pitched a new rig a few feet out, I peppered the surface with some of the gift maggots in an effort to draw fish to his bait. Easy come, easy go.

On lowering myself onto a grassy slope close enough to offer technical advice without being in casting range, which was an obvious hazard, my right hand unerringly dropped into a patch of stinging nettle. I let out a howl so blasphemous as to shock my son, not to mention the shade of the pious immortal under whose auspices we were fishing that particular day. As Walton described the four-square character of brothers of the angle with his customary embroidery, "We seldom take the name of God into our mouths but it is either to praise Him or pray to Him." My hand burned like hellfire until the youngest among us mercifully came up with some folk medicine in the form of a dockleaf, which he insisted would put an end to my torment if I'd only rub it into my wounds. To my surprise it did.

Although the bobber floating on the slack water didn't register so much as a hopeful jiggle, it was pleasant to soak in the sunshine there on a bend in Shawford Brook. A loaf of fresh bread disappeared, and some sliced ham, and a sack of potato chips, and a pint of milk, and three apples. Joan lazed further up the bank fishing for words to fill in a puzzle she was attacking with a ballpoint pen—it wasn't a matter of arrogance but the fact that she had lost her pencil, which technically happened to be my pencil, of course—while the menfolk, given nothing more serious to count as yet, kept careful track of British Rails crossing the bridge.

"Eleven, eleven trains now," Scott said before leaving the forlorn rod in my care to pelt off on what was described as a looksee for more promising water. Moments later, he returned, running hard, visibly excited. "I saw a fish, a big fish," he said. In response to my question as to how long it looked, he stretched his hands in the ancient way, narrowed the span some, compared it with a genuinely impressive trout of three pounds he once skinned out of a can't-miss commercial enterprise called the Trout Ranch in New York's Catskills.

"And how many bends down the stream did you see this walloping big fish?" I asked. With the sunshine and the bountiful picnic combining to pull the ripcord on my chronic lethargy, I was in no hurry to move any great distance, not even for a fish, which, knowing a boyish concept of size, wasn't necessarily nearly as large as he had depicted it, anyway.

But Scott's enthusiasm, his excitement, his proud sense

of discovery, were so excessive that he could not be denied. Off we went, carrying tackle, the chair, and what few remnants of lunch remained, around a right-hand turn in the river, and another, and another, until we arrived at exactly the mother-lode water, according to him. I had to admit that it looked a far better stretch, deeper than where we had been fishing, the water clear enough to see through, a nice hole hedged with weeds on the far side, just below a tumbling run—"a quiet or dead place, near to some swift," to poach a phrase from Walton. For all we knew, this might well have been the old boy's favorite spot for fishing logger-headed chub.

We hadn't worked the new site for long before abundant evidence in support of our son's evaluation briefly appeared. To this day I have no idea whether it was a roach, a rudd, or a chub, but a heavy fish nearly as long as that previous commercial word came scudding out of the weeds, flashed upstream, disappeared. "See that!" Scott yelped, so excited he missed counting another train that hurtled past. "We can catch that big one now, can't we?" He gripped the pole with both hands, just in case, pulled the bobber across the surface a foot or so, while I salted the river with another handful of maggots.

In those promising circumstances it wasn't surprising when the float soon fluttered, skinned out, and sank. Even before Scott jerked the rod and reeled in, I could see that the specimen did not begin to measure up to his idle hopes. Instead of being the genuinely impressive fish we had seen earlier, this was a tiddler to be calculated not in pounds or ounces but in drams, like some of those introductory fish I had caught myself all too many years before. The victor manfully tried to screw up his enthusiasm for a gudgeon no longer than a cigarette, quivering in the grass. "It's a pretty thing," he said with his paternal grandmother's gift for interpreting events in the most favorable light possible.

The gudgeon, despite its diminutive size, moved Walton

to a favorable, if not altogether flattering, analysis. After describing the breed right down to the black spots on its body, he wrote, "he is an excellent fish to enter a young angler, being easy to be taken with a small red worm, on or very near to the ground, he is one of those leather-mouthed fish that has teeth in his throat, and will hardly be lost off from the hook if he be once strucken." Walton generally showed a soft spot for youngsters just as I do—probably because merely two of his own nine children lived very long.

After the shoal of gudgeon noticed the Free Lunch sign dangling at the end of the line, they positively gorged themselves. The young angler being entered on the copyright holder's leisurely old stream strucken three more lookalikes, none any bigger than the first, the four together weighing little more than an ounce, every one of them with teeth so very far down in the throat that I practically had to turn the fishlets inside out extracting the hook and what was left of the maggots. Nothing any more substantial knocked at the bait, although the large fish we had seen earlier, or one very much like it, came out of the weedbed a few times, finning slowly in the water, tantalizing the two of us, resisting temptation even when it was softly cast right to its eyeballs. In the same sort of situation Walton hit on the only practical solution: "But I will meddle no more with that."

A roll of clouds blotted out the sun, and when it looked as if the colors of the day were not to return, we left the twiny brook reasonably satisfied with the four gudgeon. On our way up the crooked path we passed the gray mare, still immobile under the tree, and pitched the last of the maggots into a shallow from an antique stone footbridge. A roach bigger than anything we had seen all day squirted out from the roots of a willow, hammered at the bonanza, sweeping them up in its small mouth like a vacuum cleaner, and then slowly returned to the roots.

We loaded our gear into the car, paused for a last look at

the timbered cottage Walton occupied when he was not out back catching more fish than his newest disciple. In our different ways, right up the scale of age, the three of us realized that this was one of angling's holy places.

"Izaak Walton was famous, wasn't he, daddy?" Scott asked.

"Yes and no. He was well known while he still lived. He got famous later, after he died, when his classic book became a part of . . ."

"Twenty-six. Twenty-six trains today, and that one had thirteen coaches to it."

So much for a definition of art. We picked at the subject some later driving the M5 dual carriageway through Birmingham and Tewkesbury, catching a back road for Teddington Hands and Guiting Power, running in a light rain, the whole trip a breeze as we remembered the events of a memorable day. As Walton noted three centuries earlier, good company makes the way seem short.

We hadn't been in our transplant English digs for long that night before the phone rang. It was Nigel Wheeler, doctor, angler, trencherman, friend, who was aware of where we had been bound earlier, idly wondering how successful the expedition had been.

"How many fish?"

"Two brace." Somehow it sounded better that way.

"Good-oh. That's a nice start for the boy. What size?" Furnished with an appetite so boisterous as to make the Pittsburgh Steeler defensive line blush, only who could tell, Wheeler is generally more interested in cooking weight than in such incidentals as trout or pike.

"How's that?"

"I was asking what size the fish ran," Wheeler said, his voice as clear as a bell.

"Nigel, Nigel, are you there? I can't hear a thing except for this drumming noise. Something has gone wrong with the phone again. If you can hear me, remind me to give you details of his two brace next time I see you . . ."

IN the extravagant opinion of Izaak Walton, by all odds the most popular angling writer who ever lived, not to mention one of the most hyperbolic, fishermen as a species are truly remarkable men, decent and God-fearing, cursed with none of the character defects afflicting mere mortals who don't pursue stray pectoral fins. *The Compleat Angler* consistently depicts them as "gentlemen of tried honesty," "followers of peace," "persons of honour," and other such florid tributes generally reserved for eulogies. Halfway through his masterwork, it undoubtedly struck Walton as less self-serving to play the ventriloquist by throwing his voice in the general direction of a comely milkmaid he used as attractive background: "For she and I both love anglers, they be such honest, civil, quiet men." He lived far longer than seventeenth-century actuarial tables normally allowed for, but it's clear that Izaak Walton didn't live nearly long enough to know this particular brother of the angle.

In the best interests of my precarious reputation, it's only fair to remind any skeptics that I heed even the fine print in our bulging catalogue of law. Among many another prohibition, I never knowingly breach the resident speed limits, I uncover a head that nature has gradually been uncovering every time the band strikes up "The Star-Spangled Banner" prior to the opening kickoff, I cannot bring myself to overlook that cash honorarium for a Kiwanis Club appearance when it comes time to divulge my paltry annual income for the feds. Every once in a while I even go so far as to apply for sainthood by reminding some aging shopkeeper that he has accidentally given me change for a fiver instead of a single, although, frankly, I'm not at all certain I could pass a morality test involving larger multiples.

The exceptions to my otherwise exemplary performance as a law-abiding citizen, or a lover of virtue, in the words of Walton, invariably come about while I go a-angling. A run of shiny water posted with defiant Strictly No Fishing signs, the sight of a tempting game fish no longer in season, a hidebound local ordinance prohibiting exactly the lure I planned to use—well, while the spirit is moderately willing, the flesh is weak as sarsaparilla.

As a long-time sinner, my lapses have been so frequent that it is difficult to isolate any one of them as the most shameful. In an instance most anglers would deplore, I initiated a minor one-man crime wave by simultaneously fishing out of season, poaching private water, and casting verboten Colorado Spinners—all this with the familiar bottom-line results, I might add, which is to say not a trout all day long despite my blithe spirits.

Given a speckled blotter like that, the eventual shape of a scheduled day on the original Piscator's Hampshire Avon was clearly fixed the moment a tradesman at the Eadie

Tackle Shop in Salisbury innocuously contributed what he considered an incidental report straight out of the lower depths. The fact that this was late December meant that my friend Nigel Wheeler and I would flog the river for pike and roach, chub and perch, which come under the heading of coarse fish in England. Or at least that was the plan before we tuned in a bulletin better classified as Top Secret in our case, Wheeler's sense of law and order, while positively admirable in other regards, being little greater than my own out on the riverbank.

"Walton fished the Avon for roach, mostly, you know," the shopkeeper told us during the usual preliminaries. "But I expect he had a bit of everything, river like this. You'll be needing some smaller hooks and maggots, take about two maggots on the hook, to bottom fish under a float. You might like these new floats, too. They sort of chatter. Myself, I prefer them to the normal bungs."

"What about tinned lunch meat?" Nigel asked.

"Lunch meat is often useful."

"And sprats?"

"Yes, you'll be wanting sprats for the pike, won't you."

"Now that you mention pike, I can't help but wonder how they're running on the Avon." It seemed time for me to put the question.

"Fair, fair size. We had one recently just over twenty-six pounds." He began bagging up our purchases. "And there are a deuce of a lot of salmon running upriver right now. You might well hook into a salmon, big laddies too, now coming up on high water. It's a great pity the salmon season won't open for another few weeks."

On hearing the electrifying news I tried to get a grip on my rising blood pressure. I hated myself already, of course, and yet I knew I couldn't resist the wicked impulse to fish salmon at least part of the day. On the basis of a size-10 shoe surreptitiously sunk in my shin, it was plain that the same base program was evolving in Nigel's artful mind.

After a slight pause he picked up the conversation with a lighthearted reaction.

"I'm not very good at recognizing salmon," Nigel said. "They look a lot like pike to me."

"Well, you know when you get them to the hook," the vendor said, smiling some, obviously not aware he had pulled the cork from the bottle. "You know."

"I suppose so. Well, with the pike running well, we had better lay on more gear."

Anyone who might wonder whether it was premeditated murder the two of us had in mind need only reflect on the additional supplies we promptly ordered in our cover roles as pike fishermen. We doubled the previous ration of golden sprats and number-4 treble hooks, which theoretically are as effective with preview salmon as they are with legal in-season pike, added a spool of twenty-five-pound test nylon, which could not be used as Exhibit A, either, because pike run roughly the same size as salmon. Instead of pausing for a warm pre-lunch lunch in a snack shop, we bought a sackful of takeaway provisions to ingest along the Hampshire Avon, in the interests of allowing ourselves even more time for an assault on the pike/salmon.

Hurtling down the Fordinbridge Road for the water we had arranged to fish, exuberantly celebrating what seemed our good fortune, fixing the terms of our normal first-fish bet, Nigel and I had little interest in focusing on the picturesque landscape. "Yes, isn't it a great pity the salmon season doesn't open for another few weeks?" he cackled rhetorically. "And isn't it a great pity accidental salmon bruise so easily that it's better not to throw them back?" The drive was a blur of crisp lawns, stone cottages standing under thatched roofs, and wrinkled green land rolling south toward the ocean, which was close enough for us to actually smell and see signs of in the form of seagulls wheeling against the surprisingly warm blue skies. The weather was as out-of-season as those salmon the tacklemonger would not have mentioned if he had read his tea leaves accurately.

At a big working farm marked Burgate Manor, we backed into a makeshift carpark reserved for guests and members of the Salisbury & District Angling Club, whose abundance of leased waters—sixteen of them at last count—included that stretch of the Avon that Nigel and I were to fish. Quickly we walked a wet dirt track, crossed a footbridge stretched over a backwater, humped across a sloping meadow leading to the river.

But a closeup look at the Avon let the wind out of the daydreams we had been conjuring up ever since the salmon ahoy flash. Sheets of water standing in the fields along the roadway on our trip out were no mirage. The river was high, high and colored, a thick dark wash chuting left to right, genuine troubled water no matter what particular species we hoped to land. Unfortunately, the gear piled in the tackle box did not include a bladed odometer, although I can think of no other lapse, but Nigel, who claims to be good at such things, guessed the river was running at a speed of perhaps eight knots. As we stood there glumly watching, the flow carried kindling, whole logs, snarls of weed and, surprisingly, bread, bread cast upon the waters, three slices bobbing in one patch, seven slices more and, finally, a full bakery loaf, conceivably a profligate kind of groundbaiting by a solitary angler perched on the near bank above a suspension bridge which separates the London Angling Club beat from the Salisbury & District piece.

"The only way to take a fish today is to drop the bait right on its nose," I grumped.

"All right," said Nigel, whose spirits generally run a size or two bigger than mine. "Let us start dropping baits right on the nose."

Together we started swimming dead golden sprats on treble hooks, with enough lead to get the baits down in the boiling water and a signal float riding the surface. I like to think I was fishing strictly pike there for a while, partly because I was raised by alarmingly law-abiding parents, partly because this was pious old Walton's river I was working. Whatever it was I was beating the water for, however, I had no more success than Nigel, who was quite frankly in pursuit of something to smoke, but at least he experienced an occasional tight line. One after the other, in a melancholy pattern of failure, he hooked a nest of star weed, a scrap of wood, and the top of an orange crate.

The debris riding the crest of the river consisted of more than artifacts normally found in the back shed. All of a sudden a fish spun out of the river—a tiny fish, to be sure, no bigger than my finger, a bleak or a gudgeon, but a sample to pin our hopes to. With all the natural food in a swollen river, that single bait fish presumably had a good reason for rising clear of it, such as something bigger, far bigger, in pursuit of it, a chub, a perch, a pike, maybe even one of those laddyboy salmon the man had elliptically referred to. Nigel and I fished all the harder now, pitching our sprat into the heavy flow, following our floats with a single-minded intensity, stripping weeds off the hooks whenever necessary, casting, casting, casting.

Like the original brother of the angle, we flipped out baits into mid-stream and never forgot that the salmon is an especially itinerant fish. "And for that, first you shall observe, that usually he stays not long in a place, as trouts will, but, as I said, covets still to go nearer the spring-head," Walton remarks in his Discourse, "and that he does not, as the trout and many other fish, lie near the water-side or bank, or roots of trees, but swims in the deep and broad parts of the water, and usually in the middle, and near the ground; and that there you are to fish for him." On the kind of day we fished the Hampshire Avon, it wasn't always possible to avoid roots of trees even out in the deep and broad parts specifically prescribed.

Slowly I fished on down the bank while Nigel, who cares more about such matters, stood guard over our provisions. Below a cluster of elderberry we turned right, the river and I, and it widened some, the surge diminishing where it rolled by several oak twined against the sky. Slowly I fished on down the bank until I saw a specimen worth fishing for.

My bobber was floating the main channel when a salmon rose, big, hellish big, big by my own definitions, twenty, perhaps even twenty-five pounds, a gorgeous sight, leaping clear, climbing an invisible dam, its double-weight body arched, a great silvery shape bowed over the muddy river, not ten feet from my captive golden sprat, which I guessed or perhaps hoped had somehow triggered the jump. The sight of it lasted not nearly long enough. After that brief personal appearance, the salmon hit the water hard, with a sound like a branch breaking off a tree.

Any lingering pretense I was actually fishing nothing more than pike evaporated the moment that fish appeared. Quickly I retrieved my rig and cast again, moving up the Avon to allow for its migratory yearning for the old familiar places. In a fever to hook into the sighted salmon I twitched the sprat, heaved it close to the far bank, jerked it through the water in an effort to arouse the beast in the fish, all these special effects to absolutely no avail.

A long, if speckled, career on the waterways reminded me that the sight of a single salmon wasn't necessarily habit-forming but I couldn't help but believe the swollen Avon offered other similar fish to fry, or poach, or smoke. I strung a less shopworn bait on the hook, ran the bobber up another foot, added more lead to sink the sprat to the bottom. My pre-season quest for a salmon encouraged me to try every ruse that came to mind, yet my pre-season quest produced no more than a death-grip snag on a broken limb floating by, which cost me hook, leader, line, and sinker. Wages of sin, as I was compelled to acknowledge.

In the midst of stringing a new rig together, I heard a gunshot from across the river. Presently two hunters appeared, walking downstream, their shotguns broken open, trailing a pair of Labradors, one of them almost white, the other a handsome light brown.

"Any luck?" I called.

"Some," a short man wearing a canvas coat and modified deerstalker said. "But we haven't bagged a fisherman yet."

It wasn't long before I heard a single shot, then two more in quick succession. Far to the right, in slow motion, I saw a Labrador splash into the river to retrieve a bird, probably a pheasant at that time of year. It looked very much as though one of the hunters—Venator, I decided, the name Walton gave the model hunter in *The Compleat Angler*—had taken rather more out of the Avon than I had, so far at least.

What made my futility especially galling was the fact that the sainted river was experiencing that early run of spotted plutocrats blessed with multiple residences. Walton, while he was far from a certified authority on salmon, had studied available background material to a point where he got their migratory nature approximately right. "But if the old salmon gets to the sea, then that gristle, which shows him to be kipper, wears away, or is cast off (as the eagle is said to cast his bill), and he recovers his strength, and comes next summer to the same river," the old boy wrote, although, in view of his lapse in citing specific sources, someone else might well have written much the same thing years earlier, "if it be possible, to enjoy the former pleasures"—apparently Walton the seventeenth-century Anglican was too squeamish to identify one of those pleasures as sex—"that there possessed him; for, as one has wittily observed, he has, like some persons of honour and riches, which have both their winter and summer houses, the fresh rivers for summer, and the salt water for winter, to spend his life in." For himself, Walton, like this humble disciple, didn't care much about a range of seasonal homes provided there was abundant fishing close by.

When I rejoined Nigel at our headquarter turn on the Avon with my headline news of the big salmon I had seen sunshining out of the river, his reaction couldn't be construed as one of great surprise. "I guessed you might," he said. "I've seen two myself, biggish fish too, but antisocial, very antisocial, both of them, not nearly as friendly as they might have been. Still, the first one tickled my sprat right down to the appendix."

As we sprawled on canvas chairs diagnosing the lost morning, I checked a last plastic sack of sprats I had left behind. One lone bait remained. "What's this?" I asked with a bit of heat. "Oh, I lost a few, snagged badly, you know, couldn't be helped," he said. "Sorry." With Nigel one of the truly formidable trenchermen in the English midlands—to the tune of four ham sandwiches, two bananas, a tangerine, two chocolate bars, and a jug of coffee since I had foolishly left him with the groceries earlier, I noted—a vile suspicion that, in swinish desperation, he had also devoured the golden sprats flickered briefly in my mind.

Across the river a figure walked a long flat field, a thickset man with a collie dog, swinging a long thumbstick notched at the end, hatless, silent, visible movement in the still setting.

Nigel and I sat there gathering strength for the afternoon session and exchanging the sort of stories we often share. By Walton's rigid standards, I fear we were both hoist in a double-jeopardy situation. Not only did we intend to continue fishing for pre-season salmon, which skewered us as less than gentlemen of tried honesty, but our X-rated conversation was far too strong for his wholesome taste. "For most of his conceits were either Scripture jests or lascivious jests, for which I count no man witty," Walton reprovingly wrote of a man more tolerant brothers of the angle may have considered a genuine jackanapes.

By mutual agreement, Nigel and I abandoned any last illusions by replacing the sprat baits with artificial Devonshire Spinners, salmon lures by anybody's definition, especially any stray water bailiff who might happen to come by. But I spun myself a web of protective cover. While I was doing everything I could to breach the regulations, I would return all salmon to the river—I honestly hoped I would, anyway—once they had given me that wild, flat-out ride. So there I was, an itinerant angler far from my home waters, damned if I scored, damned if I didn't.

"This is a first-class pike bait, you know," said Nigel, his moon face a perfect blank, heaving the lure into the main channel.

"Of course it is." My own face has undergone too much wear and tear to draw a blank. "If it wasn't a first-class pike bait I wouldn't be fishing it."

No more salmon leaped out of the swollen Avon, but we did spot a scruffy consolation prize riding the crest along with the other debris—a carp, a signpost of my midwestern boyhood, a dead carp, a species Walton extolled in his Discourse as "queen of the rivers; a stately, a good, and a very subtle fish." The original's compulsion to praise even the garbage fish fouling our waters is commendable in terms of the old if-you-can't-say-something-nice axiom, I suppose, but he should have had his goose-quill pen taken away for two weeks for a distortion so shameful as that. Nigel Wheeler, who apparently shared Walton's minority assessment of the carp, jerked his rod in an effort to snag the cadaver.

For the next hour or so I worked the lower stretch, Nigel the upper, both of us changing sizes and colors of the Devonshire Spinners, before I decided that a large Mepps Spinner might also be worth a try. I heaved it out, entwined the hooks in a clump of weed, picked them clean.

Not long after that, the Hampshire Avon finally shook. During a fairly slow retrieve, the Mepps twirling below the dark surface, a bolt of lightning hit, caught hold, ran a burning live current up the line and through the rod clear to my shoulder blade. The fish felt well and truly hooked, stripping line, piling up the channel, a great invisible shape surging in the river.

"Whoo-ee, pike, a big pike fish," I whooped, preserving the code we had employed throughout the barren day. "What do we do without a gaff?"

"We improvise, that's what we do." Nigel sounded every bit as excited as I. "You wear him down and eventually beach him—or I have a go with the chancy net."

The prospect of wearing down a salmon in hostile fast water like that struck me as fairly remote, although the fish, whatever its total poundage, was plainly giving considerable weight away to me. I held the jolting rod high, let the line run, spun the reel when my adversary paused to catch a breath. The sight of a small uprooted willow washing down hardly filled me with hope—an irony, if it proved to be my doom, because I generally have trouble enough with trees positioned where they belong, up on the bank—but I pumped the rod some and the peril safely passed us by.

Just as I began to despair of my suspect vitality outlasting the salmon's, the fish showed signs of fatigue. Except for one brief leap—a tantalizing picture, wonderfully impressive specifications for a spot on my library wall, if I couldn't bring myself to pitch it back—the salmon soon demonstrated no more bounce than a walleye pike.

"Easy, easy now," Nigel advised me.

Even while he spoke the salmon resolved the qualmy moral question of freedom or a ride to some no-questions-asked taxidermist by breaking off, leaving only a tactical query. Either the fish weighed in excess of the twenty-five-pound test nylon leader it wore through or else I simply was not up to the challenge—take your choice. Personally, in the dark of the night, I have my own partisan opinion.

After breaching the parish council prohibitions concerning blasphemy, which surely would have offended Walton as much as my lapse with the salmon, at two different levels, in fact, I did my best to put the encounter into an encouraging focus. I wasn't exactly filled with wild hopes of another shot at a fish scaled to those dimensions, but now Nigel and I knew the salmon not only were running—after all, we had sighted a total of four by now—but snapping at an occasional bait as well.

Something heavy—another salmon, a pike, conceivably an overdeveloped bream—subsequently hammered at the Mepps without quite impaling itself, while my companion reported a frustrating knock from his precinct upriver. No matter how many of his other judgments I'm inclined to challenge, Piscator had it exactly right in describing "angling to be like the virtue of humility." My humility, which good friends seldom bother to mention, registered another sharp downtick when a box of lures slipped out of my pocket, floated out into the channel, and sank from sight.

If I exhibited far less self-control than a favorite uncle caught in a more tragic clutch of circumstance, it was probably because I had nobody but myself to blame. In a clumsy attempt to join the two of us in a rowboat on the Maumee River in Defiance, Ohio, a backland cousin stepped on my uncle's favorite flyrod, which is to say his late favorite flyrod, rest in peace. Somehow Carl Sprigg managed to ease our awkward relative's torment, if not his own, with a comforting cushion of rhetoric. Forty years later, I can hear him still. "It's all right, all right," Uncle Carl said. "I have two or three more at home as good as that," which he definitely did not, not with all of us feeling the winds of the Great Depression.

In the case of my own misfortune, I adjusted some on sighting a plastic bag of live maggots, which apparently

Nigel had no taste for, making maggots unique. Scaling my former dreams to a more realistic size, I skewered two of these baits on a small hook, fished a patch of relatively quiet water up against the elderberries. It made for pleasant angling, idle and aimless, and in time even produced a small roach, not over half a pound, which I unhooked and pitched back, if only to show my colors. Toward the end, the Hampshire Avon had reluctantly offered up a captive fish, in a manner of speaking.

Although Nigel predictably insisted on a long volley of farewell casts, every one of them guaranteed to be his very last, it was time to honor a firm commitment. It was time, or nearly time, to collect my wife—who forever hopes for more than I generally bring back—for a new film. Mandolin players aren't the only ones addicted to celluloid picks.

The pungent aroma of pigs was blowing in the wind, blowing in the wind, as we left the Burgate Manor Farm carpark. The last slants of the wintry sun melted down, lights flickered in a one-eyed village we passed.

"Well, we haven't measured up to Walton's version of gentlemen of tried honesty, fishing salmon before the season officially opens—fishing salmon before the season officially opens without a dead salmon to our rod too, worse luck, which makes it all the more tragic." I remarked.

"Exactly." Nigel scraped the crust from the bowl of his pipe. "Speaking of Walton, what do you suppose the father figure would do at this point?"

"What else!"

Up the track we hurried, a big foot hard on the accelerator, until we saw a country inn called the Bull, at Downton, standing off to our right. A cheery barmaid, her country accent marred by a pronounced glottal click, attended to virtually all our wishes, but the decor served to remind us of our failure. Stuffed trophy fish lined the wooden walls, big fish, fish so big, in fact, the patent-holder anglers needn't stretch them by an inch during recitals, salmon, pike, even a twelve-and-a-half-pound trout, on boards and under glass, in photographs and statistical record sheets, fish no bigger than we ourselves might have caught, with a little luck and no suspicious water bailiff prowling the beat, epic fish, every one of them, except for a novelty three-ounce gudgeon the innkeeper had whimsically mounted, or set up, as they say in English English.

Still, at the end of a day on another haunted river he used to rove with better manners than our own, Nigel and I felt at one with Walton there in the warmth of the Bull. After all, two sinners were briefly going by the book, whose mellow pages contain a restorative suggestion every busted brother of the angle ought to heed: "We'll turn into it, and refresh ourselves with a cup of drink, and a little rest."

THE late Edward R. Hewitt, an eminent American disciple of Izaak Walton, once codified the three evolving stages of the typical, card-carrying fisherman. In his view an addict begins by trying to catch all the fish he possibly can, graduates to an interest only in large trophy-sized fish and, sooner or later, arrives at a reflective state where he genuinely enjoys fishing for its own sake, with or without the traditional rewards, such as fish. At the risk of belittling my betters, it's only fair to report that Hewitt himself, stages one through three inclusive, rarely missed an opportunity to discuss his catch right down to the pennyweight with anyone who happened to ask—and, according to at least one brother of the angle, some who did not.

Unless I have read my Walton as carelessly as I've vetted the slippery fine print in, say, the warranty for our last new car, the standard reference appears to have teetered in much the same longitude. While his appreciation of the subtler flavors of the sport gradually enlarged, he was constantly caught up in all three stages simultaneously. As everyone familiar with *The Compleat Angler* knows, Walton was captivated—some might say even obsessed—with the attendant birdsong, pretty milkmaids, and honeysuckle. The lark at break of day arising was a gorgeous sight, all right, especially if Walton had some fish up on the grass as well.

Few, if any, of the rivers he roved offered him a greater opportunity to straddle Hewitt's three categories than the Thames. The river has been best described by Walton, who knew it well where it washed through London, past Windsor and under Henley Bridge. "The chief is Thamisis, compounded of two rivers, Thame and Isis," he wrote, "whereof the former, rising somewhat beyond Thame in Buckinghamshire, and the latter near Cirencester in Gloucestershire, meet together about Dorchester in Oxfordshire; the issue of which happy conjunction is the Thamisis, or Thames; hence it flieth between Berks, Buckinghamshire, Middlesex, Surrey, Kent, and Essex; and so weddeth itself to the Kentish Medway, in the very jaws of the ocean. This glorious river feeleth the violence and benefit of the sea more than any river in Europe, ebbing and flowing twice a day, more than sixty miles; about whose banks are so many fair towns and princely palaces." Whether he was extolling the virtues of fish, rivers, or anglers, Walton was seldom given to understatement.

Despite that chronic gift for hyperbole, the Thames was and is indeed a glorious river, although it took a $200 million, fifteen-year clean-up program to put it right not long ago after a century of vile pollution. The river is so healthy today that it has produced a total of eighty-nine different species, including Atlantic salmon, an eight-and-a-quarter-pound specimen of which was trapped in the screens at a power station in 1974. Long-view Britishers promptly dumped five thousand salmon parr in the River Eye, a small Thames tributary, at Upper Slaughter in Gloucestershire in hopes of establishing a trend. Meanwhile, the river is filled with tench, barbel, carp, bream, chub, pike, dace, perch, roach, rudd, trout, and other fish.

Given a bonanza so assorted as that, I finally chose to fish pike on my first trip to the Thames, not because I'm especially keen on the vicious, slack-jawed fish, but rather because relatively few of the other Walton waters I was scheduled to sample assayed much in the way of pike. So there I was, on a left-hand turn in the river, standing in sheeting rain on a Sunday morning shortly before Christmas, swimming a live minnowlike bleak on a number-8 treble hook, winding slack twelve-pound monofilament line onto an open-faced Mitchell 420 reel, hoping, hoping, hoping the prospects were better than they looked.

"The river is still a bit on the naughty side," observed Peter Stone, a vigorous little full-time bookbinder and part-time angling writer, who had kindly offered to let me come fish with him. "We won't take any pike on a day like this, but as long as we're here we might just as well give it a blinking go." After readjusting his plastic float, Stone expanded on that gloomy theme. "Some people think a hellish rain doesn't bother fish. But it does. As my friend Dick Walker once said, to a fish, rain is like cannonballs falling on a tin roof."

For half an hour the bouncy little year-round angler's forecast proved maddeningly accurate. We fished in the rain without so much as a touch, although, as Stone went to some pains to explain, we couldn't have chosen a more promising stretch of water. "The river is absolutely crawling with pike here," he told me. "Not long ago, I caught seventy-four pounds of pike right here, including a very big one, for a BBC television show they wanted me to fish for." From the looks of things, the riches to be had amounted to no great secret. Despite the adverse weather, two coarse fishermen huddled under green umbrellas a few yards upstream, their long rods set in brackets, bobbers showing on the colored water, while two more worked the far bank probably forty feet away.

"We'll get no pike today," Stone repeated, in case I was in any doubt about the prospects.

Two casts later, he spoke again, his voice thinned to an intriguing whisper. "I've a pike tickling at my bait now," he said. His shiny green-and-yellow-striped float quivered, sank, bobbed to the surface again. Stone tightened his line by arching the rod, his bony face screwed into an expression of "well, maybe," before he let out an emphatic grump: "He didn't ever really take." On reeling in, he found the scales of his dead bleak badly raked, like someone had taken a cheese grater to it. A fresh bleak hooked through the top lip drifted down what Walton used to call the swift of the river, once, twice, three times. "I've something tickling me again."

The fish visibly tickled the bait several times, pulled the float underwater. Using familiar old techniques, Stone tightened the line again and then, after what struck me as a perilously long time, jerked the rod far back and wound the reel. "He's smallish," he exclaimed. "He's definitely a smallish pike." As British pike go, the fish was positively smallish, three or four pounds, eighteen to twenty inches, not even worth pulling up on the grass. Stone shook it off in the shallows, dipped into the plastic bucket, strung on another bleak no longer than his landmark nose.

After that first fish broke the melancholy spell, I was able to enlarge my awareness to a point where I could register some of the essential background that Walton was often moved to comment on. Three black rooks perched on the bare limbs of a twisted oak tree, a flock of geese waddled over the muddy meadow toward a bend in the river, two bay horses rubbed against one another in the wet behind us. Down the river, behind a high door decorated with the heraldic crest of one of the Oxford colleges, several thin racing shells were carefully stacked upside down. Across the field the spires of Oxford rose in the steady rain, slim and perfect, standing forever over the haunted old city.

On the far bank, one of the neighboring anglers left his protective umbrella briefly to shake the contents of a battered cooking pan in the river. "What's that?" I asked my mentor. "Groundbait," Stone said. "I use groundbait myself many a time, maggots, usually, very helpful too, especially if the fishing is slow. The maggots attract small feed fish to the piece of water you're fishing, and the small feed fish, in turn, attract the more sizable lads, but a driving rain like this isn't what we want."

Moments later, the groundbaiter took the Lord's name in vain—Walton would not have approved—and pumped at his glass rod. Peter Stone and I watched the sequence in slow motion, the Blimey working the rod, reeling line, scooping the fish into his long-handled net, lifting it ashore, warily reaching into the net. "Not much of a fish, that," Stone informed me in a voice that clearly did not intend to belittle our brother of the angle across the river. "Maybe five pounds of pike, at a guess." The victor stroked the sides of the fish like a trout, gently put it back.

Stone took another pike not quite that size while I caught an infant myself, which caused me to reflect that things really weren't so bad, however negative the authority's earlier forecast, three pike to our own rods, another across the river, four fish in just over an hour in the heavy weather. The rain began to diminish and then disappeared altogether. Once the clouds peeled back, exposing a hazy sun, several dog-walkers appeared, and a man with two children, and a family of five who spread a canvas groundcloth and opened a wicker picnic basket in the gathering sunshine.

The dramatic improvement put Stone in a jubilant mood.

"Oh, we'll have some real fishing now that the weather has turned," he said. "Our baits probably have passed over fifty pike on this piece of water already, but they wouldn't take because of the sour weather. We'll have some real fishing, all right."

Unfortunately, we fished for nearly two hours in the sunshine with no success, although I did lose a bleak when my impatience got the better of me. "You lost your bait," Stone said, rather chidingly, I thought, but perhaps I was merely feeling self-conscious about the gaffe. A large swan came winging up the river, right to left, the powerful beat of its wings making a rackety sound, before planing down, raking a sheet of water, not ten yards out.

On our way back to the village parking lot, a stalwart looking man in a thick turtleneck sweater waved from the far bank. "He's a world-class pike fisherman," Stone told me, and raised his voice a few notches. "Good day, there, Geoff. Are you having a lovely season?" Geoff cupped his hands together. "Oh yes, lovely," he said. "Three hundred seventeen pounds of pike to date, and the season not half over yet." Edward R. Hewitt would not have had any trouble pigeonholing Geoff.

In the parking lot I did what I could to thank Peter Stone for the trouble he had gone to on my behalf. His dark eyes bulged some as I handed over a quart of wonderfully expensive whisky.

"No need for that, you know," he said, getting a firm grip on the bottle. "I like a touch now and then, same as anyone else, but a bottle this size, no need for a bottle this size, really, last me a good long while. And remember, if you have another go for pike, you can use almost any bait you want, like Walton wrote."

The pike isn't especially selective when it comes to a choice of groceries, which is putting it mildly, as readers have reason to know. Walton extols the potluck feeding habits of the fish commencing with the very first edition of

135

The Compleat Angler. He subsequently altered, revised, and expanded several other sections in four later editions without ever scaling down his view of the pike's voracious character. "To be called the tyrant of the rivers, or the fresh-water wolf, by reason of his bold, greedy, devouring disposition; which is so keen, as Gesner relates, a man going to a pond (where it seems a pike had devoured all the fish) to water his mule, had a pike bit his mule by the lips; to which the pike hung so fast that the mule drew him out of the water, and by that accident the owner of the mule angled out the pike," the old boy wrote with his usual gusto. "And the same Gesner observes, that a maid in Poland had a pike bit her by the foot, as she was washing clothes in a pond. And I have heard the like of a woman in Killingworth pond, not far from Coventry."

On the basis of reliable returns from several precincts, things have not changed much since Walton's day. Among other entrees, chicken, duck, squirrels, even venomous snakes have been found inside dead pike during the usual post-mortems. Perhaps the most aching variation on that theme recently occurred in Bemidji, Minnesota, when a man discovered the remains of his son's two missing pet rabbits in a sixteen-pound fish he pulled out of a nearby lake.

In view of the pike's eclectic taste, it isn't surprising that anglers both now and then have filled in their daydreams with a wildly assorted range of feed. Walton recommended frogs, roach, dace, perch, and so on, but, typically, he amended the menu to include some condiments for the occasional gourmet fish as well. "Dissolve gum of ivy in oil of spike, and therewith anoint your dead bait," he wrote, following a graphic play-by-play account of exactly how to wire a live frog onto the hook. Such elaborate detail, while immensely helpful for fishermen, of course, couldn't help but offend squeamish individuals who don't happen to spend their spare time on the water. More than anything else, that reference to frogs was said to have inflamed Lord Byron, whose recreations took another form, to a point of boiling censure:

And angling too, that solitary vice,
Whatever Izaak Walton sings or says:
The quaint, old, cruel coxcomb, in his gullet
Should have a hook, and a small trout to pull it.
Don Juan

When I reread Walton's chapter on the pike during my Thames experience, I was reminded of a rumpled little black man soaking in the sunshine in the tall grasses of long ago, his long rod propped in a forked stick on the bank of the Fox River in Illinois back when the Fox used to be my home water. At the risk of intruding on his torpor, which seemed a remote possibility, a friend and I put the Big Question in hopes of gathering some useful information before we rigged up and started fishing ourselves. Impressed by an expression of interest, our brother of the angle promptly reeled in to show us exactly what he was using to bamboozle any stray pike in a waterway assaying mostly carp and bass. Once we saw the lure he was fishing, the two of us had to get a grip on our good manners. It lingers still on the edge of my memory, a big jointed Pikie-Minnow plug, which was status quo except for a couple of bizarre refinements. He'd covered both triple gang hooks with a snarl of nightcrawlers, and he let the rig lie motionless on the surface instead of winding it in at various rates of speed, as the manufacturer's directions suggested. I hadn't read my Walton at the time, still being in a basic Robin Hood literary phase, but I suppose our minority chum half-dozing on the riverbank had as much chance as we had—maybe more.

Whatever the seventeenth-century angler's credentials otherwise, his evaluation of the pike's all-consuming feeding habits seems in no way extravagant. After all, in my own case, I managed to hook—hook, not always land, mind you—English-accented pike with live gudgeon, dead herring, cardboard lunch meat, and Daredevil spoons in different sizes. One January morning on the Thames near the Compleat Angler at Marow in Buckinghamshire, a comfortable inn where Walton reportedly composed great swatches of his masterwork when he was not working the river twining so close by, I found myself completely out of surefire lures and baits due to a hellish assortment of misfortunes, among them hanging my last Daredevil high in a horse chestnut tree. Since it was not yet the time I promised to take my wife shopping, I rummaged through a cluttered tackle box searching for anything that might arouse a pike. In the end I chose an old red-and-white Heddon River Runt, a Made-in-America plug designed largely for bass, although sportsmen on the Wye in Wales hook a surprising number of oh-boy salmon with the same plastic jimcrack. Idly I started casting without much hope of anything more than a sore elbow before I had to pack it in. But it felt good all the same, I had to admit, a sense of transatlantic continuity, the import River Runt quivering some on the retrieve, the familiar red-and-white shape summoning up visions of my lost youth, the sun warming me despite the gritty temperature, a vagabond angler adrift on alien waters.

"Any luck?" An alarmingly fit-looking native in a red jogging suit appeared at my side.

"No, same old thing, no luck at all. Anti-American, these pike," I said by way of station identification.

He paused for a moment, thankfully accepted the apple I offered, focused on the plug twitching through the water. "Well, if it's pike you're fishing, you'll be wanting live baitfish, won't you." He bit a hole in the apple. "You'll be wanting live baitfish, preferably gudgeon, about . . . Hello, hello"—his voice rode up the scale—"look at that!"

Not thirty feet out, a long sullen shape was following the River Runt with what Walton once described as "more than common eagerness." If my nerve ends didn't flutter some at the looming sight, it was merely because they have been worn smooth over the years. The fish hit like the edge of doom, engorging the plug, straightening the line, bowing the stiff rod. Despite the fact that I had seldom formally been introduced to a double-weight fresh-water fish before, I'd anticipated the magical moment for so long that I knew precisely what to do. Rod tip high, the twenty-pound test line fairly taut but not under any excessive strain, I let the monstrous pike show its stuff. It boiled toward the far bank, a great speckled blur in the water, shaking the hated iron in its lean jaws, hitting the bottom with a whiplash crack.

For a long manic moment it looked as if I might finally have some walk-in business for a nearby taxidermist, whose price, however stiff for a man of my modest means, I would be genuinely delighted to pay. The pike turned, ascended and, wallowing some, or so it seemed, came straight at us, while my companion the jogger grabbed for the landing net in hopes he'd have an opportunity to properly thank me for that apple. Unfortunately, such was not to be. All of a sudden the fish came catapulting out of the Thames, shook its malevolent head, broke off. Exit pike, exit Heddon River Runt, exit several feet of line, exit all those lingering dreams that I would land something big enough to brag about. As a bone-deep native Illinoisian, I was in the situation Lincoln once found himself: it hurt too much to laugh and I was too old to cry.

"Fifteen pounds, fifteen pounds if he would scale an ounce, a great pity." The physical-fitness freak showed the customary English gift for understatement.

"Twenty," I said with a bit more heat than I intended or he deserved.

Several weeks after what constituted that hazy moral victory—why is it that my life abounds with moral rather than explicit victories?—with the River Runt, I enlarged on the usual menu fishing the Thames at Wolvercote just outside of Oxford, where Walton must have cast a horsehair line, at least on the basis of strong circumstantial evidence. It is perfectly true that his sprawling dialogue specifically mentions the English mother water only at Henley bridge and Windsor. But it is also perfectly true that he had a son at the university, whom Walton, a doting father as well as a traveling man of comfortable means, undoubtedly visited on a number of occasions. As anyone even dimly familiar with his book ought to know, the original couldn't possibly have done time around Oxford without nipping down to so tempting a river, which is to say he may very well have fished the same grassy run I was walking that late February morning.

Without in any way intending to inflame the Save the Goldfish lobby, I must confess to having stopped by a pet shop in nearby Witney for a dozen of the beleaguered species, which ran me twenty English pence apiece, because a pikemonger friend emphatically urged me to fish live baits. It wasn't difficult to resolve the choice of catching my own baitfish or buying goldfish. On hearing how I planned to use the merchandise, however, a squeamish saleslady became audibly upset—only not so upset, I noticed, as to cancel the transaction.

Beyond a bend in the river, at the edge of a large flat pasture several horses were grazing, the Thames bellied into a channel fed by a roily backwater. In my view, the offbeat bait might have a splendid utilitarian value. If goldfish don't exactly glow in muddy water, at least they show more color than gudgeon, bleak, small roach, and other less ornamental charity-bait fish.

Once the small hook, lead-shot weights, and plastic bobber were assembled, I delicately hooked a doomed goldfish through the lip and flipped out my first cast. Sadly, sadly, it was not altogether a success. The weighted rig spun into the dark channel while forty cents worth of bait, shaken loose by the cast, arched completely across the river in an imprudent, utterly separate parabola. There was more togetherness when I threaded on another goldfish, the bobber floating downriver with the current until it was time to lift it out and throw upstream again. Almost mechanically I cast, cast again, the brown wash of the Thames before me, several university racing shells racked on the far bank. On the second cast the float abruptly jiggled, stopped, moved a few inches upstream before I leaned into the rod too late. At the rate I was spending them, my twelve goldfish would not last until lunchtime.

As I dipped into the bucket for another, I couldn't help but recall to mind the peckish paragraph from Brooks Roberts, a dear friend with whom I have fished away many a tantalizing summer on the Neversink in New York, whose letter was still burning a hole in my memory. Weeks before, I had made the mistake of explaining how I was fishing several of Izaak Walton's favorite rivers. Roberts, a fine angler with a rigid regard for the sporting code—except for the legal closing date of trout season, anyway—felt compelled to express himself a bit sharply, I thought, on what struck him as an anomaly.

"Have you no shame, and have you considered, Robert, the price you will pay for publicizing such base fishing? Drummed out of The Anglers' Club, struck from the rolls of The Flyfishers' Club of London, banned from the Beaverkill, snubbed on the Neversink."

Very little, I told myself. While taking a brown trout on a dry fly amounts to fishing in its most exalted form for me, and, given a choice, is my preference every time, my speckled past also thrums with other approaches, other techniques, other concepts. I've swum doughballs for carp, speared suckers, drilled holes through the ice in pursuit of pickerel, and even allowed a companion whose judgment I generally respect to persuade me that it wasn't a mortal sin to use a night line festooned with thirty or forty baited hooks in Arkansas. Over the years I have tried virtually everything except dynamite and a thrownet. I don't suppose I have caught my proper share of fish, not if one considers all the time and effort involved, but it wasn't for lack of a venturesome nature.

In view of those and other youthful indiscretions, it struck me as relatively sporting to be fishing nothing more base than live goldfish there on the Thames, although, to be perfectly frank, it must be said that I was still fishing at no profit by mid-morning, as I curtly told an old shipwreck of a man who made the usual inquiries during a shuffling ramble past my station. In a toneless effort to buoy my spirits, the oldtimer informed me that a schoolboy— couldn't be more than twelve years old, mind you—had killed a fourteen-pound pike upriver earlier in the day.

Any moral qualms I may have nourished about an experimental last resort evaporated on learning that I was being badly outfished even by undergraduates. Quickly I weighted my line with a battery-fed gimcrack emitting a gritty metallic buzz, like the sound of a coin telephone before the dime drops, which plainly has caught more fishermen than fish, a gift from a Milwaukee manufacturer who sent it along in case I might want to say a few kind words in print, such as Fishcaller and ten dollars plus sales tax. Here's hoping Brooks Roberts doesn't read this book, which he probably will not, unless he's signed on for a speed-reading course.

While Roberts's reaction, if and when, is likely to be acerbic, I cast these sound effects into the water convinced that the patron saint looking down on all of us—from where he probably uses groundbait in the River Styx—certainly would not mind. After all, Walton took advantage of the high technology of the seventeenth century, metal hooks, horsehair lines, and greenheart rods, while I was merely

142

exploiting those innovations mad scientists of our own era have developed for bottom-line returns, either way you look at it. "Or these live baits may make sport, being tied about the body or wings of a goose or duck and she chased over a pond," Walton wrote in his chapter on pike, for example. A few paragraphs later he revealed further abracadabra: "And some affirm, that any bait anointed with the marrow of the thigh-bone of an hern [heron] is a great temptation to any fish."

Since I was unaccountably out of marrow of the thigh-bone of the hern, I had to make do with the goldfish and Fishcaller, which looked a formidable combination. Sure enough, on my fourth cast, the second of which cost me another forty cents in mid-flight, something tuned to the proper wave length hammered my bait hard, sinking the plastic float, stripping line off the reel, arching the glass rod. The fish surged through the dark water, whooshed toward a weedbed on the far side. I thought I had lost it when the line briefly went slack, but the pike was only gathering strength for some deceitful calisthenics.

Up it came, thrashing out of the river, sawing its brute head, desperately trying to shake the treble hook hopefully locked in that long mouth, the buzzer clearly audible in the frosty morning, another fish on yet another river trying to break me off. But in this instance, at least, it was man who conquered nature, if only for the sake of novelty. The pike put up token resistance while I reeled in, less bold than melancholy, as Walton once wrote, and, except for a thunderclap roll at the very end, when I scooped the net into the water, the conflict was no more dramatic than a friendly talk with the banker.

The fish, while hardly the biggest I had seen close up, was respectable enough, long and deep, sunburst dots showing above the white belly, heaving in the folds of the net. The official audit awaited the arrival of a coarse fisherman attired in the fashion of Admiral Peary, who, aware of the activity, came drumming up the bank from his own stretch down near a dam and, after a meticulous weigh-in, said it scaled just over eight pounds. His eyeballs bulged some on examining first the tattered remains of the goldfish and then the buzzing Fishcaller. I extracted the hook with the protective help of a heavy glove and heaved the pike back into the Thames, which put me in conflict with the master, of course.

After establishing the fact that the pike feeds on nearly anything, which is true, Walton proceeded to describe the fish as a three-star meal, which it emphatically is not. "Out of these, take his guts, and keep his liver, which you are to shred very small, with thyme, sweet marjoram, and a little winter-savory," he wrote, "to these put some pickled oysters, and some anchovies, two or three, both these last whole; for the anchovies will melt and the oysters should not; to these you must add also a pound of sweet butter, which you are to mix with the herbs that are shred, and let them all be well salted." In elaborate detail Walton described how the fish should be skewered on a spit, slowly roasted, basted with claret wine, and laced with garlic and orange juice before serving. "This dish of meat is too good for any but anglers, or very honest men," he concluded, aware of a distinction he generally ignored. Any writer who can manage to make pike sound that appetizing ought to be writing advertising for the National Turnip Institute.

It may be my poor but honest origins, but I must admit that I have fed on pike in Illinois, Wisconsin, and Minnesota, where they are caught far more than they are cooked. No matter how long the fish are soaked beforehand, no matter how crisp they are baked on a plank, no matter how much inventive seasoning is added, this particular dish of meat never loses its tough, oily, cardboard quality. Either the British version of the pike has a very different taste, or else, as Walton wrote elsewhere in his dialogue, "the belly has no ears when hunger comes upon it."

Shortly after my successful trial spin with the enterprising rig, traffic picked up on the Thames. Two swan settled onto my beat, a roach fisherman braced under an umbrella started casting his maggots a few yards upstream, some Oxford mesomorphs lowered their racing shell into the dirty water just across from me. The spires still showed against the gray skies beyond the pasture, life still had a leisurely beat to it. But with only two surviving goldfish in the bucket and the wind whistling right through my corduroys, it was obviously time to take on a round of anti-freeze.

At the Old New Inn in Bourton-on-the-Water, a log fire cracked in the stone hearth. When he did the proper thing by pulling me a long pint of lager and lime, the publican, a gregarious mogul who occasionally fishes in his restricted spare time, seated himself beside me.

"Take any pike today?" he asked.

"Yes, yes, I did."

"How many did you take?"

"Half a brace." Somehow the English English sounded more impressive than admitting to merely the one fish.

"Any size?"

"Nice size. It ran just over eight pounds."

"A tiddler." Slowly shaking his head, he bored a hole in my ego. "A pike that small is only a tiddler."

So it was, of course, as I learned on subsequently talking with a school of coarse fishermen and skimming through the literature. Twenty-, twenty five- and even thirty-pound pike are horsed out of U.K. waters right through the long season without causing anyone to bother ringing the churchbells. The week I caught my tiddler, in fact, *The Angling Times*, a wetback periodical which doesn't pretend to enshrine all the walloping big fish caught the previous season days, cited three thirty-pounders, not one of them,

145

I couldn't help but notice, taken on anything so exotic as goldfish. The official British record remains a matter of rackety controversy. While the largest listed fresh-water wolf, as Walton called them, comes to forty-three pounds, several reliable eyewitnesses swear to seeing Tommy Morgan weigh in a forty-seven-pound, eleven-ounce trophy on the bonny bonny banks of Loch Lomond in 1945.

Still, I had had what was for me a relatively successful time of it fishing the sprawling Thames. No doubt I missed some of the birdsong, the lambs gamboling in green fields, the lavender scent of country inns that Izaak Walton painted in as background any time he wasn't too caught up indexing the ample bill-of-fare suitable for pike once they tie on their bibs. But at least I had not missed every fish I tentatively hooked, not quite, anyway, which is all I ever ask when I go a-angling, same as my antique master, not to mention Edward R. Hewitt, despite all that twaddle about a day on the river healing the soul with or without any accompanying fish.

$\mathbb{A}$n angler, a proper angler, I see." The scarecrow of a milkman who had just sold me a healing pint of gold top there in Abbott's Worthy could not help but notice my booted feet, the Fisherman's Friend clippers strung to my jacket, a big hat adorned with small flies. "Off to fish the Itchen, are you?"

"Yes, I am." Since I was officially certified to fish a piece of the Itchen, a prudence not always the case, I saw no reason to deny it.

"Special river, the Itchen."

"Oh."

My monosyllabic response could hardly be construed as an invitation to prolong our tête-à-tête. Yet the familiar old storm warnings were audibly gathering. Blame it on my general air of blank wonder, but strangers frequently seem to take me for an inquisitive alien anxious to tune in on whatever artless smalltalk they can manage. A dated encounter with an assistant District Commissioner in East Africa, whose personal views of a missionary station a few miles up the track I had in no way solicited, was merely frustrating; an experience with a faded lady who innocently accosted me—at least I guessed it to be innocent, else she ought to have set a markdown price for used merchandise—on the street not two blocks from my apartment and treated me to a windy, disjointed account of life in east Manhattan was downright maddening.

"Special river, you know." The milkman leaned against a figurative farm gate. "Izaak Walton, he used to fish the Itchen in olden times."

"That doesn't make the Itchen special." I felt compelled to play the devil's advocate, although I knew I would hate myself in the morning. "Old Walton fished every river he ever saw—and he saw a good many."

His bony face registered mild shock at my flippant irreverence. "Yes, right, dead right, I suppose. But the Itchen was Walton's very last river, wasn't it?"

At the risk of offending the dairy lobby, whose produce is essential to me in view of a hellish adolescent taste for milk, I abruptly concluded our dialogue in favor of locating a particular roadway described as pitching down a tumbling hill. Abbott's Worthy is a small English village, total population nobody I asked could tell me, situated on the edge of memory in Hampshire. It is little different from such neighboring settlements as Charity and Long Parish, Leachford and Nether Wallop, except for one thing. It happens to stand along the Itchen where I was to fish it as part of my systematic campaign to cover the rivers Walton especially enjoyed.

It was perfectly true that Izaak Walton wet a line in waters beyond any count during his ninety years, not only because he loved fishing, of course, but also because he was seldom critical of any river so long as it held fish. A kind and pious individual who wrote *The Compleat Angler* mostly for his own pleasure after producing some wartless, transparently partisan biographies of eminent Englishmen, Walton invariably viewed rivers much as he did people, sunny side up. On the basis of available research, it also seems true that the Itchen was the last river Walton roved before he himself was scooped into the net in nearby Winchester in 1683. Appropriately, a gift window from English and American brethren of the angle lighting his tomb in Winchester Cathedral shows the Itchen turning toward St. Catherine's Hill, Walton seated alongside his fishing tackle, a favorite Biblical quotation, Study to Be Quiet, lettered across the bottom, the whole scene frozen in muted stained glass.

It was good to return to Hampshire for reasons that went beyond my impending day on the Itchen. The small-scale geography also gave me another shot at the Sheriff House Hotel in neighboring Stockbridge, whose kitchen I regard as the most impressive in England. A takeaway picnic signed by E. F. Fisher, the proprietor, lay in the trunk of my hired car as I eased down the hillside. Like the master, I knew the hour would toll when the river keeper and I would be "hungry as hawks," as Piscator described the situation in the flavorful pages of his Discourse.

At a thatch-roofed Tudor house not a day over four hundred years old, I put myself in the hands of Len Bishop, who had been awaiting me while I fraternized with the milkman. Bishop is a formidable specimen, big, thickset, with a bull neck and fingers thick as sausages, a man who plainly was not born so much as he was quarried, which ought to give him some edge in his constant guard against poachers and stray romantics foolish enough to trespass on the water he patrols. He wrung my hand harder than circumstances demanded, led me down the last of the hill to a wooden fence we scrambled over.

"A stack of Yankees come through this area looking for a spot of fishing," Bishop said. "Last season I gillied for three different lots of Yanks all in the same week, poor fishing too. I hope we can do better for you."

Exactly my sentiments, although one look at the Itchen shook my faith. Even in a thin rain the river was transparent, clear as glass, a window through which fish could easily focus on a gawky outlander working a rod on the high bank. It ran in an easy glide, turning in a series of slow loops, a fairly deep mirror of a chalkstream rooted with green mare's-tail weedbed. Altogether, the prospects struck me as alarmingly bleak.

On the advice of counsel I commenced the challenge by fishing a tiny Ginger Quill. I fished it for exactly five casts before it snapped off during a truant backcast in a strand of barbed wire. Len Bishop, a good frugal countryman who had tied the fly himself, got down on his hands and knees searching the matted ground under the fencing until he finally managed to find it—"more sharp-eyed than any hawk you have named," Walton wrote.

Later the rain dried up; the fickle English sun, which flickers on and off like trick lights on a Christmas tree, warmed our necks. Later I saw I was casting something more than the number-16 fly. In the glaring light I was also casting a bulky shadow the original of which measured six-three and weighed in at 220 pounds, as much substance as shadow, as the resident trout undoubtedly observed, if only briefly. Once again I had violated a stiff old stricture laid down by the maestro: "For the sight of any shade amazes the fish, and spoils your sport—of which you must take great care." Determined not to amaze the fish, at least in that melancholy context, I moved back on the bank some and cast, cast, cast from a half crouch, with no greater success.

Briefly, very briefly, Len Bishop and I relaxed on a fishing bench awaiting the next cloudburst hatch of flies. While the river keeper nourishes a buoyant view of many contemporary fixtures, he admits to some reservations regarding the closeup problems we all of us worry about. "Inflation, not a stick better, is it, not enough jobs to go round, either, crime, rolling up every year, isn't it, nothing like things used to be," Bishop remarked glumly. His preliminaries were more valid than his summary. Bishop and I both tend to look back on a previous generation, a previous century, through a wistful prism. According to the gospel of history, however, his specific grumps—rising prices, unemployment, violence—echo similar defects from the seventeenth century that Walton inhabited. The chronic optimist who saw virtually everything, even fish, as larger than life, in fact, abandoned London because it was "dangerous for honest men to be there."

At a bend in the river where the far bank sloped up a garden to another thatch-roofed house, we came upon a deafish old native. In a dry toneless voice he reminded us that Walton had fished the river to the tune of a sixteen-pound pike, among other things, he reportedly wrestled out of a deep pool just ahead. All the while I kept casting for trout at absolutely no profit.

With a pair of magnifying spectacles perched on the end of my broken nose, I tied different flies to the light leader, dry flies and nymphs, in sizes scaled to the bottom line of an ophthalmologist's eye chart, most of them, and still nothing happened. In my desperation I even introduced a number-18 Hairwing Coachmen in the hopes that Piscator, who, in another brief sermon to his disciple, said, "And note, that the smallest flies are the best," was not simply riffling the air. But after almost wearing my arm off pitching into fast water churning below a six-foot dam, I asked my companion if we ought to push on.

"No," Bishop said. "There's fish right here."

"What in heaven's name do they take?"

"Funnily enough, I got a two-pounder here on a special

home-made fly last autumn. I saw him, nipped right up to my house, pinched a bit of my wife's knitting wool, black and yellow, it was, tied it to the hook, got the fish very first cast."

A man who can improvise like that shouldn't be standing empty-handed. Silently, I passed Bishop my rod. He covered the river in a lovely pattern, left to right, every cast perhaps a foot from the last, lengthening the distance some until he grunted and lifted the top of the rod, and a fish came thrashing out of the water. I hadn't scored on the Itchen yet, but my rod had. The fish ran about the size of a brown trout that Steve Collett, a devoted transatlantic friend of our son Scott, had carried to our doorway a few days earlier, asking if we would be kind enough to weigh it for him. Since his family's flourishing bakery and general store was positively stiff with scales, I saw through his grandstand subterfuge—but I played out the game all the same by carefully notarizing the shiny trophy on a spring balance originally acquired for bigger things.

Outside a small shed on up the river, we paused to gather strength for the afternoon. The nearby fields lighted with sunshine, small English robins singing on a hedge behind us, Bishop and I sat on a bench feeding on a picnic lunch that Walton would have appreciated: home-made bread lathered with fresh-churned country butter, thin slices of ham, bright red tomatoes, apples, bananas, an orange, cookies not long out of the oven, mellow local beer. One way and another we were "as merry as beggars," in the familiar words.

On the far side of the Itchen, a long cast from where we lazed, a pretty lady was quietly fishing during our lunch. She would creep up to the water on all fours and then, doubled up like a sideshow contortionist, flick a moderately long line onto the water. She was so still, so well camouflaged, so passive even when she scored that Bishop and I scarcely noticed she had taken two fish before our very eyes.

The sight of the compleat angleperson putting a brace in the grass triggered a hazy memory. All too many years ago, a shirt-tail relative named Ralph Batten sometimes used to quietly joint a rod, quietly knot a fly to a light leader, and quietly catch some breakfast-size trout as several canoe-loads of family drifted Michigan's shiny Manistee River without quite realizing how well he was actually producing. Any skeptics in the party were convinced next morning when the fish sputtered in a heavy iron skillet set over a wood fire.

Later Len Bishop and I followed the river as it turned toward the end of the beat beyond a stand of oak trees. Every so often trout came to the surface and snapped at the natural fly hatch, "a leash of trouts," to lift a phrase, generally just out of casting range, although one of them, a heavy brownie dark with age, did show not thirty feet away. It wasn't the biggest trout in Hampshire, not with a wizard named Sam Howard, who uses a computer to short-circuit approximately twenty thousand years of normal evolution in his dramatic refinement of selective breeding, recently exhibiting several four-year-old fish scaling more than thirty pounds each, but it was big enough to set me spinning relatively heroic dreams.

"Gently, gently, gently," Bishop cautioned.

My first cast fell far short of the fish. My second was what the British often describe as bang-on, two-three feet above, gentle enough, with no wrinkles in the leader. The big trout moved slightly, considering the Pheasant Tail nymph, decided against it.

"Try again," Bishop said.

The memory of that next cast haunts me still. The fly ruffled the water, the leader coiled. Spooked, badly spooked, the trout worked its fins and tailed upriver until we lost sight of it in weedbed along the far bank, another missing fish to join the multitude, another busted dream.

"Blank," I said, more or less. "Blank, blank, blankety-blank."

Despite the lost opportunity, there was no reason to despair, with a possible fish always awaiting me around the next bend. Occasional trout dimpled the surface and stirred against weeds in water so perfect it actually looked painted on the tumbling land. Until Bishop, whose charter it is to make certain no such predators invade the holy water, emphatically assured me that it could not possibly be, I swore I saw a small forbidden pike too.

On such a mellow day an angler can be forgiven the wistful hope there is something to the proverb "The gods do not subtract from the allocated span of Men's lives the Hours spent in Fishing," graven on an Assyrian Tablet, 200 B.C. A man wants as many such days as he can accumulate, with or without fish.

Every time the fly hatch on the river diminished or disappeared, Len Bishop and I got to yarning. It was pleasurable slowly walking the grass, resting for a while, splitting a last tin of beer, comfortably yarning. Mostly we yarned of trout, brown trout, epic brown trout, so long and deep they might splinter my light rod if I ever had the good fortune to hook into one.

In the end I hooked nothing at all on the Itchen. Somehow the empty creel did not seem important as we hiked a roll in the land toward a timbered old pub. The river, the songbirds, the glassy green meadows, the picnic and the company of a friendly guide, not to mention the giddy prospect—prospect, mind you—of taking a nice fish on the very next cast, were sufficient.

Besides, I suspect that the original brother of the angle whose dated text we all of us love, if not swear by, drew an occasional blank too, when he was roving the Itchen, the Dove, and the Trent. Like it or not, angling would not

154

offer such wonderfully challenging sport—"For angling may be said to be so like the mathematics, that it can never be fully learnt; at least not so fully, but that there will still be more new experiences left for the trial of other men that succeed us"—if the only losers were invariably the fish.